Universitext

Dirk van Dalen

Logic and Structure

Second Edition

Springer-Verlag
Berlin Heidelberg New York Tokyo 1983

Dirk van Dalen
Rijksuniversiteit Utrecht, Mathematisch instituut
Budapestlaan 6, Postbus 80.010
3508 TA Utrecht, The Netherlands

AMS Subject Classification (1980): 03-01

ISBN 3-540-12831-X Springer-Verlag Berlin Heidelberg New York Tokyo
ISBN 0-387-12831-X Springer-Verlag New York Heidelberg Berlin Tokyo

ISBN 3-540-09893-3 1. Auflage Springer-Verlag Berlin Heidelberg New York
ISBN 0-387-09893-3 1st Edition Springer-Verlag New York Heidelberg Berlin

Printed in Germany

Printing and bookbinding: Beltz, Offsetdruck, Hemsbach
2141/3140-543210

Preface

Logic appears in a 'sacred' and in a 'profane' form. The sacred form is dominant in proof theory, the profane form in model theory. The phenomenon is not unfamiliar, one observes this dichotomy also in other areas, e.g. set theory and recursion theory. For one reason or another, such as the discovery of the set theoretical paradoxes (Cantor, Russell), or the definability paradoxes (Richard, Berry), a subject is treated for some time with the utmost awe and diffidence. As a rule, however, sooner or later people start to treat the matter in a more free and easy way.

Being raised in the 'sacred' tradition, I was greatly surprised (and somewhat shocked) when I observed Hartley Rogers teaching recursion theory to mathematicians as if it were just an ordinary course in, say, linear algebra or algebraic topology. In the course of time I have come to accept his viewpoint as the didactically sound one: before going into esoteric niceties one should develop a certain feeling for the subject and obtain a reasonable amount of plain working knowledge.

For this reason I have adopted the profane attitude in this introductory text, reserving the more sacred approach for advanced courses. Readers who want to know more about the latter aspect of logic are referred to the immortal texts of Hilbert-Bernays or Kleene.

The present book has developed out of courses given at the University at Utrecht in the mathematics department to undergraduates. The experience drawn from these courses and the reactions of the participants was that one should try to incorporate bits of real mathematics as soon as possible. For that reason the well-known structures, such as groups, partially ordered sets, projective planes, are introduced at the earliest possible occasion.

By now, it is generally agreed that a mathematician should know how to formalize his language and his semantics. One of the traditional stumbling blocks in any logic course is the awkward business of actually proving theorems. As a rule, one gets over this part as quickly as possible and ignores formal proof. I have, in an effort to stimulate the students, introduced Gentzen's system of natural deduction, without going into the esoteric issues of proof theory. As an extra benefit, Gentzen's natural deduction represents intuitive reasoning quite faithfully. In this system students can fairly easily construct derivations for

themselves, and what is more: they generally like it. The technical details, required for the proof of the completeness theorem, are kept to a minimum in this approach. In the third chapter we initiate the study of models of various theories. The basic theorems, e.g. the compactness theorem, the Skolem-Löwenheim theorems, are applied to a number of 'real life' examples, such as arithmetic and analysis. It is shown how to obtain non-standard models, and how to exploit infinitely large numbers and infinitesimals. Skolem functions are also introduced, and the introduction of definable functions and predicates is studied. Finally, using the already gathered knowledge, a quick exposition of second-order logic is given; a topic that has regained some attention after being overshadowed for a time by set theory. We have refrained from treating the incompleteness theorems and recursion theory; however important those subjects are, they are not of central importance for mathematicians who do not intend to specialize in logic or computer science. Neither have we included intuitionistic logic. Again, the subject deserves a treatment, but not (yet?) in an introduction for general mathematicians.
Strictly speaking there are hardly any prerequisites for the reader; the first chapter can be understood by everybody. The second chapter uses a few elementary facts about algebra for the sake of illustrating the logical notions. In the last chapter some facts from algebra are used, but certainly not more than one would find in any introductory text.
As a matter of fact the reader does not have to be an accomplished algebraist, as long as he is to a certain degree familiar with the main notions and structures of elementary mathematics. One should recognize certain structures as old friends, and one should be prepared to make new friends.

In a text on logic one has the choice of slipping over tedious, technical details, or elaborating them ad nauseam. I have tried to avoid both extremes by covering some proofs in full detail, and leaving some routine matters to the reader. It should be stressed, however, that the majority of the proofs is trivial, but that the reader should not take my word for it and convince himself by devising proofs by himself, only consulting the book when stuck or when not certain of the correctness.

In particular the reader is urged to do the exercises, some of which are merely a training ground for definitions, etc. There are also a number of problems that constitute minor (or even major) theorems, but that can be handled strictly on the basis of the material in the text. Finally, some problems require a bit of knowledge of such subjects as set theory, algebra or analysis. Since the latter kind of problems present a glimpse of the use of logic in the real world, they should not be neglected.

Some of the material in this book is optional, e.g. one can safely skip the parts that deal with normal forms, duality, functional completeness, switching and (when in a hurry) the sections on the missing connectives (1.7 and 2.9).

In section 3.1 it is advisable to skip at first reading the proof of the completeness theorem and to go straight for the applications in 3.2. After getting the right feeling for this kind of material it is wise to get a thorough grasp of the proof of the completeness theorem, as the technique is very basic indeed.

Various people have contributed to the shaping of the text at one time or another. I wish to thank *Henk Barendregt*, who also tested the material in class, *Dana Scott* and *Jane Bridge* for their advice and criticism, and in particular *Jeff Zucker* who offered criticism and advice in a most unselfish way. It was he who suggested to incorporate the conjunction in our treatment of natural deduction.

Finally I want to express my gratitude and appreciation to *Sophie van Sterkenburg* for her patient typing and retyping.

Maccagno - De Meern 1979

Contents

0. Introduction

Without adopting one of the various views advocated in the foundations of mathematics, we may agree that mathematicians need and use a language, if only for the communication of their results and their problems. Whereas mathematicians have been claiming the greatest possible exactness for their methods, they should also be sensitive as to their means of communication. It is well known that Leibniz proposed to put the practice of mathematical communication and mathematical reasoning on a firm base; it was, however, not before the nineteenth century that those enterprises were (more) successfully undertaken by G. Frege and G. Peano. No matter how successfully and rigorously Frege, Russell, Hilbert, Bernays and others developed mathematical logic, it was only in the second half of this century that logic and its language showed any features of interest to the general mathematician. The sophisticated results of Gödel were valued of course, but any pratical use was not made of them. Even Tarski's result on the decidability of elementary algebra and geometry had to bide its time before any applications turned up.

Nowadays the application of logic to algebra, analysis, topology, etc. are numerous and well-recognized. It seems strange that quite a number of simple facts, within the grasp of any student, were overlooked for such long time. It is not possible to give proper credit to all those who opened up this new territory, any list would inevitably show the preferences of the author, and neglect some fields and persons.

Let us note that mathematics has a fairly regular, canonical way of formulating its material, partly by its nature, partly under the influence of strong schools, like the one of Bourbaki. Furthermore the crisis at the beginning of this century has forced mathematicians to pay attention to the finer details of their language and to their assumptions concerning the nature and the extent of the mathematical universe. This attention started to pay off when it was discovered that there was in some cases a close connection between a class of mathematical structures and its syntactical description.

We will give some examples.

It is well known that a subset of a group G which is closed under multiplication and inverse, is a group; however, a subset of an algebraically closed field F which is closed under sum, product, minus, and inverse, is in general not an algebraically closed field. This phenomenon is an instance of something quite general: an axiomatizable class of structures is axiomatized by a set of universal sentences (of the form $\forall x_1,\ldots,x_n\varphi$, with φ quantifier free) iff it is closed under substructures. If we check the axioms of group theory we see that indeed all axioms are universal, while not all the axioms of the theory of algebraically closed fields are universal. The latter fact could of course be accidental, it could be the case that we were not clever enough to discover a universal axiomatization of the class of algebraically closed fields. The above theorem of Tarski and Łos tells us, however, that it is impossible to find such an axiomatization!

The point of interest is that we have a simple syntactic criterion for some property of a class of structures. We can, so to speak, read the behaviour of the real mathematical world (in some simple cases) off from its syntactic description.

There are numerous examples of the same kind, e.g. *Lyndon's Theorem*: if a class of structures is axiomatizable then it is closed under homomorphisms iff it can be axiomatized by a set of positive sentences (i.e. sentences which, in prenex normal form with the open part in disjunctive normal form, do not contain negations).

The most basic and at the same time monumental example of such a connection between syntactical notions and the mathematical universe is of course *Gödel's completeness theorem*, which tells us that provability in any of the many available formal systems is extensionally identical with *truth* in all structures. That is to say, although provability and truth are totally different notations, (the first is combinatorial in nature, the latter set theoretical), they determine the same class of sentences: φ is provable iff φ is true in all structures.

Given the fact the study of logic involves a great deal of syntactical toil, we will set out by presenting an efficient machinery for dealing with syntax. We use the technique of *inductive definitions* and as a consequence we are rather inclined to see trees wherever possible e.g. we prefer natural deduction in the tree form to the linear versions that are here and there in use.

One of the amazing phenomena in the development of the foundations of mathematics is the discovery that the language of mathematics itself can be studied by mathematical means. This is far from a futile play: Gödel's incompleteness theorems, for instance, lean heavily on a mathematical analysis of the language of arithmetic, and the work of Gödel and Cohen in the field of the independence proofs in set theory requires a thorough knowledge of the mathematics of mathematical language. These topics are not in the scope of the present book, so we can confine ourselves to the simpler parts of the syntax. Nonetheless we will aim at a thorough treatment, in the hope that the reader will realize that all these things which he suspects to be trivial, but cannot see why, are perfectly amenable to proof. It may help the reader to think of himself as a computer with great mechanical capabilities, but with no creative insight, in those cases where he is puzzled because 'why should we prove something so utterly evident!' On the other hand the reader should keep in mind that he is not a computer and that, certainly when he gets to chapter 3, certain details should be recognized as trivial.

For the actual practice of mathematics predicate logic is doubtlessly the perfect tool, since it allows us to handle individuals. All the same we start this book with an exposition of propositional logic. There are various reasons for this choice.

In the first place propositional logic offers in miniature the problems that we meet in predicate logic, but there the additional difficulties obscure some of the relevant features e.g. the completeness theorem for propositional logic already uses the concept of 'maximal consistent set', but without the complications of the Henkin axioms.

In the second place there are a number of truly propositional matters that would be difficult to treat in a chapter on predicate logic without creating an impression of discontinuity that borders on chaos. Finally it seems a matter of sound pedagogy to let propositional logic precede predicate logic. The beginner can in a simple context get used to the proof theoretical, algebraic and model theoretic skills that would be overbearing in a first encounter with predicate logic.

1. Propositional Logic

1.1. PROPOSITIONS AND CONNECTIVES

Traditionally, logic is said to be the art (or study) of reasoning; so in order to describe logic in this tradition, we have to know what 'reasoning' is. According to some traditional views reasoning consists of the building of chains of linguistic entities by means of a certain relation '... follows from ....', a view which is good enough for our present purpose. The linguistic entities occurring in this kind of reasoning are taken to be *sentences*, i.e. entities that express a complete thought, or state of affairs. We call those sentences *declarative*. This means that, from the point of view of natural language, our class of acceptable linguistic objects is rather restricted.

Fortunately this class is wide enough when viewed from the mathematician's point of view. So far logic has been able to get along pretty well under this restriction. True, one cannot deal with questions, or performative statements, but the role of these entities is negligible in pure mathematics. I must make an exception for performative statements, which play an important role in programming; think of instructions as "goto, if ... then, else ...", etc. For reasons given below, we will, however, leave them out of consideration.

The sentences we have in mind are of the kind "25 is a square number", "every positive integer is the sum of four squares", "there is only one empty set". A common feature of all those declarative sentence is the possibility of assigning them a truth value, *true* or *false*. We do not require the actual determination of the truth value in concrete cases, such as for instance Fermat's last problem of Riemann's hypothesis. It suffices that we can "in principle" assign a truth value.

Our so-called *two-valued* logic is based on the assumption that every sentence is either true or false, it is the cornerstone of the practice of truth tables.

Some sentences are minimal in the sense that there is no proper part which is also a sentence, e.g. $5 \in \{0,1,2,5,7\}$, or $2 + 2 = 5$; others can be taken apart into smaller parts, e.g. 'ρ is rational or ρ is irrational' (where ρ is some constant). Conversely, we can build larger sentences from smaller ones by using *connectives*. We know many connectives in natural language; the following list is by no means meant to be exhaustive: *and*, *or*, *not*, *if* ... *then* ..., *but*, *since*, *as*, *for*, *although*, *neither* ... *nor* ... . In ordinary discourse, and also in informal mathematics, one uses these connectives incessantly; however, in formal mathematics we will economize somewhat on the connectives we admit. This is mainly for reasons of exactness. Compare, for example, the following two sentences: "π is irrational, but it is not algebraic", "Max is a Marxist, but he is not humorless". In the second statement we may discover a suggestion of some contrast, as if we should be surprised that Max is not humorless. In the first case such a surprise cannot be so easily imagined (unless, e.g. one has just read that almost all irrationals are algebraic); without changing the meaning one can transform this statement into "π is irrational and π is not algebraic".

So why use (in a formal text) a formulation that carries vague, emotional undertones? For these and other reasons (e.g. of economy) we stick in logic to a limited number of connectives, in particular those that have shown themselves to be useful in the daily routine of formulating and proving.

Note, however, that even here ambiguities loom. Each of the connectives has already one or more meanings in natural language. We will give some examples:

1. John drove on and hit a pedestrian.
2. John hit a pedestrian and drove on.
3. If I open the window then we'll have fresh air.
4. If I open the window then 1 + 3 = 4.
5. If 1 + 2 = 4, then we'll have fresh air.
6. John is working or he is at home.
7. Euclid was a Greek or a mathematician.

From 1 and 2 we conclude that 'and' may have an ordering function in time. Not so in mathematics; "π is irrational and 5 is positive" simply means that both parts are the case. Time just does not play a role in formal mathematics. We could not very well say "π was neither rational nor irrational before 1882". What we would want to say is "before 1882 it was unknown whether π was rational or irrational".

In the examples 3 - 5 we consider the implication. Example 3 will be generally accepted, it displays a feature that we have come to accept as inherent to implication: there is a relation between the premise and the conclusion. This feature is lacking in the examples 4 and 5. Nonetheless we will allow cases such as 4 and 5 in mathematics. There are various reasons to do so. One is the consideration that meaning should be left out of syntactical considerations. Otherwise syntax would become unwieldy and we would run into an esoteric practice of exceptional cases. This general implication, in use in mathematics, is called *material implication*. The other implications have been studied under the names of *strict implication*, *relevant implication*, etc.

Finally 6 and 7 demonstrate the use of 'or'. We tend to accept 6 and to reject 7. One mostly thinks of 'or' as something exclusive. In 6 we more or less expect John not to work at home, while 7 is unusual in the sense that we as a rule do not use 'or' when we could actually use 'and'. There is also a habit of not using a disjunction if we already know which of the two parts is the case e.g. "32 is a prime or 32 is not a prime" will be considered artificial (to say the least) by most of us, since we already know that 32 is not a prime. Yet mathematics freely uses such superfluous disjunctions, for example "$2 \geqslant 2$" (which stands for "$2 > 2$ or $2 = 2$").

In order to provide mathematics with a precise language we will create an artificial, formal language, which will lend itself to mathematical treatment. First we will define a language for propositional logic, i.e. the logic which deals only with *propositions* (sentences, statements). Later we will extend our treatment to a logic which also takes properties of individuals into account.

The process of *formalization* of propositional logic consists of two stages: (1) present a formal language, (2) specify a procedure for obtaining *valid* or *true* propositions.

We will first describe the language, using the technique of *inductive definitions*. The procedure is quite simple:

First give the smallest propositions, which are not decomposable into smaller propositions; next describe how composite propositions are constructed out of already given propositions.

1.1.1. Definition. The language of propositional logic has an alphabet consisting of
(i) proposition symbols: $p_0, p_1, p_2, \dots$,
(ii) connectives : $\wedge$, $\vee$, $\rightarrow$, $\neg$, $\leftrightarrow$, $\bot$,
(iii) auxilliary symbols : (,).

The connectives carry traditional names:

$\wedge$	-	and	-	conjunction
$\vee$	-	or	-	disjunction
$\rightarrow$	-	if ..., then ...	-	implication
$\neg$	-	not	-	negation
$\leftrightarrow$	-	iff	-	equivalence, bi-implication
$\bot$	-	falsity	-	falsum, absurdum

The proposition symbols and $\bot$ stand for the indecomposable propositions, which we call *atoms*, or *atomic propositions*.

1.1.2. Definition. The set PROP of propositions is the smallest set X with the properties.

(i) $p_i \in X \quad (i \in N), \bot \in X$,

(ii) $\varphi,\psi \in X \Rightarrow (\varphi \wedge \psi), (\varphi \vee \psi), (\varphi \to \psi), (\varphi \leftrightarrow \psi) \in X$,

(iii) $\varphi \in X \Rightarrow (\neg \varphi) \in X$.

The clauses describe exactly the possible ways of building propositions. In order to simplify clause (ii) we write $\varphi,\psi \in X \Rightarrow (\varphi \square \psi) \in X$, where $\square$ is one of the connectives $\wedge$, $\vee$, $\to$, $\leftrightarrow$.

A warning to the reader is in order here. We have used Greek letters φ,ψ in the definition; are they propositions?
Clearly we did not intend them to be so, as we want only those strings of symbols obtained by combining symbols of the alphabet in a correct way. Evidently no Greek letters come in at all! The explanation is as follows: φ and ψ are used as variables for propositions. Since we want to study logic, we must use a language to discuss it in. As a rule this language is plain, everyday English. We call the language used to discuss logic our *meta-language* and φ and ψ are *meta variables* for propositions. We could do without meta-variables by handling (ii) and (iii) verbally: if two propositions are given, then a new proposition is obtained by placing the connective $\wedge$ between them and by adding brackets in front and at the end, etc. This verbal version should suffice to convince the reader of the advantage of the mathematical machinery.

Note that we have added a rather unusual connective, $\bot$. Unusual, in the sense that it does not connect anything. *Logical constant* would be a better name. For uniformity we stick to our present usage. $\bot$ is added for convenience, one could very well do without it, but it has certain advantages.

Examples. $(p_7 \to p_0), ((\bot \vee p_{32}) \wedge (\neg p_2)) \in$ PROP.
$p_1 \leftrightarrow p_7, \neg\neg \bot, ((\to \wedge \notin$ PROP.

It is easy to show that something belongs to PROP (just carry out the construction according to 1.1.2); it is much harder to show that something does not belong to PROP. We will do one example:

$$\neg\neg \bot \notin \text{PROP}.$$

Suppose $\neg\neg \bot \in X$ and X satisfies (i), (ii), (iii) of definition 1.1.2.

We claim that $Y = X - \{\neg\neg \bot\}$ also satisfies (i), (ii) and (iii). Since $\bot, p_i \in X$, also $\bot, p_i \in Y$. If $\varphi, \psi \in Y$, then $\varphi, \psi \in X$. Since X satisfies (ii) $(\varphi \square \psi) \in X$. From the form of the expressions it is clear that $(\varphi \square \psi) \neq \neg\neg \bot$ (look at the brackets), so $(\varphi \square \psi) \in X - \{\neg\neg \bot\} = Y$. Likewise one shows that Y satisfies (iii). Hence X is not the smallest set satisfying (i), (ii) and (iii), so $\neg\neg \bot$ cannot belong to PROP.

Properties of propositions are established by an inductive procedure analogous to definition 1.1.2: first deal with the atoms, and then go from the parts to the composite propositions. This is made precise in

1.1.3. Theorem. Let A be a property, then $A(\varphi)$ holds for all $\varphi \in$ PROP if

(i) $A(p_i)$, for all i, and $A(\bot)$,

(ii) $A(\varphi), A(\psi) \Rightarrow A((\varphi \square \psi))$,

(iii) $A(\varphi) \Rightarrow A((\neg \varphi))$.

Proof. Let $X = \{\varphi \in \text{PROP} \mid A(\varphi)\}$, then X satisfies (i), (ii) and (iii) of definition 1.1.2. So PROP $\subseteq$ X, i.e. for all $\varphi \in$ PROP $A(\varphi)$ holds. □

We call an application of theorem 1.1.3 a *proof by induction on* φ. The reader will note an obvious similarity between the above theorem and the principle of complete induction in arithmetic.

1.1.4. Definition. (a) A sequence $\varphi_1, \ldots, \varphi_n$ is called a *formation sequence* of φ if $\varphi_n = \varphi$ and for all $i \leqslant n$

(i) φ_i = atomic, or

(ii) $\varphi_i = (\varphi_j \square \varphi_k)$ for certain $j,k < i$, or

(iii) $\varphi_i = (\neg \varphi_j)$ for certain $j < i$.

(b) φ is a *subformula* (cf. exercise 9) of ψ if

(i) $\varphi = \psi$, or

(ii) $\psi = (\psi_1 \square \psi_2)$ and φ is a subformula of ψ_1 or of ψ_2, or

(iii) $\psi = (\neg \psi_1)$ and φ is a subformula of ψ_1.

Examples. (a) $\bot, p_2, p_3, (\bot \vee p_2), (\neg(\bot \vee p_2)), (\neg p_3)$ and $p_3, (\neg p_3)$ are both formation sequences of $(\neg p_3)$. Note that formation sequences may contain 'garbage'.
(b) p_2 is a subformula of $((p_7 \vee (\neg p_2)) \rightarrow p_1)$. $(p_1 \rightarrow \bot)$ is a subformula of $(((p_2 \vee (p_1 \wedge p_0)) \leftrightarrow (p_1 \rightarrow \bot))$.

We now give some trivial examples of proof by induction.

1. *Each proposition has an even number of brackets.*

Proof. (i) Each atom has 0 brackets and 0 is even.

(ii) Suppose φ and ψ have 2n, resp. 2m brackets, then $(\varphi \square \psi)$ has $2(n+m+1)$ brackets.

(iii) Suppose φ has 2n brackets, then $(\neg \varphi)$ has $2(n+1)$ brackets.

2. *Each proposition has a formation sequence.*

Proof. (i) If φ is an atom, then the sequence consisting of just φ is a formation sequence of φ.

(ii) Let $\varphi_1,\ldots,\varphi_n$ and $\psi_1,\ldots,\psi_m$ be formation sequences of φ and ψ, then one easily sees that $\varphi_1,\ldots,\varphi_n, \psi_1,\ldots,\psi_m, (\varphi_n \square \psi_m)$ is a formation sequence of $(\varphi \square \psi)$.

(iii) Left to the reader.

We can improve on 2:

1.1.5. Theorem. PROP is the set of all expressions having formation sequences.

Proof. Let F be the set of all expressions (i.e. strings of symbols) having formation sequences. We have shown that PROP $\subseteq$ F.
Let φ have a formation sequence $\varphi_1,\ldots,\varphi_n$, we show $\varphi \in$ PROP by induction on n.
$n = 1$: $\varphi = \varphi_1$ and by definition φ is atomic, so $\varphi \in$ PROP. Suppose that all expressions with formation sequences of length $m < n$ are in PROP. By definition $\varphi_n = (\varphi_i \square \varphi_j)$ for $i,j < n$, or $\varphi_n = (\neg \varphi_i)$ for $i < n$, or φ_n is atomic. In the first case φ_i and φ_j have formation sequences of length $i,j < n$, so by induction hypothesis $\varphi_i,\varphi_j \in$ PROP. As PROP satisfies the clauses of definition 1.1.2, also $(\varphi_i \square \varphi_j) \in$ PROP. Treat negation likewise. The atomic case is trivial. Conclusion F $\subseteq$ PROP. $\square$

Theorem 1.1.5 is in a sense a justification of the definition of formation sequence. It also enables us to establish properties of propositions by ordinary induction on the length of formation sequences.

In arithmetic one often defines functions by recursion, e.g. exponentiation is defined by $x^0 = 1$ and $x^{y+1} = x^y \cdot x$, or the factorial function by $0! = 1$ and $(x + 1)! = x! \cdot (x + 1)$.
The justification is rather immediate: each value is obtained by using the preceding values (for positive arguments). There is an analogous principle in our

syntax.

Example: the number $b(\varphi)$, of brackets of φ, can be defined as follows:

$$b(\varphi) = 0 \text{ for } \varphi \text{ atomic,}$$
$$b((\varphi \,\square\, \psi)) = b(\varphi) + b(\psi) + 2,$$
$$b((\neg\, \varphi)) = b(\varphi) + 2.$$

The value of $b(\varphi)$ can be computed by successively computing $b(\psi)$ for its subformulae ψ.

We now formulate the general principle of

Definition by Recursion. Let mappings $H_\square : A^2 \to A$ and $H_\neg : A \to A$ be given and let H be a mapping from the set of atoms into A, then there exists exactly one mapping $F : PROP \to A$ such that

$$F(\varphi) = H(\varphi) \text{ for } \varphi \text{ atomic,}$$
$$F((\varphi \,\square\, \psi)) = H_\square(F(\varphi), F(\psi)),$$
$$F((\neg\, \varphi)) = H_\neg(F(\varphi)).$$

In concrete applications it is usually rather easily seen to be a correct principle. However, in general one has to prove the existence of a unique function satisfying the above equations. For the moment we will simply accept the principle; a proof will be presented in the Appendix.

We give some examples of definition by recursion:

1. The *rank* $r(\varphi)$ of a proposition φ is defined by

$$r(\varphi) = 0 \text{ for atomic } \varphi,$$
$$r((\varphi \,\square\, \psi)) = \max(r(\varphi), r(\psi)) + 1,$$
$$r((\neg\, \varphi)) = r(\varphi) + 1.$$

2. The (parsing) *tree* of a proposition φ is defined by

$T(\varphi) = \cdot\varphi$ for atomic

$T((\varphi \,\square\, \psi)) =$

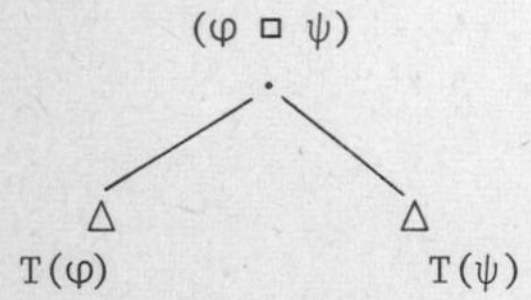

$T((\neg\, \varphi)) =$

Examples. $\varphi_1 = (p_1 \to (\bot \vee (\neg p_3)))$

$T(\varphi_1)$:

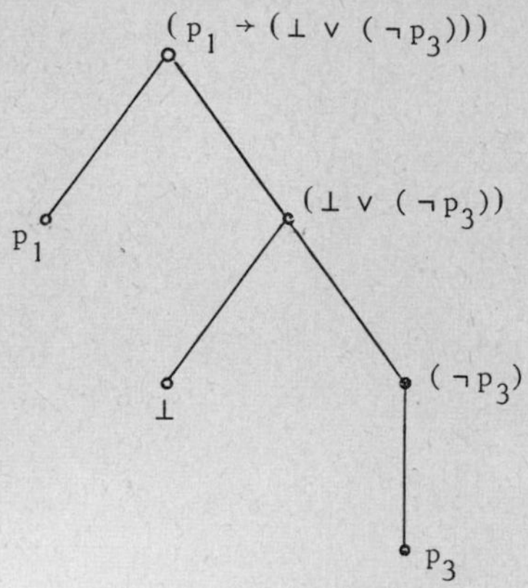

$\varphi_2 = (\neg(\neg(p_1 \wedge (\neg p_1))))$

$T(\varphi_2)$:

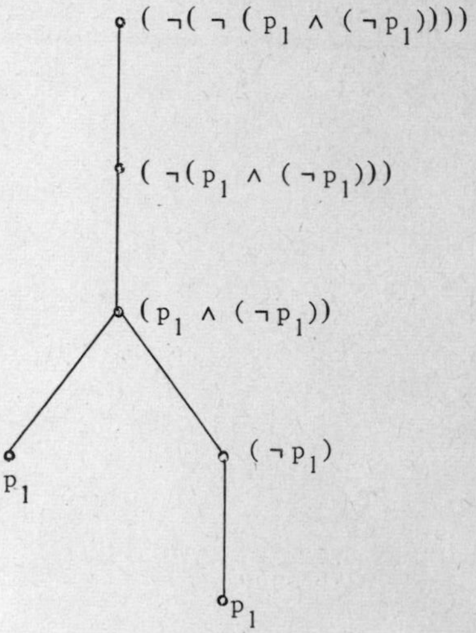

A simpler way to exhibit the trees consists of listing the atoms at the bottom, and indicating the connectives at the nodes.

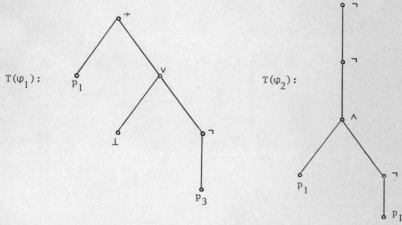

$T(\varphi_1)$:

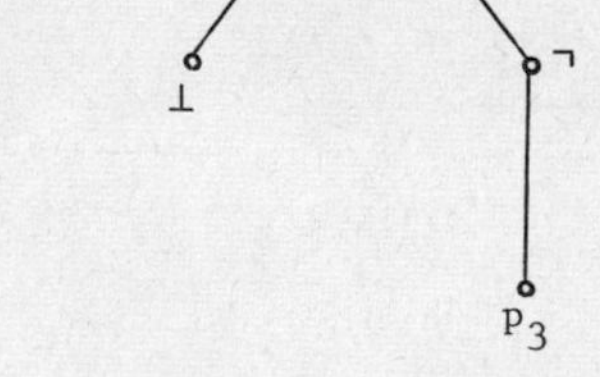

$T(\varphi_2)$:

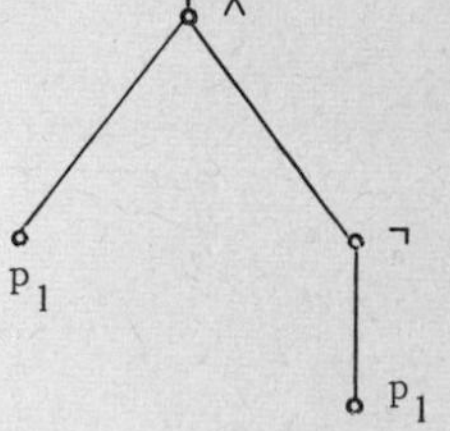

In order to simplify our notation we will economize on brackets. We will always discard the brackets at the ends and we will discard brackets in the case of negations. Furthermore we will use the convention that $\wedge$ and $\vee$ bind more strongly than $\rightarrow$ and $\leftrightarrow$ (cf. $\cdot$ and + in arithmetic), and that $\neg$ binds more strongly than the other connectives.

Examples. $\neg\varphi \vee \varphi$ stands for $((\neg\varphi) \vee \varphi)$,
$\neg(\neg\neg\neg\varphi \wedge \bot)$ stands for $(\neg((\neg(\neg(\neg\varphi))) \wedge \bot))$,
$\varphi \vee \psi \rightarrow \varphi$ stands for $((\varphi \vee \psi) \rightarrow \varphi)$,
$\varphi \rightarrow \varphi \vee (\psi \rightarrow \chi)$ stands for $(\varphi \rightarrow (\varphi \vee (\psi \rightarrow \chi)))$.

Warning: note that those abbreviations are, properly speaking, no propositions.

EXERCISES.

1. Give formation sequences of
   $(\neg p_2 \rightarrow (p_3 \vee (p_1 \leftrightarrow p_2))) \wedge \neg p_3$,
   $(p_7 \rightarrow \neg\bot) \leftrightarrow ((p_4 \wedge \neg p_2) \rightarrow p_1)$,
   $(((p_1 \rightarrow p_2) \rightarrow p_1) \rightarrow p_2) \rightarrow p_1$.

2. Show that $((\rightarrow \notin PROP$.

3. Let φ be a subformula of ψ. Show that φ occurs in each formation sequence of ψ.

4. If φ occurs in a shortest formation sequence of ψ then φ is a subformula of ψ.

5. Let r be the rank function.
   (a) Show that $r(\varphi) \leqslant$ number of connectives of φ,
   (b) Give examples of φ such that $<$ or $=$ holds in (a),
   (c) Find the rank of the propositions in exercise 1.

6. (a) Determine the trees of the propositions in exercise 1,
   (b) Determine the propositions with the following trees.

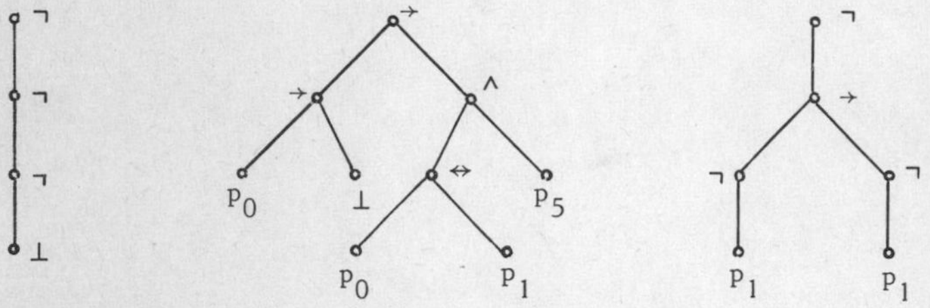

7. Let $|T(\varphi)|$ be the number of nodes of $T(\varphi)$. By the "number of connectives in φ" we mean the number of occurrences of connectives in φ.

   (a) If φ does not contain $\perp$, show: number of connectives of φ + number of atoms of $\varphi \leqslant |T(\varphi)|$,

   (b) The number of subformulas of $\varphi \leqslant |T(\varphi)|$,

   (c) A branch of a tree is a maximal linearly ordered set.
   The length of a branch is the number of its nodes minus one. Show that $r(\varphi)$ is the length of a longest branch in $T(\varphi)$.

   (d) Let φ not contain $\perp$. Show: the number of connectives in φ + the number of atoms of $\varphi \leqslant 2^{r(\varphi)+1} - 1$.

8. Show that a proposition with n connectives has at most $2n + 1$ subformulas.

9. Recast definition 1.1.4(b) in the form of a definition by recursion of the function sub: PROP $\to \mathcal{P}$(PROP) which assigns to each proposition φ the set sub(φ) of its subformulas.

1.2. SEMANTICS

The task of interpreting propositional logic is simplified by the fact that the entities considered have a simple structure. The propositions are built up from rough blocks by adding connectives.
The simplest parts (atoms) are of the form "grass is green", "Mary likes Goethe", "6 - 3 = 2", which are simply *true* or *false*. We extend this assignment of *truth values* to composite propositions, by reflection on the meaning of the logical connectives.

Let us agree to use 1 and 0 instead of 'true' and 'false'. The problem we are faced with is how to interprete $\varphi \square \psi$, $\neg \varphi$, given the truth values of φ and ψ.

We will illustrate the solution by considering the in-out-table for Messrs. Smith and Jones.

Conjunction.

	in	out
Smith	×	
Jones	×	

A visitor who wants to see both Smith and Jones wants the table to be in the position shown here, i.e.

"Smith is in" $\wedge$ "Jones is in" is true iff
"Smith is in" is true and "Jones is in" is true.

We write $v(\varphi) = 1$ (resp. 0) for "φ is true" (resp. false). Then the above consideration can be stated as $v(\varphi \wedge \psi) = 1$ iff $v(\varphi) = v(\varphi) = 1$, or $v(\varphi \wedge \psi) = \min(v(\varphi), v(\psi))$.
One can also write it in the form of a *truth table*:

$\wedge$	0	1
0	0	0
1	0	1

Disjunction.

If a visitor wants to see one of the partners, no matter who, he wants the table to be in one of the positions

	in	out
Smith	×	
Jones		×

	in	out
Smith		×
Jones	×	

	in	out
Smith	×	
Jones	×	

In the last case he can make a choice, but that is no problem, he wants to see at least one of the gentlemen.
In our notation, the interpretation of $\vee$ is given by

$$v(\varphi \vee \psi) = 1 \quad \text{iff} \quad v(\varphi) = 1 \quad \text{or} \quad v(\psi) = 1.$$

Shorter: $v(\varphi \vee \psi) = \max(v(\varphi), v(\psi))$.

In truth table form:

$\vee$	0	1
0	0	1
1	1	1

Negation.

The visitor who is solely interested in our Smith will state that "Smith is not in" if the table is in the position

	in	out
Smith		×

So "Smith is not in" is true if "Smith is in" is false. We write this as $v(\neg\varphi) = 1$ iff $v(\varphi) = 0$, or $v(\neg\varphi) = 1 - v(\varphi)$.

In truth table form:

$\neg$	
0	1
1	0

Implication.

Our legendary visitor has been informed that "Jones is in if Smith is in". Now he can at least predict the following positions of the table

	in	out
Smith	×	
Jones	×	

	in	out
Smith		×
Jones		×

If the table is in the position

	in	out
Smith	×	
Jones		×

,

then he knows that the information was false.

The remaining case

	in	out
Smith		×
Jones	×	

cannot be dealt with in such a simple way. There evidently is no reason to consider the information false, rather 'not very helpful', or 'irrelevant'. However, we have committed ourselves to the position that each statement is true or false, so we decide to call "If Smith is in, then Jones is in" true in the present case. The reader should realize that we have made a deliberate choice here; a choice that will prove a happy one in view of the elegance of the system that results. There is no compelling reason, however, to stick to the notion of implication that we just introduced. Various other notions have been studied in the literature, for mathematical purposes our notion (also called 'material implication') is however perfectly suitable.

Note that there is just one case in which an implication is false (see the truth table below), one should keep this observation in mind for future application.

In our notation the interpretation of implication is given by $v(\varphi \to \psi) = 0$ iff $v(\varphi) = 1$ and $v(\psi) = 0$.

Its truth table is:

$\to$	0	1
0	1	1
1	0	1

Equivalence.

If our visitor knows that "Smith is in if and only if Jones is in, then he knows that they are either both in, or both out. Hence $v(\varphi \leftrightarrow \psi) = 1$ iff $v(\varphi) = v(\psi)$.

The truth table of $\leftrightarrow$ is:

$\leftrightarrow$	0	1
0	1	0
1	0	1

Falsum.

An absurdity, such as "$0 \neq 0$", "some odd numbers are even", "I am not myself", cannot be true. So we put $v(\bot) = 0$.

We collect the foregoing in

1.2.1. Definition. A mapping $v : \text{PROP} \to \{0,1\}$ is a *valuation* if

$$v(\varphi \wedge \psi) = \min(v(\varphi), v(\psi))$$
$$v(\varphi \vee \psi) = \max(v(\varphi), v(\psi))$$
$$v(\varphi \to \psi) = 0 \Leftrightarrow v(\varphi) = 1 \text{ and } v(\psi) = 0$$
$$v(\varphi \leftrightarrow \psi) = 1 \Leftrightarrow v(\varphi) = v(\psi)$$
$$v(\neg \varphi) = 1 - v(\varphi)$$
$$v(\bot) = 0$$

If a valuation is only given for atoms then it is, by virtue of the definition by recursion, possible to extend it to all propositions.

1.2.2. Theorem. If v' is a mapping from the atoms in $\{0,1\}$, satisfying $v'(\bot) = 0$, then there exists a unique valuation v, such that $v(\varphi) = v'(\varphi)$ for atomic φ.

From this theorem it appears that there are many valuations (cf. exercise 4).

The *value* $v(\varphi)$ *of* φ *under* v only depends on the values of v on atomic subformulae of φ:

1.2.3. Lemma. If $v(p_i) = v'(p_i)$ for all p_i occurring in φ, then $v(\varphi) = v'(\varphi)$.

Proof. An easy induction on φ. □

An important subset of PROP is that of all propositions φ which are *always true*, i.e. true under all valuations.

1.2.4. Definition. (i) φ is a *tautology* if $v(\varphi) = 1$ for all valuations v,

(ii) $\models \varphi$ stands for 'φ is a tautology',

(iii) Let Γ be a set of propositions, then $\Gamma \models \varphi$ iff for all v:

$(v(\psi) = 1 \text{ for all } \psi \in \Gamma) \Rightarrow v(\varphi) = 1.$

In words: $\Gamma \models \varphi$ holds iff φ is true under all valuations that make all ψ in Γ true. We say that φ is a semantical consequence of Γ. We write $\Gamma \not\models \varphi$ if $\Gamma \models \varphi$ is not the case.

Examples.

1) $\models \varphi \to \varphi$; $\models \neg\neg\varphi \to \varphi$; $\models \varphi \vee \psi \leftrightarrow \psi \vee \varphi$,

2) $\varphi, \psi \models \varphi \wedge \psi$; $\varphi, \varphi \to \psi \models \psi$; $\varphi \to \psi, \neg\psi \models \neg\varphi$.

It is often convenient to substitute propositions for subformulae; it turns out to be sufficient to define substitution for atoms only.

We write $\varphi[\psi/p_i]$ for the proposition obtained by replacing all occurrences of p_i in φ by ψ. As a matter of fact, substitution of ψ for p_i defines a mapping of PROP into PROP, which can be given by recursion (on φ):

$$\varphi[\psi/p_i] = \begin{cases} \varphi \text{ if } \varphi \text{ atomic and } \varphi \neq p_i \\ \psi \text{ if } \varphi = p_i \end{cases}$$

$$(\varphi_1 \square \varphi_2)[\psi/p_i] = \varphi_1[\psi/p_i] \square \varphi_2[\psi/p_i]$$

$$(\neg\varphi)[\psi/p_i] = \neg\varphi[\psi/p_i].$$

The following theorem tells us that by substituting equivalent parts we obtain equivalent propositions.

1.2.5. Substitution theorem. If $\models \varphi_1 \leftrightarrow \varphi_2$, then $\models \psi[\varphi_1/p] \leftrightarrow \psi[\varphi_2/p]$, where p is an atom.

Proof. Induction on ψ.

1. ψ atomic. If $\psi \neq p$, then $\psi[\varphi_1/p] = \psi = \psi[\varphi_2/p]$, and for each valuation $v(\psi \leftrightarrow \psi) = 1$ (see def. 1.2.1) so $\models \psi[\varphi_1/p] \leftrightarrow \psi[\varphi_2/p]$.
   If $\psi = p$, then $\psi[\varphi_i/p] = \varphi_i$, and the result follows from the premise.

2. $\psi = \psi_1 \square \psi_2$. Induction hypothesis: $\models \psi_i[\varphi_1/p] \leftrightarrow \psi_i[\varphi_2/p]$, or $v(\psi_i[\varphi_1/p]) = v(\psi_i[\varphi_2/p])$. Since the value
   $v((\psi_1 \square \psi_2)[\varphi_j/p]) = v(\psi_1[\varphi_j/p] \square \psi_2[\varphi_j/p])$ is uniquely determined by the values of its parts we immediately conclude
   $v((\psi_1 \square \psi_2)[\varphi_1/p]) = v((\psi_1 \square \psi_2)[\varphi_2/p])$ for all v. So
   $\models (\psi_1 \square \psi_2)[\varphi_1/p] \leftrightarrow (\psi_1 \square \psi_2)[\varphi_2/p]$.

3. $\psi = \neg \psi_1$. Induction hypothesis: $\models \psi_1[\varphi_1/p] \leftrightarrow \psi_1[\varphi_2/p]$, or $v(\psi_1[\varphi_1/p]) = v(\psi_1[\varphi_2/p])$ for all v.
   Now $v((\neg \psi_1)[\varphi_1/p]) = v(\neg \psi_1[\varphi_1/p]) = 1 - v(\psi_1[\varphi_1/p]) = 1 - v(\psi_1[\varphi_2/p]) =$
   $= v(\neg \psi_1[\varphi_2/p])$ for all v.
   So $\models (\neg \psi_1)[\varphi_1/p] \leftrightarrow (\neg \psi_1)[\varphi_2/p]$.

There are various techniques for testing tautologies. One such (rather slow) technique uses truth tables. We give one example:

$$(\varphi \to \psi) \leftrightarrow (\neg \psi \to \neg \varphi)$$

φ	ψ	$\neg \varphi$	$\neg \psi$	$\varphi \to \psi$	$\neg\psi \to \neg \varphi$	$(\varphi \to \psi) \leftrightarrow (\neg \psi \to \neg\varphi)$
0	0	1	1	1	1	1
0	1	1	0	1	1	1
1	0	0	1	0	0	1
1	1	0	0	1	1	1

The last column consists of 1's only. Since, by lemma 1.2.3 only the values φ and ψ are relevant, we had to check 2^2 cases. If there are n (atomic) parts we need

2^n lines.

One can compress the above table a bit, by writing it in the following form:

$(\varphi$	$\rightarrow$	$\psi)$	$\longleftrightarrow$	$(\neg\,\psi$	$\rightarrow$	$\neg\,\varphi)$
0	1	0	1	1	1	1
0	1	1	1	0	1	1
1	0	0	1	1	0	0
1	1	1	1	0	1	0

EXERCISES.

1. Check by the truth table method which of the following propositions are tautologies
   (*a*) $(\neg\varphi \vee \psi) \leftrightarrow (\psi \rightarrow \varphi)$
   (*b*) $\varphi \rightarrow ((\psi \rightarrow \sigma) \rightarrow ((\varphi \rightarrow \psi) \rightarrow (\varphi \rightarrow \sigma)))$
   (*c*) $(\varphi \rightarrow \neg\varphi) \leftrightarrow \neg\varphi$
   (*d*) $\neg(\varphi \rightarrow \neg\varphi)$
   (*e*) $(\varphi \rightarrow (\psi \rightarrow \sigma)) \leftrightarrow ((\varphi \wedge \psi) \rightarrow \sigma)$
   (*f*) $\varphi \vee \neg\varphi$ (principle of the excluded third)
   (*g*) $\bot \leftrightarrow (\varphi \wedge \neg\varphi)$
   (*h*) $\bot \rightarrow \varphi$ (ex falso sequitur quodlibet)

2. Show (*a*) $\varphi \models \varphi$;
   (*b*) $\varphi \models \psi$ and $\psi \models \sigma \Rightarrow \varphi \models \sigma$;
   (*c*) $\models \varphi \rightarrow \psi \Rightarrow \varphi \models \psi$.

3. Determine $\varphi[\neg p_0 \rightarrow p_3/p_0]$ for $\varphi = p_1 \wedge p_0 \rightarrow (p_0 \rightarrow p_3)$;
   $\varphi = (p_3 \leftrightarrow p_0) \vee (p_2 \rightarrow \neg p_0)$.

4. Show that there are $2^{\aleph_0}$ valuations.

5. Show $v(\varphi \wedge \psi) = v(\varphi) \cdot v(\psi)$
   $v(\varphi \vee \psi) = v(\varphi) + v(\psi) - v(\varphi) \cdot v(\psi)$
   $v(\varphi \rightarrow \psi) = 1 - v(\varphi) + v(\varphi) \cdot v(\psi)$
   $v(\varphi \leftrightarrow \psi) = 1 - |v(\varphi) - v(\psi)|$

6. Show $v(\varphi \rightarrow \psi) = 1 \Leftrightarrow v(\varphi) \leqslant v(\psi)$.

1.3. SOME PROPERTIES OF PROPOSITIONAL LOGIC

On the basis of the previous sections we can already prove a lot of theorems about propositional logic. One of the earliest discoveries concerning propositional logic was its similarity with algebra.
Following Boole, an extensive study of the algebraic properties was made by a number of logicians. The purely algebraic aspects have since then been studied in the so-called *Boolean Algebra*.

We will just mention a few of those algebraic laws.

1.3.1. Theorem. The following propositions are tautologies

$(\varphi \vee \psi) \vee \sigma \leftrightarrow \varphi \vee (\psi \vee \sigma)$ $\quad$ $(\varphi \wedge \psi) \wedge \sigma \leftrightarrow \varphi \wedge (\psi \wedge \sigma)$

associativity

$\varphi \vee \psi \leftrightarrow \psi \vee \varphi$ $\quad$ $\varphi \wedge \psi \leftrightarrow \psi \wedge \varphi$

commutativity

$\varphi \vee (\psi \wedge \sigma) \leftrightarrow (\varphi \vee \psi) \wedge (\varphi \vee \sigma)$ $\quad$ $\varphi \wedge (\psi \vee \sigma) \leftrightarrow (\varphi \wedge \psi) \vee (\varphi \wedge \sigma)$

distributivity

$\neg(\varphi \vee \psi) \leftrightarrow \neg\varphi \wedge \neg\psi$ $\quad$ $\neg(\varphi \wedge \psi) \leftrightarrow \neg\varphi \vee \neg\psi$

De Morgan's laws

$\varphi \vee \varphi \leftrightarrow \varphi$ $\quad$ $\varphi \wedge \varphi \leftrightarrow \varphi$

idempotency

$\neg\neg\varphi \leftrightarrow \varphi$

double negation law

Proof. Check the truth tables or do a little computation.
E.g. De Morgan's law: $v(\neg(\varphi \vee \psi)) = 1 \Leftrightarrow v(\varphi \vee \psi) = 0 \Leftrightarrow v(\varphi) = v(\psi) = 0$
$\Leftrightarrow v(\neg\varphi) = v(\neg\psi) = 1 \Leftrightarrow v(\neg\varphi \wedge \neg\psi) = 1$.
So $v(\neg(\varphi \vee \psi)) = v(\neg\varphi \wedge \neg\psi)$ for all v, i.e. $\models \neg(\varphi \vee \psi) \leftrightarrow \neg\varphi \vee \neg\psi$.
The reader should prove the remaining tautologies by himself. □

In order to apply the previous theorem in "logical calculations" we need a few more equivalences. This is demonstrated in the simple equivalence $\models \varphi \wedge (\varphi \vee \psi) \leftrightarrow \varphi$ (exercise for the reader). For, by the distributive law $\models \varphi \wedge (\varphi \vee \psi) \leftrightarrow (\varphi \wedge \varphi) \vee (\varphi \wedge \psi)$ and $\models (\varphi \wedge \varphi) \vee (\varphi \wedge \psi) \leftrightarrow \varphi \vee (\varphi \wedge \psi)$, by idempotency and the substitution theorem. So $\models \varphi \wedge (\varphi \vee \psi) \leftrightarrow \varphi \vee (\varphi \wedge \psi)$: just applying the above laws will not eliminate ψ!

We list a few more convenient properties.

1.3.2. Lemma. If $\models \varphi \rightarrow \psi$, then $\models \varphi \wedge \psi \leftrightarrow \varphi$ and
$\models \varphi \vee \psi \leftrightarrow \psi$

Proof. By exercise 6 of section 1.2 , $\models \varphi \rightarrow \psi$ implies $v(\varphi) \leqslant v(\psi)$ for all v.
So $v(\varphi \wedge \psi) = \min(v(\varphi), v(\psi)) = v(\varphi)$ and $v(\varphi \vee \psi) = \max(v(\varphi), v(\psi)) = v(\psi)$ for all v. □

1.3.3. Lemma. (a) $\models \varphi \Rightarrow \models \varphi \wedge \psi \leftrightarrow \psi$
(b) $\models \varphi \Rightarrow \models \neg\varphi \vee \psi \leftrightarrow \psi$
(c) $\models \bot \vee \psi \leftrightarrow \psi$
(d) $\models \neg\bot \wedge \psi \leftrightarrow \psi$

Proof. Left to the reader.

The following theorem establishes some equivalences involving various connectives.

1.3.4. Theorem. (a) $\models (\varphi \leftrightarrow \psi) \leftrightarrow (\varphi \rightarrow \psi) \wedge (\psi \rightarrow \varphi)$
(b) $\models (\varphi \rightarrow \psi) \leftrightarrow (\neg\varphi \vee \psi)$
(c) $\models \varphi \vee \psi \leftrightarrow (\neg\varphi \rightarrow \psi)$
(d) $\models \varphi \vee \psi \leftrightarrow \neg(\neg\varphi \wedge \neg\psi)$
(e) $\models \varphi \wedge \psi \leftrightarrow \neg(\neg\varphi \vee \neg\psi)$
(f) $\models \neg\varphi \leftrightarrow (\varphi \rightarrow \bot)$
(g) $\models \bot \leftrightarrow \varphi \wedge \neg\varphi$

Proof. Compute the truth values of the left-hand and right-hand sides. □

The above theorem tells us that we can "define" up to logical equivalence all connectives in terms of $\{\vee,\neg\}$, or $\{\rightarrow,\neg\}$, or $\{\wedge,\neg\}$, or $\{\rightarrow,\bot\}$.
That is, we can find e.g. a proposition involving only $\vee$ and $\neg$, which is equivalent to $\varphi \leftrightarrow \psi$, etc.

We now have enough material to handle logic as if it were algebra. For convenience we write φ eq. ψ for $\models \varphi \leftrightarrow \psi$.

1.3.5. Lemma. eq. is an equivalence relation on PROP,
i.e. φ eq. φ (reflexivity),
φ eq. $\psi \Rightarrow \psi$ eq. φ (symmetry),
φ eq. ψ and ψ eq. $\sigma \Rightarrow \varphi$ eq. σ (transitivity).

Proof. Use $\models \varphi \leftrightarrow \psi$ iff $v(\varphi) = v(\psi)$ for all v. $\square$

We give some examples of algebraic computations, which establish a chain of equivalences.

1. $\models [\varphi \rightarrow (\psi \rightarrow \sigma)] \leftrightarrow [\varphi \wedge \psi \rightarrow \sigma]$,

$\varphi \rightarrow (\psi \rightarrow \sigma)$	eq.	$\neg \varphi \vee (\psi \rightarrow \sigma)$,	(1.3.4(b))
$\neg \varphi \vee (\psi \rightarrow \sigma)$	eq.	$\neg \varphi \vee (\neg \psi \vee \sigma)$,	(1.3.4(b) and subst. thm.)
$\neg \varphi \vee (\neg \psi \vee \sigma)$	eq.	$(\neg \varphi \vee \neg \psi) \vee \sigma$,	(ass.)
$(\neg \varphi \vee \neg \psi) \vee \sigma$	eq.	$\neg (\varphi \wedge \psi) \vee \sigma$,	(*De Morgan* and subst. thm.)
$\neg (\varphi \vee \psi) \vee \sigma$	eq.	$(\varphi \wedge \psi) \rightarrow \sigma$,	(1.3.4(b))
So $\varphi \rightarrow (\psi \rightarrow \sigma)$	eq.	$(\varphi \wedge \psi) \rightarrow \sigma$.	

We now leave out the references to the facts used, and make one long string.

2. $\models (\varphi \rightarrow \psi) \leftrightarrow (\neg \psi \rightarrow \neg \varphi)$,

$\neg \psi \rightarrow \neg \varphi$ eq. $\neg\neg \psi \vee \neg \varphi$ eq. $\psi \vee \neg \varphi$ eq. $\neg \varphi \vee \psi$ eq. $\varphi \rightarrow \psi$

3. $\models \varphi \rightarrow (\psi \rightarrow \varphi)$,

$\varphi \rightarrow (\psi \rightarrow \varphi)$ eq. $\neg \varphi \vee (\neg \psi \vee \varphi)$ eq. $(\neg \varphi \vee \varphi) \vee \neg \psi$.

Since the last one is a tautology so also is the first one.

We have seen that $\vee$ and $\wedge$ are associative, therefore we adopt the convention, also used in algebra, to delete brackets in iterated disjunction and conjunctions; i.e. we write $\varphi_1 \vee \varphi_2 \vee \varphi_3 \vee \varphi_4$, etc.
No matter how we restore (syntactically correctly) the brackets, the resulting formula is determined uniquely up to equivalence.

Have we introduced *all* connectives so far? Obviously not. We can always invent new ones. Here is a famous one, introduced by Sheffer; $\varphi|\psi$ stands for "not both φ and ψ". More precise: $\varphi|\psi$ is given by the following truth table

|	0	1
0	1	1
1	1	0

Let us say than an n-ary logical connective \$ is *defined* by its truth table, or by its valuation function, i.e. $v(\$(\varphi_1,\dots,\varphi_n)) = f(v(\varphi_1),\dots,v(\varphi_n))$. Although we can apparently introduce many new connectives in this way, there are no surprises in stock for us, as all of those connectives are definable in terms of $\vee$ and $\neg$:

1.3.6. Theorem. For each n-ary connective \$ defined by its valuation function, there is a proposition τ, containing only $\varphi_1,\dots,\varphi_n$, $\vee$ and $\neg$, such that $\models \tau \leftrightarrow \$(\varphi_1,\dots,\varphi_n)$.

Proof. Induction on n.
For n = 1 there are 4 possible connectives with truth tables

1	
0	0
1	0

2	
0	1
1	1

3	
0	0
1	1

4	
0	1
1	0

One easily checks that the propositions $\neg(\varphi \vee \neg\varphi)$, $\varphi \vee \neg\varphi$, φ and $\neg\varphi$ will meet the requirements.

Suppose that for all n-ary connectives propositions have been found. Consider $\$(\varphi_1,\dots,\varphi_n, \varphi_{n+1})$ with truth table:

φ_1	φ_2	φ_n	φ_{n+1}	$\$(\varphi_1,\dots,\varphi_n, \varphi_{n+1})$
0	0	0	0	i_1
.	.	0	1	i_2
.	0	1	.	.
.	1	1	.	.
0	.	.	.	.
.	1	.	.	.
1	0	.	.	.
.	.	.	.	.
.	.	.	.	.
.	0	.	.	.
.	1	0	.	.
.	.	0	.	.
1	.	1	0	.
.	.	1	1	$i_{2^{n+1}}$

where $i_k \leqslant 1$.

We consider two auxilliary connectives $\$_1$ and $\$_2$ defined by $\$_1(\varphi_2,\dots,\varphi_{n+1}) = \$(\varphi_1 \wedge \neg\varphi_1, \varphi_2,\dots,\varphi_{n+1})$ and $\$_2(\varphi_2,\dots,\varphi_{n+1}) = \$(\varphi_1 \vee \neg\varphi_1,\varphi_2,\dots,\varphi_{n+1})$ (given by the upper and lower half of the above table).

By the induction hypothesis there are propositions σ_1 and σ_2, containing only $\varphi_2,\dots,\varphi_{n+1}$, $\vee$ and $\neg$ so that $\models \$_i(\varphi_2,\dots,\varphi_{n+1}) \leftrightarrow \sigma_i$.
From those two propositions we can construct the proposition τ:
$\tau := (\varphi_1 \to \sigma_2) \wedge (\neg\varphi_1 \to \sigma_1)$. Claim: $\models \$(\varphi_1,\dots,\varphi_{n+1}) \leftrightarrow \tau$.
If $v(\varphi_1) = 0$, then $v(\varphi_1 \to \sigma_2) = 1$, so $v(\tau) = v(\neg\varphi_1 \to \sigma_1)$, and since $v(\neg\varphi_1) = 1$: $v(\neg\varphi_1 \to \sigma_1) = v(\sigma_1) = v(\$_1(\varphi_2,\dots,\varphi_{n+1})) = v(\$(\varphi_1,\varphi_2,\dots,\varphi_{n+1}))$, using $v(\varphi_1) = 0 = v(\varphi_1 \wedge \neg\varphi_1)$.

The case $v(\varphi_1) = 1$ is similar.
Now, expressing $\to$ and $\wedge$ in terms of $\vee$ and $\neg$ (1.3.4), we have $v(\tau') = v\,\$(\varphi_1,\dots,\varphi_{n+1})$ for all v (another use of lemma 1.2.3), where τ' eq. τ and τ' contains only the connectives $\vee$ and $\neg$.

For another solution see exercise 7.

The above theorem and theorem 1.3.4 are pragmatic justifications for our choice of the truth table for $\to$: we get an extremely elegant and useful theory. Theorem 1.3.6 is usually expressed by saying that $\vee$ and $\neg$ form a *functionally complete* set of connectives. Likewise $\wedge,\neg$ and $\to,\neg$ and $\perp,\to$ form functionally complete sets.

In analogy to the Σ and Π from algebra we introduce finite disjunctions and conjunctions.

1.3.7. <u>Definition.</u>

$$\bigwedge_{i\leq 0} \varphi_i = \varphi_0$$

$$\bigwedge_{i\leq n+1} \varphi_i = \bigwedge_{i\leq n} \varphi_i \wedge \varphi_{n+1}$$

$$\bigvee_{i\leq 0} \varphi_i = \varphi_0$$

$$\bigvee_{i\leq n+1} \varphi_i = \bigvee_{i\leq n} \varphi_i \vee \varphi_{n+1}$$

1.3.8. <u>Definition.</u> If $\varphi = \bigwedge_{i\leq n} \bigvee_{j\leq m_i} \varphi_{ij}$, where φ_{ij} is atomic or the negation of an atom, then φ is a *conjunctive normal form*.

If $\varphi = \bigvee_{i \leq n} \bigwedge_{j \leq m_i} \varphi_{ij}$, where φ_{ij} is atomic or the negation of an atom, then φ is a *disjunctive normal form*.

The normal forms are analogous to the well-known normal forms in algebra: $ax^2 + byx$ is "normal", whereas $x(ax + by)$ is not. One can obtain normal forms by simply "multiplying", i.e. repeated application of distributive laws. In algebra there is only one "normal form"; in logic there is a certain duality between $\wedge$ and $\vee$, so that we have two normal form theorems.

1.3.9. Theorem. For each φ there are conjunctive normal forms φ^c and disjunctive normal forms φ^d, such that $\models \varphi \leftrightarrow \varphi^c$ and $\models \varphi \leftrightarrow \varphi^d$.

Proof. First eliminate all connectives other then $\wedge$, $\vee$ and $\neg$. Then prove the theorem by induction on the resulting proposition in the restricted language of $\wedge$, $\vee$ and $\neg$.

(a) φ is atomic. Then $\varphi^c = \varphi^d = \varphi$.

(b) $\varphi = \psi \wedge \sigma$. Then $\varphi^c = \psi^c \wedge \sigma^c$. In order to obtain a disjunctive normal form we consider $\psi^d = \bigvee \psi_i$, $\sigma^d = \bigvee \sigma_j$, where the ψ_i's and σ_j's are conjunctions of atoms and negations of atoms.

Now $\varphi = \psi \wedge \sigma$ eq. $\psi^d \wedge \sigma^d$ eq. $\bigvee_{i,j} (\psi_i \wedge \sigma_j)$.

The last proposition is in normal form, so we equate φ^d to it.

(c) $\varphi = \psi \vee \sigma$. Similar to *(b)*.

(d) $\varphi = \neg \psi$. By the induction hypothesis ψ has normal forms ψ^d and ψ^c.

$\neg \psi$ eq. $\neg \psi^c$ eq. $\neg \bigwedge \bigvee \psi_{ij}$ eq. $\bigvee \bigwedge \neg \psi_{ij}$ eq. $\bigvee \bigwedge \psi'_{ij}$, where $\psi'_{ij} = \neg \psi_{ij}$ if ψ_{ij} is atomic, and $\psi_{ij} = \neg \psi'_{ij}$ if ψ_{ij} is the negation of an atom.

(Observe $\neg\neg \psi_{ij}$ eq. ψ_{ij}). Clearly $\bigvee \bigwedge \psi'_{ij}$ is a disjunctive normal form for φ. The conjunctive normal form is left to the reader. □

For another proof of the normal form theorems see exercise 7.

When looking at the algebra of logic in theorem 1.3.1, we saw that $\vee$ and $\wedge$ behaved in a very similar way, to the extent that the same laws hold for both. We will make this 'duality' precise. For this purpose we consider a language with only the connectives $\vee$, $\wedge$ and $\neg$.

1.3.10. Definition. Define a mapping $* : \text{PROP} \to \text{PROP}$ recursively by

$$\varphi^* = \neg \varphi \text{ if } \varphi \text{ is atomic,}$$

$$(\varphi \wedge \psi)^* = \varphi^* \vee \psi^*,$$

$(\varphi \vee \psi)^* = \varphi^* \wedge \psi^*,$
$(\neg \varphi)^* \quad = \neg \varphi^*.$

Example. $((p_0 \wedge \neg p_1) \vee p_2)^* = (p_0 \wedge \neg p_1)^* \wedge p_2^* =$
$(p_0^* \vee (\neg p_1)^*) \wedge \neg p_2 = (\neg p_0 \vee \neg p_1^*) \wedge \neg p_2 = (\neg p_0 \vee \neg\neg p_1) \wedge \neg p_2$
eq. $(\neg p_0 \vee p_1) \wedge \neg p_2$.

Note that the effect of the $*$-translation boils down to taking the negation and applying De Morgan's laws.

1.3.11. Lemma. $v(\varphi^*) = 1 - v(\varphi)$

Proof. Induction on φ.
For φ atomic $v(\varphi^*) = v(\neg \varphi) = 1 - v(\varphi)$.
$v((\varphi \wedge \psi)^*) = v(\varphi^* \vee \psi^*) = \max(v(\varphi^*), v(\psi^*)) = \max(1 - v(\varphi), 1 - v(\psi)) =$
$\max(v(\neg \varphi), v(\neg \psi)) = v(\neg \varphi \vee \neg \psi) = v(\neg (\varphi \wedge \psi)) = 1 - v(\varphi \wedge \psi)$.
$v((\varphi \vee \psi)^*)$ and $v((\neg\varphi)^*)$ are left to the reader. □

1.3.12. Corollary. $\models \varphi^* \leftrightarrow \neg \varphi$.

Proof. Immediate from lemma 1.3.11. □

So far this is not the proper duality we have been looking for. We really just want to interchange $\wedge$ and $\vee$. So we introduce a new translation.

1.3.13. Definition. The duality mapping ^{d} : PROP $\to$ PROP is recursively defined by

$\varphi^d \quad = \varphi$ for atomic,
$(\varphi \wedge \psi)^d = \varphi^d \vee \psi^d,$
$(\varphi \vee \psi)^d = \varphi^d \wedge \psi^d,$
$(\neg \varphi)^d \quad = \neg \varphi^d$

1.3.14. Duality theorem. $\models \varphi \leftrightarrow \psi \Leftrightarrow \models \varphi^d \leftrightarrow \psi^d$.

Proof. We use the $*$-translation as an intermediate step. Let us introduce the notion of simultaneous substitution to simplify the proof.
$\sigma[\tau_0,\ldots,\tau_n / p_0,\ldots,p_n]$ is obtained by substituting τ_i for p_i for all $i \leqslant n$ simultaneously (see exercise 15).

$$\varphi^d[\neg\neg p_0,\ldots,\neg\neg p_n / p_0,\ldots,p_n] = \varphi^*[\neg p_0,\ldots,\neg p_n / p_0,\ldots,p_n].$$

By the substitution theorem $\models \varphi^d \leftrightarrow \varphi^*[\neg p_0,\ldots,\neg p_n / p_0,\ldots,p_n]$. The same

equivalence holds for ψ.
By corollary 1.3.12 $\models \varphi^* \leftrightarrow \neg \varphi$, $\models \psi^* \leftrightarrow \neg \psi$. Since $\models \varphi \leftrightarrow \psi$, also $\models \neg \varphi \leftrightarrow \neg \psi$.
Hence $\models \varphi^* \leftrightarrow \psi^*$, and therefore
$\models \varphi^*[\neg p_0,\dots,\neg p_n \;/\; p_0,\dots,p_n] \leftrightarrow \psi^*[\neg p_0,\dots,\neg p_n \;/\; p_0,\dots,p_n]$.
Using the above relation between φ^d and φ^* we now obtain $\models \varphi^d \leftrightarrow \psi^d$.
The converse follows immediately, as $\varphi^{dd} = \varphi$. □

The duality theorem gives us one identity for free for each identity we establish.

EXERCISES.

1. Show by 'algebraic' means
   - $\models (\varphi \to \psi) \leftrightarrow (\neg \psi \to \neg \varphi)$, contraposition
   - $\models (\varphi \to \psi) \wedge (\psi \to \sigma) \to (\varphi \to \sigma)$, transitivity of $\to$
   - $\models (\varphi \to (\psi \wedge \neg \psi)) \to \neg \varphi$,
   - $\models (\varphi \to \neg \varphi) \to \neg \varphi$,
   - $\models \neg (\varphi \wedge \neg \varphi)$,
   - $\models \varphi \to (\psi \to \varphi \wedge \psi)$
   - $\models ((\varphi \to \psi) \to \varphi) \to \varphi$. Peirce's law.

2. Simplify the following propositions (i.e. find a simpler equivalent proposition.
   (a) $(\varphi \to \psi) \wedge \varphi$,
   (b) $(\varphi \to \psi) \vee \neg \varphi$,
   (c) $(\varphi \to \psi) \to \psi$,
   (d) $\varphi \to (\varphi \wedge \psi)$,
   (e) $(\varphi \wedge \psi) \vee \varphi$,
   (f) $(\varphi \to \psi) \to \varphi$.

3. Show that $\{\neg\}$ is not a functionally complete set of connectives.
   Idem for $\{\to,\vee\}$ (hint: show that each valuation has for at least one string of arguments the value 1).

4. Show that the Sheffer stroke, $|$, forms a functionally complete set (hint: $\models \neg \varphi \leftrightarrow \varphi|\varphi$).

5. Show that the connective $\downarrow$, with valuation function $v(\varphi \downarrow \psi) = 1$ iff $v(\varphi) = v(\psi) = 0$, forms a functionally complete set (neither φ, nor ψ).

6. Show that | and ↓ are the only binary connectives \$ such that {\$} is functionally complete.

7. The functional completeness of $\{\vee,\neg\}$ can be shown in an alternative way. Let \$ be an n-ary connective with valuation function $v(\$(\varphi_1,\dots,\varphi_n)) = f(v(\varphi_1),\dots,v(\varphi_n))$. We want a proposition τ such that
$v(\tau) = 1 \Leftrightarrow f(v(\varphi_1),\dots,v(\varphi_n)) = 1$.
Suppose $f(v(\varphi_1),\dots,v(\varphi_n)) = 1$, at least once.
Form conjunctions $\varphi_1 \wedge \bar{\varphi}_2 \wedge \dots \wedge \bar{\varphi}_n$ such that $\bar{\varphi}_i = \varphi_i$ if $v(\varphi_i) = 1$, $\bar{\varphi}_i = \neg\varphi_i$ if $v(\varphi_i) = 0$, and $f(v(\varphi_1),\dots,v(\varphi_n)) = 1$. Then show $(\bar{\varphi}_1^1 \wedge \bar{\varphi}_2^1 \dots \wedge \bar{\varphi}_n^1) \vee \dots \vee (\bar{\varphi}_1^k \wedge \bar{\varphi}_2^k \wedge \dots \wedge \bar{\varphi}_n^k) \leftrightarrow \$(\varphi_1,\dots,\varphi_n)$ where the disjunction is taken over all n-tuples such that $f(v(\varphi_1),\dots,v(\varphi_n)) = 1$.
Alternatively, we can look for a proposition σ such that $v(\sigma) = 0 \Leftrightarrow f(v(\varphi_1),\dots,v(\varphi_n)) = 0$. Carry out the details.
Note that this proof of the functional completeness at the same time proves the normal form theorems.

8. Let the ternary connective \$ be defined by
$v(\$(\varphi_1,\varphi_2,\varphi_3)) = 1 \Leftrightarrow v(\varphi_1) + v(\varphi_2) + v(\varphi_3) \geqslant 2$ (the majority connective).
Express \$ in terms of $\vee$ and $\neg$.

9. Let the binary connective # be defined by
Express # in terms of $\vee$ and $\neg$.

#	0	1
0	0	1
1	1	0

10. Determine conjunctive and disjunctive normal forms for
$\neg(\varphi \leftrightarrow \psi)$, $((\varphi \to \psi) \to \psi) \to \psi$, $(\varphi \to (\varphi \wedge \neg\psi)) \wedge (\psi \to (\psi \wedge \neg\varphi))$.

11. Give a criterion for a conjunctive normal form to be a tautology.

12. Prove $\bigwedge\limits_{i\leqslant n} \varphi_i \vee \bigwedge\limits_{j\leqslant m} \psi_j$ eq. $\bigwedge\limits_{\substack{i\leqslant n\\ j\leqslant m}} (\varphi_i \vee \psi_j)$ and

$\bigvee\limits_{i\leqslant n} \varphi_i \wedge \bigvee\limits_{j\leqslant m} \psi_j$ eq. $\bigvee\limits_{\substack{i\leqslant n\\ j\leqslant m}} (\varphi_i \wedge \psi_j)$.

13. The set of all valuations, thought of as the set of all 0-1-sequences, forms a topological space, the so-called Cantor space.

The basic open sets are of the form $\{v \mid v(p_{i_1}) = \ldots = v(p_{i_n}) = 1$ and $v(p_{j_1}) = \ldots = v(p_{j_m}) = 0\}$, $i_k \neq j_p$ for $k \leqslant n$; $p \leqslant m$.

Define a function $[\![\ ]\!] : PROP \to P(C)$ (subsets of Cantor space) by: $[\![\varphi]\!] = \{v \mid v(\varphi) = 1\}$.

(a) Show that $[\![\varphi]\!]$ is a basic open set (which is also closed),

(b) $[\![\varphi \vee \psi]\!] = [\![\varphi]\!] \cup [\![\psi]\!]$; $[\![\varphi \wedge \psi]\!] = [\![\varphi]\!] \cap [\![\psi]\!]$; $[\![\neg \varphi]\!] = [\![\varphi]\!]^c$,

(c) $\models \varphi \Leftrightarrow [\![\varphi]\!] = C$; $[\![\bot]\!] = \emptyset$; $\models \varphi \to \psi \Leftrightarrow [\![\varphi]\!] \subseteq [\![\psi]\!]$.

Extend the mapping to sets of propositions Γ by $[\![\Gamma]\!] = \{v \mid v(\varphi) = 1$ for all $\varphi \in \Gamma\}$. Note that $[\![\Gamma]\!]$ is closed.

(d) $\Gamma \models \varphi \Leftrightarrow [\![\Gamma]\!] \subseteq [\![\varphi]\!]$.

14. We can view the relation $\models \varphi \to \psi$ as a kind of ordering. Put $\varphi \lhd \psi := \models \varphi \to \psi$ and $\not\models \psi \to \varphi$.
    (i) for each φ, ψ such that $\varphi \lhd \psi$, find σ with $\varphi \lhd \sigma \lhd \psi$,
    (ii) find $\varphi_1, \varphi_2, \varphi_3, \ldots$ such that $\varphi_1 \lhd \varphi_2 \lhd \varphi_3 \lhd \varphi_4 \lhd \ldots$,
    (iii) show that for each φ, ψ there is a least σ with $\varphi, \psi \lhd \sigma$.

15. Give a recursive definition of the simultaneous substitution $\varphi[\psi_1, \ldots, \psi_n / p_1, \ldots, p_n]$ and formulate and prove the appropriate analogue of the substitution theorem (1.2.5).

1.4. LOGIC AND SWITCHING

A simple network, consisting of two terminals connected through a switch, stands for a function that can take two values: 1 for switch on, 0 for switch off. By combining those basic networks in a suitable way one can build up networks that bear a close resemblance to propositions. Below are indicated the two main modes of composing circuits

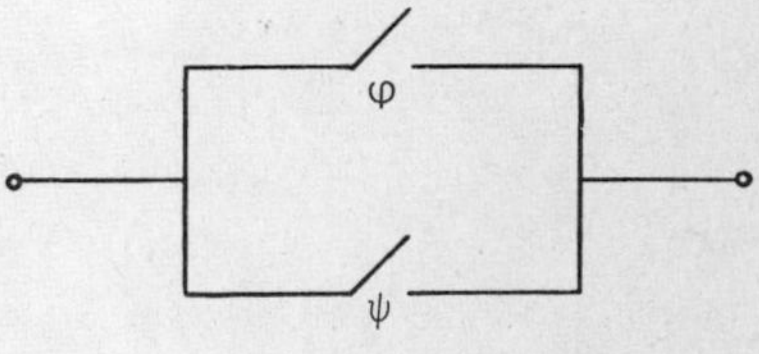

$\varphi \wedge \psi$ $\qquad\qquad$ $\varphi \vee \psi$

In the case that φ and ψ are in series, a current passes iff φ and ψ are both on. In the parallel case, a current passes iff at least one switch is on. By $\neg\varphi$ we denote a switch that is on iff φ is off.
We can now make various networks, corresponding to propositions in which only atoms can be negated.

We present a few examples

1.

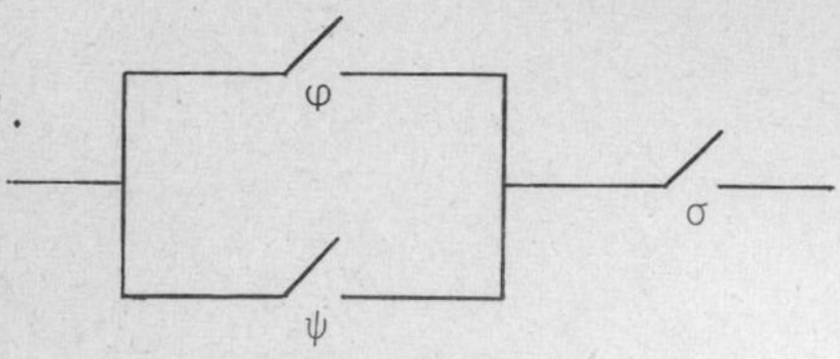

2.

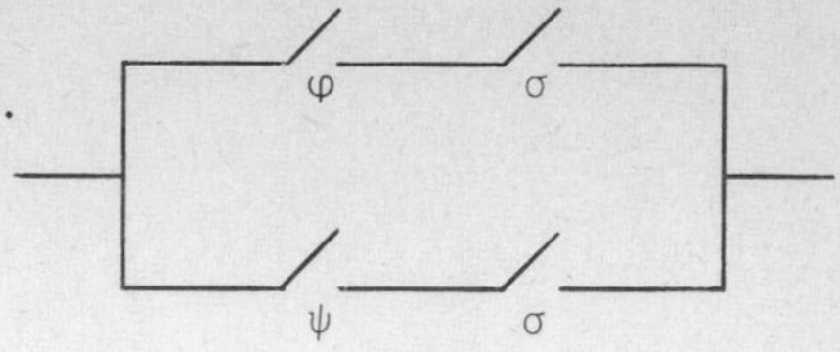

3.

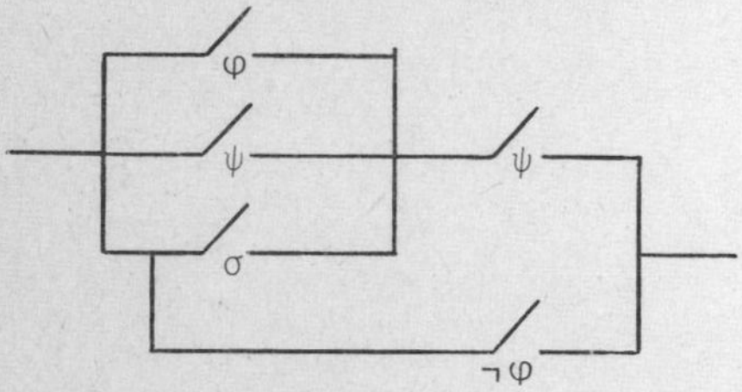

4.

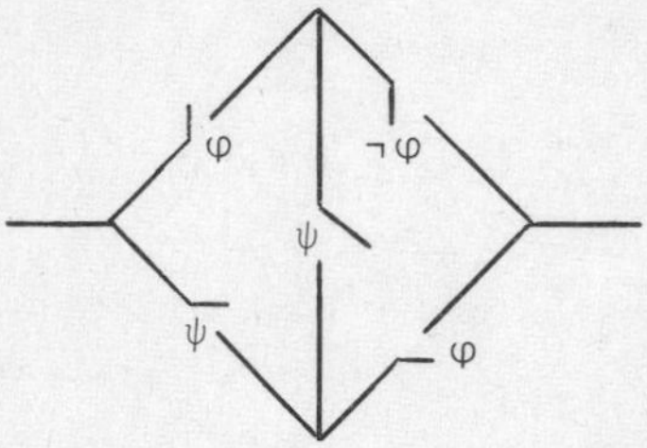

The corresponding propositions are:

(1) $(\varphi \vee \psi) \wedge \sigma$,

(2) $(\varphi \vee \sigma) \vee (\psi \wedge \sigma)$,

(3) $((\varphi \vee \psi \vee \sigma) \wedge \psi) \vee \neg\varphi$,

(4) $(\varphi \wedge \neg\varphi) \vee (\varphi \wedge \psi \wedge \varphi) \vee (\psi \wedge \psi \wedge \neg\varphi) \vee (\psi \wedge \varphi)$.

The last one is a bit tricky, because we have not built it with $\wedge$ and $\vee$ components as in the other examples. The trick is to consider all possible paths from left to right. We note that the networks (1) and (2) are equivalent. (3) is equivalent to $\psi \vee \neg\varphi$ and (4) is equivalent to $(\varphi \wedge \psi) \vee (\psi \wedge \neg\varphi) = \psi \wedge (\varphi \vee \neg\varphi) = \psi$. Both equivalents are, in one sense or another, more economic than (3) and (4).

Logic can be useful in constructing networks with prescribed input-output behaviour. In principle one can realize all switching networks because of the functional completeness of propositional logic,
Example: design a circuit with two switches such that when either switch is pulled the output changes (from on to off, or vice versa).

The truth table for the corresponding proposition looks like:

φ	ψ	
0	0	1
0	1	0
1	0	0
1	1	1

(or with a last column 0 1 1 0).

Using the technique of exercise 7, section 1.3 we find that $(\varphi \wedge \psi) \vee (\neg \varphi \wedge \neg \psi)$ corresponds to the truth table. So a required circuit is:

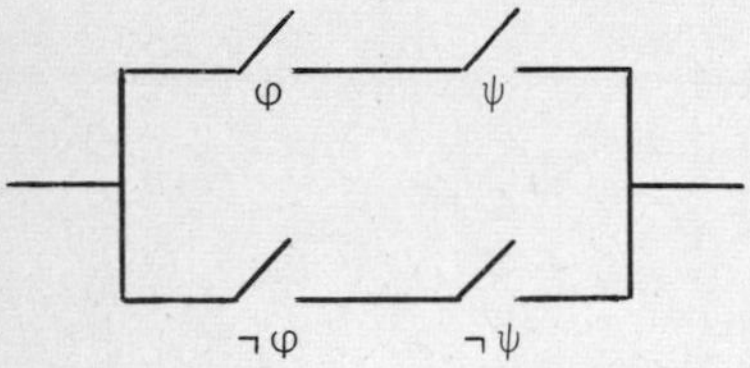

We think of one switch operating both φ and $\neg \varphi$, the same for ψ and $\neg \psi$.

The study of switching circuits is a discipline in its own right, cf. M.A. Harrison. *Introduction to switching and automata theory*, New York 1965.

1.5. NATURAL DEDUCTION

In the preceding sections we have adopted the view that propositional logic is based on truth tables, i.e. we have looked at logic from a semantical point of view. This, however, is not the only possible point of view. If one thinks of logic as a codification of (exact) reasoning, then it should stay closed to the practice of inference making, instead of basing itself on the notion of truth. We will now explore the non-semantic approach, by setting up a system for deriving conclusions from premises. Although this approach is of a formal nature, i.e. it abstains from interpreting the statements and rules, it is advisable to keep some interpretation in mind. We are going to introduce a number of derivation rules, which are, in a way, the atomic steps in a derivation. These derivations rules are designed (by Gentzen), to render the intuitive meaning of the connectives as faithfully as possible.

There is one minor problem, which at the same time is a major advantage, namely: our rules express the constructive meaning of the connectives. This advantage will not be exploited, but it is good to keep it in mind when dealing with logic (it is exploited in intuitionistic logic).

One small example: the principle of the excluded third tells us that $\models \varphi \vee \neg \varphi$, i.e., assuming that φ is a definite mathematical statement, either it or its negation must be true. Now consider some unsolved problem, e.g. Fermat's conjecture, call it F. Then either F is true, or $\neg$ F is true. However, we do not know which of the two is true, so the constructive content of $F \vee \neg F$ is nil. Constructively, one would require a method to find out which of the alternatives holds.

The propositional connective which has a strikingly different meaning in a constructive and in a non-constructive approach is the disjunction.
Therefore we restrict our language for the moment to the connectives $\wedge, \rightarrow$ and $\bot$. This is no real restriction as $\{\rightarrow, \bot\}$ is a functionally complete set.

Our derivations consist of very simple steps, such as "from φ and $\varphi \rightarrow \psi$ conclude ψ", written as

$$\frac{\varphi \qquad \varphi \rightarrow \psi}{\psi} \qquad \text{or} \qquad \varphi, \varphi \rightarrow \psi \vdash \psi.$$

The propositions above the line are *premises*, and the one below the line is the *conclusion*. The above example *eliminated* the connective $\rightarrow$. We can also *introduce* connectives.
The derivation rules for $\wedge$ and $\rightarrow$ are separated into

INTRODUCTION RULES | *ELIMINATION RULES*

$$(\wedge\, I)\ \frac{\varphi \qquad \psi}{\varphi \wedge \psi} \qquad\qquad (\wedge\, E)\ \frac{\varphi \wedge \psi}{\varphi} \qquad \frac{\varphi \wedge \psi}{\psi}$$

$$(\rightarrow I)\ \frac{\begin{array}{c}\not\varphi \\ \vdots \\ \psi\end{array}}{\varphi \rightarrow \psi} \qquad\qquad (\rightarrow E)\ \frac{\varphi \qquad \varphi \rightarrow \psi}{\psi}$$

For $\bot$ we have two rules, both of which eliminate.

$$(\bot)\ \frac{\bot}{\varphi} \qquad\qquad (RAA)\ \frac{\begin{array}{c}\not\neg\varphi \\ \vdots \\ \bot\end{array}}{\varphi}$$

As usual '$\neg \varphi$' is used here as an abbreviation for '$\varphi \to \bot$'.

The rules for $\wedge$ are evident: if we have φ and ψ we may conclude $\varphi \wedge \psi$, and if we have $\varphi \wedge \psi$ we may conclude φ (or ψ). The introduction rule for implication has a different form. It states that, if we can derive φ from ψ (as a hypothesis), then we may conclude $\varphi \to \psi$ (without the hypothesis φ).
This agrees with the intuitive meaning of implication: $\varphi \to \psi$ means "ψ follows from φ". We have written the rule ($\to$ I) in the above form to suggest a derivation. The notation will become clearer after we have defined derivations.

The rule ($\to$ E) is also evident on the meaning of implication. If φ is given and we know that ψ follows from φ, then we have also ψ.

The *falsum rule*, ($\bot$), expresses that from an absurdity we can derive everything (ex falso sequitur quodlibet), and the *reductio ad absurdum rule*, (RAA), is a formulation of the *principle of proof by contradiction:* if one derives a contradiction from the hypothesis $\neg \varphi$, then one has a derivation of φ (without the the hypothesis $\neg \varphi$, of course). In both ($\to$ I) and (RAA) hypotheses disappear, this is indicated by the striking out of the hypothesis. We say that such a hypothesis is *cancelled*.

Let us digress for a moment on the cancellation of hypotheses. We first consider implication introduction. There is a well-known theorem in plane geometry which states that "if a triangle is isosceles, then the angles at the base are equal to one another" (Euclid's Elements, Book I, proposition 5). This is shown as follows: we suppose that we have an isosceles triangle and then, in a number of steps, we deduce that the angles at the base are equal. Thence we conclude that *the angles at the base are equal if the triangle is isosceles.*

Query 1: do we still need the hypothesis that the triangle is isosceles? Of course not! We have, so to speak, incorporated this condition in the statement itself. It is precisely the role of conditional statements, such as "if it rains I will use my umbrella", to get rid of the obligation to require (or verify) the condition. In abstracto: if we can deduce ψ using the hypothesis φ, then $\varphi \to \psi$ is the case *without the hypothesis* φ (there may be other hypotheses, of course).

Query 2: is it forbidden to maintain the hypothesis? Answer: no, but it clearly is superfluous. As a matter of fact we usually experience superfluous conditions as confusing or even misleading, but that is rather a matter of the psychology of problem solving than of formal logic. Usually we want the best possible result, and it is intuitively clear that the more hypotheses we state for a theorem, the weaker our result is. Therefore we will as a rule cancel as many hypotheses as possible.

In the case of reductio ad absurdum we also deal with cancellation of hypotheses. Again, let us consider an example.

In analysis we introduce the notion of a *convergent sequence* (a_n) and sub-sequently the notion "a is a limit of (a_n)". The next step is to prove that for each convergent sequence there is a unique limit; we are interested in the part of the proof that shows that there is at most one limit. Such a proof may run as follows: we suppose that there are two distinct limits a and a', and from this hypothesis, a ≠ a', we derive a contradiction.
Conclusion: a = a'. In this case we of course drop the hypothesis a ≠ a', this time it is not a case of being superfluous, but of being in conflict!

So, both in the case (→ I) and of (RAA), it is sound practice to cancel all occurrences of the hypothesis concerned.

In order to master the technique of Natural Deduction, and to get familiar with the technique of cancellation, one cannot do better than to look at a few concrete cases. So before we go on to the notion of *derivation* we consider a few examples.

$$
\text{I.} \quad
\cfrac{
  \cfrac{\dfrac{\overset{①}{\varphi \wedge \psi}}{\psi} \wedge E \qquad \dfrac{\overset{①}{\varphi \wedge \psi}}{\varphi} \wedge E}{\dfrac{\psi \wedge \varphi}{\varphi \wedge \psi \to \psi \wedge \varphi} \to I} \wedge I
}{}
$$

$$
\text{II.} \quad
\cfrac{
  \cfrac{
    \cfrac{\dfrac{\overset{②}{\varphi} \qquad \overset{①}{\varphi \to \bot}}{\bot} \to E}{(\varphi \to \bot) \to \bot} \to I \;①
  }{\varphi \to [(\varphi \to \bot) \to \bot]} \to I \;②
}{}
$$

$$
\text{III.} \quad
\cfrac{
  \cfrac{
    \dfrac{\overset{①}{\varphi \wedge \psi}}{\psi} \wedge E \qquad
    \cfrac{\dfrac{\overset{①}{\varphi \wedge \psi}}{\varphi} \wedge E \qquad \overset{②}{\varphi \to (\psi \to \sigma)}}{\psi \to \sigma} \to E
  }{
    \cfrac{\dfrac{\sigma}{\varphi \wedge \psi \to \sigma} \to I \;①}{[\varphi \to (\psi \to \sigma)] \to [\varphi \wedge \psi \to \sigma]} \to I \;②
  } \to E
}{}
$$

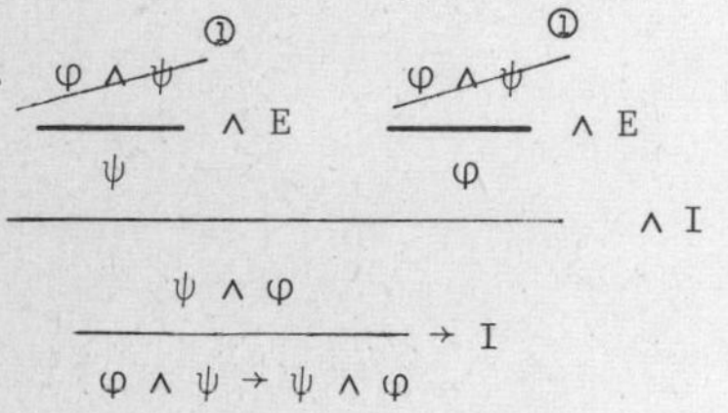

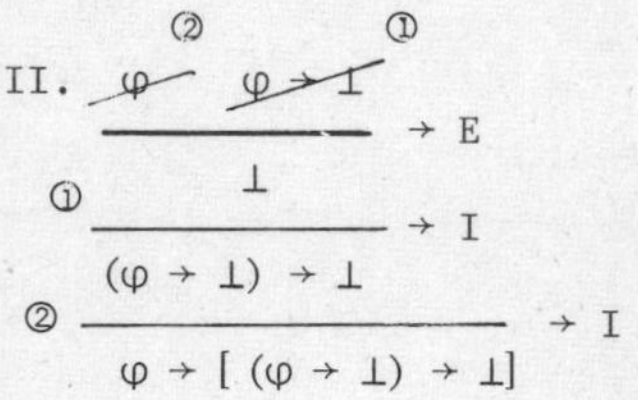

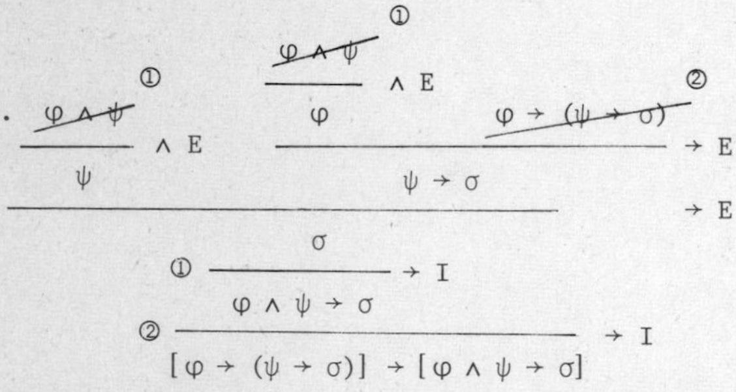

If we use the customary abbreviation '¬ φ' for '$\varphi \to \bot$' we can bring some derivations into a more convenient form. (We know that ¬ φ and $\varphi \to \bot$, as given in 1.2., are semantically equivalent).

We rewrite derivation II using the abbreviation:

II'.

$$\dfrac{\dfrac{\dfrac{\overset{②}{\not\varphi} \qquad \overset{①}{\not{\neg\varphi}}}{\bot}\ \to E}{\neg\neg\varphi}\ \to I\ ①}{\varphi \to \neg\neg\varphi}\ \to I\ ②$$

In the following example we use the negation sign and also the bi-implication; $\varphi \leftrightarrow \psi$ stands for $(\varphi \to \psi) \wedge (\psi \to \varphi)$.

IV.

$$\dfrac{\dfrac{\dfrac{\dfrac{\dfrac{\overset{①}{\not\varphi} \quad \dfrac{\overset{③}{\not{(\varphi \leftrightarrow \neg\varphi)}}}{\varphi \to \neg\varphi}\ \wedge E}{\neg\varphi}\ \to E \qquad \overset{①}{\not\varphi}}{\bot}\ \to E}{\neg\varphi}\ \to I\ ① \qquad \dfrac{\overset{③}{\not{(\varphi \leftrightarrow \neg\varphi)}}}{\neg\varphi \to \varphi}\ \wedge E}{\varphi}\ \to E \qquad \dfrac{\dfrac{\dfrac{\overset{②}{\not\varphi} \quad \dfrac{\overset{③}{\not{(\varphi \leftrightarrow \neg\varphi)}}}{\varphi \to \neg\varphi}\ \wedge E}{\neg\varphi}\ \to E \qquad \overset{②}{\not\varphi}}{\bot}\ \to E}{\neg\varphi}\ \to I\ ②}{\dfrac{\bot}{\neg(\varphi \leftrightarrow \neg\varphi)}\ \to I\ ③}\ \to E$$

The examples show us that derivations have the form of trees. We show the trees below

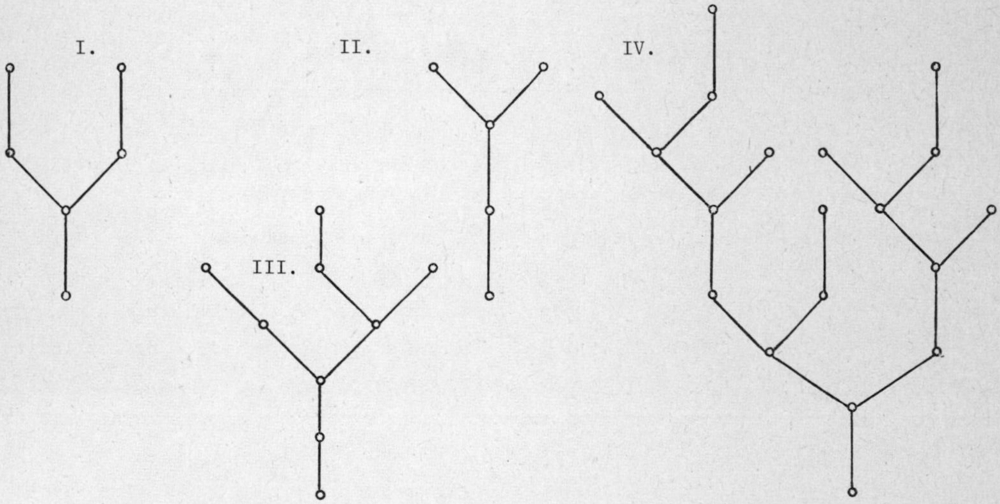

One can just as well present derivations as (linear) strings of propositions: we will stick, however, to the tree form.

We now have to define the notion of *derivation* in general. We will use an inductive definition to produce trees. Notation: if $\begin{matrix} D \\ \varphi \end{matrix}$, $\begin{matrix} D' \\ \varphi' \end{matrix}$ are derivations with conclusions φ , φ' , then

$$\dfrac{\begin{matrix} D \\ \varphi \end{matrix}}{\psi} \qquad \dfrac{\begin{matrix} D \\ \varphi \end{matrix} \quad \begin{matrix} D' \\ \varphi' \end{matrix}}{\psi}$$

are derivations obtained by applying a derivation rule to φ (and φ and φ').

The cancellation of a hypothesis is indicated as follows: if $\begin{matrix} \psi \\ D \\ \varphi \end{matrix}$ is a derivation with hypothesis ψ, then $\dfrac{\begin{matrix} \not\psi \\ D \\ \varphi \end{matrix}}{\sigma}$ is a derivation with ψ cancelled.

With respect to the cancellation of hypotheses, we note that one does not necessarily cancel all occurrences of some proposition φ. This clearly is justified, as one feels that adding hypotheses does not make a proposition underivable (irrelevant information may always be added).
Furthermore one may apply ($\rightarrow$ I) if there is no hypothesis available for cancellation e.g. $\dfrac{\varphi}{\psi \rightarrow \varphi} \rightarrow \text{I}$ is a correct derivation, using just ($\rightarrow$ I).
To sum it up: given a derivation tree of ψ (or $\perp$), we obtain a derivation tree of $\varphi \rightarrow \psi$ (or φ) by adding $\varphi \rightarrow \psi$ (or φ) at the bottom of the tree and striking out some (or all) occurrences, if any, of φ (or $\neg\varphi$) on top of the tree.

A few words on the practical use of natural deduction: if you want to give a derivation for a proposition it is advisable to devise some kind of strategy, just like in a game. Suppose that you want to show $[\varphi \rightarrow (\psi \rightarrow \sigma)] \rightarrow [\varphi \wedge \psi \rightarrow \sigma]$ (example III), then (since the proposition is an implicational formula) the rule ($\rightarrow$ I) suggests itself. So try to derive $\varphi \wedge \psi \rightarrow \sigma$ from $\varphi \rightarrow (\psi \rightarrow \sigma)$.
Now we know where to start and where to go to. To make use of $\varphi \wedge \psi \rightarrow \sigma$ we want $\varphi \wedge \psi$ (for ($\rightarrow$ E)), and to get $\varphi \rightarrow (\psi \rightarrow \sigma)$ we want to derive $\psi \rightarrow \sigma$ from φ. So we may add φ as a hypothesis and look for a derivation of $\psi \rightarrow \sigma$. Again, this asks for a derivation of σ from ψ, so add ψ as a hypothesis and look for a derivation of σ. By now we have the following hypotheses available: $\varphi \wedge \psi \rightarrow \sigma$, φ and ψ. Keeping in mind that we want to eliminate $\varphi \wedge \psi$ it is evident what we should do. The derivation III shows in detail how to carry out the derivation.

After making a number of derivations one gets the practical conviction that one should first take propositions apart, and then construct the required propositions by putting together the parts in a suitable way. This practical conviction is confirmed by the *normalization theorem*, which is beyond the scope of this book. The reader should consult *Prawitz, 1965*.

There is a particular point which tends to confuse novices:

$$\dfrac{\begin{array}{c}\not{\varphi}\\ \vdots\\ \bot\end{array}}{\neg\varphi}\rightarrow I \qquad \text{and} \qquad \dfrac{\begin{array}{c}\not{\neg\varphi}\\ \vdots\\ \bot\end{array}}{\varphi}\,\text{RAA}$$

look very much alike. Are they not both cases of Reductio ad absurdum? As a matter of fact the leftmost derivation tells us (informally) that the assumption of φ leads to a contradiction, so φ *cannot be the case*. This is in our terminology the meaning of "not φ".

The rightmost derivation tells us that the assumption of $\neg\varphi$ leads to a contradiction, hence (by the same reasoning) $\neg\varphi$ *cannot be the case*.

So, on account of the meaning of negation, we only would get $\neg\neg\varphi$. It is by no means clear that $\neg\neg\varphi$ is equivalent to φ (indeed, this is denied by the intuitionists), so it is an extra property of our logic. (This is confirmed in a technical sense: $\neg\neg\varphi\rightarrow\varphi$ is not derivable in the system without RAA, cf. *Prawitz, 1965*).

We now return to our theoretical notions.

1.5.1. Definition. The set of derivations is the smallest set X such that

(1) The one element tree φ belongs to X for all $\varphi \in$ PROP.

(2 $\wedge$) If $\begin{array}{c}D\\ \varphi\end{array}, \begin{array}{c}D'\\ \varphi'\end{array} \in X$, then $\dfrac{\begin{array}{cc}D & D'\\ \varphi & \varphi'\end{array}}{\varphi\wedge\varphi'} \in X$

If $\begin{array}{c}D\\ \varphi\wedge\psi\end{array} \in X$, then $\dfrac{\begin{array}{c}D\\ \varphi\wedge\psi\end{array}}{\varphi}, \dfrac{\begin{array}{c}D\\ \varphi\wedge\psi\end{array}}{\psi} \in X$

(2 $\rightarrow$) If $\begin{array}{c}\varphi\\ D\\ \psi\end{array} \in X$, then $\dfrac{\begin{array}{c}\not{\varphi}\\ D\\ \psi\end{array}}{\varphi\rightarrow\psi} \in X$

$$\text{If } \begin{array}{cc} \mathcal{D} & \mathcal{D}' \\ \varphi & \varphi \to \psi \end{array} \in X, \text{ then } \dfrac{\begin{array}{cc} \mathcal{D} & \mathcal{D}' \\ \varphi & \varphi \to \psi \end{array}}{\psi} \in X,$$

$$(2\bot)\ \text{If } \begin{array}{c} \mathcal{D} \\ \bot \end{array} \in X, \text{ then } \dfrac{\begin{array}{c} \mathcal{D} \\ \bot \end{array}}{\varphi} \in X.$$

$$\text{If } \begin{array}{c} \neg\varphi \\ \mathcal{D} \\ \bot \end{array} \in X, \text{ then } \dfrac{\begin{array}{c} \not{\neg\varphi} \\ \mathcal{D} \\ \bot \end{array}}{\varphi} \in X.$$

The bottom formula of a derivation is called its *conclusion*. Since the class of derivations is inductively defined, we can mimic the results of section 1.1.

E.g. we have a *principle of induction on* $\mathcal{D}$: let A be a property. If A(D) for one element derivations and A is preserved under the clauses $(2\wedge)$ $(2\to)$ and $(2\bot)$, then A(D) holds for all derivations. Likewise we can define mappings on the set of derivations by recursion. (cf. exercises 6,8).

1.5.2. Definition. The relation $\Gamma \vdash \varphi$ between sets of propositions and propositions is defined by: there is a derivation with conclusion φ and with all (uncancelled) hypotheses in Γ.

We say that φ is *derivable* from Γ. Note that by definition Γ may contain many superfluous "hypotheses". The symbol $\vdash$ is called *turnstile*.

If $\Gamma = \emptyset$, we write $\vdash \varphi$, and we say that φ is a *theorem*.

We could have avoided the notion of 'derivation' and taken instead the notion of 'derivability' as fundamental, see exercise 9. The two notions, however, are closely related.

1.5.3. Lemma.
1. $\Gamma \vdash \varphi$ if $\varphi \in \Gamma$,
2. $\Gamma \vdash \varphi,\ \Gamma' \vdash \psi \Rightarrow \Gamma \cup \Gamma' \vdash \varphi \wedge \psi$,
3. $\Gamma \vdash \varphi \wedge \psi \Rightarrow \Gamma \vdash \varphi$ and $\Gamma \vdash \psi$,
4. $\Gamma \cup \{\varphi\} \vdash \psi \Rightarrow \Gamma \vdash \varphi \to \psi$,
5. $\Gamma \vdash \varphi,\ \Gamma' \vdash \varphi \to \psi \Rightarrow \Gamma \cup \Gamma' \vdash \psi$,
6. $\Gamma \vdash \bot \Rightarrow \Gamma \vdash \varphi$,
7. $\Gamma \cup \{\neg\varphi\} \vdash \bot \Rightarrow \Gamma \vdash \varphi$.

Proof. Immediate from the definition of derivation. □

We now list some theorems. $\neg$ and $\leftrightarrow$ are used as abbreviations.

1.5.4. <u>Theorem</u>.
1. $\vdash \varphi \to (\psi \to \varphi)$,
2. $\vdash \varphi \to (\neg \varphi \to \psi)$,
3. $\vdash (\varphi \to \psi) \to [(\psi \to \sigma) \to (\varphi \to \sigma)]$,
4. $\vdash (\varphi \to \psi) \leftrightarrow (\neg \psi \to \neg \varphi)$
5. $\vdash \neg\neg \varphi \leftrightarrow \varphi$,
6. $\vdash [\varphi \to (\psi \to \sigma)] \leftrightarrow [\varphi \wedge \psi \to \sigma]$,
7. $\vdash \bot \leftrightarrow (\varphi \wedge \neg \varphi)$.

Proof. 1.

$$\textcircled{1}\ \dfrac{\dfrac{\cancel{\varphi}^{\,1}}{\psi \to \varphi}\ \to I}{\varphi \to (\psi \to \varphi)}\ \to I$$

2.

$$\textcircled{2}\ \dfrac{\textcircled{1}\ \dfrac{\dfrac{\dfrac{\cancel{\varphi}^{\,2} \quad \cancel{\neg\varphi}^{\,1}}{\bot}\ \to E}{\psi}\ \bot}{\neg \varphi \to \psi}\ \to I}{\varphi \to (\neg \varphi \to \psi)}\ \to I$$

3.

$$\textcircled{3}\ \dfrac{\textcircled{2}\ \dfrac{\textcircled{1}\ \dfrac{\dfrac{\dfrac{\cancel{\varphi}^{\,1} \quad \cancel{\varphi \to \psi}^{\,3}}{\psi} \quad \cancel{\psi \to \sigma}^{\,2}}{\sigma}}{\varphi \to \sigma}\ \to I}{(\psi \to \sigma) \to (\varphi \to \sigma)}\ \to I}{(\varphi \to \psi) \to [(\psi \to \sigma) \to (\varphi \to \sigma)]}\ \to I$$

4. Substitute $\bot$ for σ in 3, then $\vdash (\varphi \to \psi) \to (\neg \psi \to \neg \varphi)$.

Conversely:

$$\textcircled{3}\ \dfrac{\textcircled{2}\ \dfrac{\textcircled{1}\ \dfrac{\dfrac{\dfrac{\cancel{\neg\psi}^{\,1} \quad \cancel{\neg \psi \to \neg \varphi}^{\,3}}{\neg \varphi} \quad \cancel{\varphi}^{\,2}}{\bot}}{\psi}\ \mathrm{RAA}}{\varphi \to \psi}}{(\neg \psi \to \neg \varphi) \to (\varphi \to \psi)}$$

$$\text{So we have}\quad \dfrac{\overset{D}{(\varphi \to \psi) \to (\neg \psi \to \neg \varphi)} \qquad \overset{D'}{(\neg \psi \to \neg \varphi) \to (\varphi \to \psi)}}{(\varphi \to \psi) \leftrightarrow (\neg \psi \to \neg \varphi)}$$

5. We already proved $\varphi \to \neg\neg\varphi$ as an example.

$$\text{Conversely}\quad \dfrac{\dfrac{\dfrac{\cancel{\neg\varphi} \quad \cancel{\neg\neg\varphi}}{\bot}\ \text{RAA}}{\varphi}}{\neg\neg\varphi \to \varphi}$$

The result now follows.

Examples 6, 7 are left to the reader.

The system, outlined in this section, is called the "calculus of natural deduction" for a good reason. That is: its manner of making inferences corresponds to the reasoning we intuitively use. The rules present means to take formulas apart, or to put them together. A derivation then consists of a skilful manipulation of the rules, the use of which is usually suggested by the form of the formula we want to prove.

We will discuss one example in order to illustrate the general strategy of building derivations. Let us consider the converse of our previous example III.

To prove $(\varphi \wedge \psi \to \sigma) \to [\varphi \to (\psi \to \sigma)]$ there is just one initial step: assume $\varphi \wedge \psi \to \sigma$ and try to derive $\varphi \to (\psi \to \sigma)$. Now we can either look at the assumption or at the desired result. Let us consider the latter one first: to show $\varphi \to (\psi \to \sigma)$, we should assume φ and derive $\psi \to \sigma$, but for the latter we should assume ψ and derive σ.
So, altogether we may assume $\varphi \wedge \psi \to \sigma$ and φ and ψ. Now the procedure suggests itself: derive $\varphi \wedge \psi$ from φ and ψ, and σ from $\varphi \wedge \psi$ and $\varphi \wedge \psi \to \sigma$.

Put together, we get the following derivation

$$\dfrac{\dfrac{\dfrac{\dfrac{\dfrac{\overset{②}{\cancel{\varphi}} \quad \overset{①}{\cancel{\psi}}}{\varphi \wedge \psi} \qquad \overset{③}{\cancel{\varphi \wedge \psi \to \sigma}}}{\sigma}}{\psi \to \sigma}\,①}{\varphi \to (\psi \to \sigma)}\,②}{(\varphi \wedge \psi \to \sigma) \to [\varphi \to (\psi \to \sigma)]}\,③$$

Had we considered $\varphi \wedge \psi \to \sigma$ first, then the only way to proceed is to add $\varphi \wedge \psi$ and apply $\to$ E. Now $\varphi \wedge \psi$ either remains an assumption, or it is obtained from something else. It immediately occurs to the reader to derive $\varphi \wedge \psi$ from φ and ψ. But now he will build up the derivation we obtained above.

Simple as this example seems, there are complications. In particular the rule of reductio ad absurdum is not nearly as natural as the other ones. Its use must be learned by practice; also a sense for the distinction between *constructive* and *non-constructive* will be helpful when trying to decide on when to use it.

Finally, we introduce $\top$ as an abbreviation for $\neg \bot$ (i.e. $\bot \to \bot$).

EXERCISES.

1. Show that the following propositions are derivable.
   (*a*) $\varphi \to \varphi$,
   (*b*) $\bot \to \varphi$,
   (*c*) $\neg(\varphi \wedge \neg \varphi)$,
   (*d*) $(\varphi \to \psi) \leftrightarrow \neg(\varphi \wedge \neg \psi)$,
   (*e*) $(\varphi \wedge \psi) \leftrightarrow \neg(\varphi \to \neg \psi)$,
   (*f*) $\varphi \to (\psi \to \varphi \wedge \psi)$.

2. Idem for (*a*) $(\varphi \to \neg \varphi) \to \neg \varphi$,
   (*b*) $[\varphi \to (\psi \to \sigma)] \leftrightarrow [\psi \to (\varphi \to \sigma)]$,
   (*c*) $(\varphi \to \psi) \wedge (\varphi \to \neg \psi) \to \neg \varphi$,
   (*d*) $(\varphi \to \psi) \to [(\varphi \to (\psi \to \sigma)) \to (\varphi \to \sigma)]$.

3. Show (*a*) $\varphi \vdash \neg(\neg \varphi \wedge \neg \psi)$,
   (*b*) $\neg(\varphi \wedge \neg \psi), \varphi \vdash \psi$,
   (*c*) $\neg \varphi \vdash (\varphi \to \psi) \leftrightarrow \neg \varphi$,
   (*d*) $\vdash \varphi \Rightarrow \vdash \psi \to \varphi$.

4. Show $\vdash [(\varphi \to \psi) \to (\varphi \to \sigma)] \to [(\varphi \to (\psi \to \sigma))]$,
   $\vdash ((\varphi \to \psi) \to \varphi) \to \varphi$.

5. Show (*a*) $\Gamma \vdash \varphi \Rightarrow \Gamma \cup \Delta \vdash \varphi$,
   (*b*) $\Gamma \vdash \varphi \; ; \; \Delta, \varphi \vdash \psi \Rightarrow \Gamma \cup \Delta \vdash \psi$.

6. Analogous to the substitution operator for propositions we define a substitution operator for derivations.
   $D[\varphi/p]$ is obtained by replacing each occurrence of p in each proposition in D by φ. Give a recursive definition of $D[\varphi/p]$.

Show that $D[\varphi/p]$ is a derivation if D is one, and that
$\Gamma \vdash \sigma \Rightarrow \Gamma[\varphi/p] \vdash \sigma[\varphi/p]$.
Remark: for several purposes finer notions of substitution are required, but this one will do for us.

7. *Substitution theorem.* $\vdash \varphi_1 \leftrightarrow \varphi_2 \Rightarrow \vdash \psi[\varphi_1/p] \leftrightarrow \psi[\varphi_2/p]$.
Hint: induction on ψ (the theorem will also follow from the substitution theorem for $\models$, once we have proved the completeness theorem).

8. The *size*, s(D), of a derivation is the number of all proposition occurrences in D. Give a recursive definition of s(D). Show that one can prove properties of derivations by *induction on the size.*

9. Give an inductive definition of the relation $\vdash$ (use the list of lemma 1.5.3), show that this relation coincides with the derived relation of definition 1.5.2. Conclude that each Γ, with $\Gamma \vdash \varphi$, contains a minimal, finite Γ' such that also $\Gamma' \vdash \varphi$.

10. Show (a) $\vdash \top$,
(b) $\vdash \varphi \quad \Leftrightarrow \quad \vdash \varphi \leftrightarrow \top$,
(c) $\vdash \neg\varphi \quad \Leftrightarrow \quad \vdash \varphi \leftrightarrow \bot$.

11. Use the clauses of lemma 1.5.3 for an inductive definition of the relation $\vdash$. Show that for this relation we have $\Gamma \vdash \varphi \Leftrightarrow$ there is a derivation of φ from Γ.

1.6. COMPLETENESS

In the present section we will show that "truth" and "derivability" coincide. To be precise: the relations " $\models$ " and " $\vdash$ " coincide. The easy part of the claim is: "derivability" implies "truth"; for derivability is established by the existence of a derivation.
The latter notion is inductively defined, so we can prove the implication by induction on the derivation.

1.6.1. Lemma (soundness). $\Gamma \vdash \varphi \Rightarrow \Gamma \models \varphi$.

Proof. Since, by definition 1.5.2, $\Gamma \vdash \varphi$ iff there is a derivation D with all its hypotheses in Γ, it suffices to show: For each derivation D with conclusion φ and hypotheses in Γ we have $\Gamma \models \varphi$. We now use induction on D.

1. If D has one element, then evidently $\varphi \in \Gamma$. The reader easily sees that $\Gamma \models \varphi$.

2. ($\wedge$ I). Induction hypothesis: $\begin{matrix} D \\ \varphi \end{matrix}$ and $\begin{matrix} D' \\ \varphi' \end{matrix}$ are derivations and for each Γ, Γ'

containing the hypotheses of D, D' $\Gamma \models \varphi$, $\Gamma' \models \varphi'$.

Now let Γ'' contain the hypotheses of
$$\dfrac{\begin{array}{cc} D & D' \\ \varphi & \varphi' \end{array}}{\varphi \wedge \varphi'}$$

Choosing Γ and Γ' to be precisely the set of hypotheses of D, D', we see that $\Gamma'' \supseteq \Gamma \cup \Gamma'$.

So $\Gamma'' \models \varphi$ and $\Gamma'' \models \varphi'$. Let $v(\psi) = 1$ for all $\psi \in \Gamma''$, then $v(\varphi) = v(\varphi') = 1$, hence $v(\varphi \wedge \varphi') = 1$.

This shows $\Gamma'' \models \varphi \wedge \varphi'$.

($\wedge$E). Induction hypothesis: For any Γ containing the hypothesis of $\begin{array}{c} D \\ \varphi \wedge \psi \end{array}$ we have $\Gamma \models \varphi \wedge \psi$. Evidently Γ contains all hypotheses of $\dfrac{\begin{array}{c} D \\ \varphi \wedge \psi \end{array}}{\varphi}$ and $\dfrac{\begin{array}{c} D \\ \varphi \wedge \psi \end{array}}{\psi}$. It is left to the reader to show $\Gamma \models \varphi$ and $\Gamma \models \psi$.

($\rightarrow$I). Induction hypothesis: For any Γ containing all hypotheses of $\begin{array}{c} \varphi \\ D \\ \psi \end{array}$, $\Gamma \models \psi$.

Let Γ' contain all hypotheses of $\dfrac{\begin{array}{c} \cancel{\varphi} \\ D \\ \psi \end{array}}{\varphi \rightarrow \psi}$. Suppose $\Gamma' \not\models \varphi \rightarrow \psi$, then there is a valuation v such that $v(\sigma) = 1$ for all $\sigma \in \Gamma'$ and $v(\varphi \rightarrow \psi) = 0$, i.e. $v(\varphi) = 1$ and $v(\psi) = 0$. But then $\Gamma' \cup \{\varphi\}$ contains all hypotheses of the first derivation and thus $\Gamma' \cup \{\varphi\} \models \psi$. Contradiction.

So $\Gamma' \models \varphi \rightarrow \psi$.

($\rightarrow$E). An exercise for the reader.

($\perp$). Induction hypothesis: For each Γ containing all hypothesis of $\begin{array}{c} D \\ \perp \end{array}$, $\Gamma \models \perp$.

Since $v(\perp) = 0$ for all v, there is no valuation v such that $v(\psi) = 1$ for all $\psi \in \Gamma$.

Let Γ' contain all hypothesis of $\dfrac{\begin{array}{c} D \\ \perp \end{array}}{\varphi}$ and suppose that $\Gamma' \not\models \varphi$, then $v(\psi) = 1$ for all $\psi \in \Gamma'$ and $v(\varphi) = 0$, for some v. Since Γ' contains all hypotheses of the first derivation we have a contradiction.

(RAA). Induction hypothesis: For each Γ containing all hypotheses of $\begin{array}{c} \neg\varphi \\ D \\ \perp \end{array}$, we have $\Gamma \models \perp$. Let Γ' contain all hypotheses of $\dfrac{\begin{array}{c} \cancel{\neg\varphi} \\ D \\ \perp \end{array}}{\varphi}$ and suppose $\Gamma' \not\models \varphi$, then there exists

a v such that $v(\psi) = 1$ for all $\psi \in \Gamma'$ and $v(\varphi) = 0$, i.e. $v(\neg\varphi) = 1$.
But then $\Gamma'' = \Gamma' \cup \{\neg \varphi\}$ contains all hypotheses of the first derivation and $v(\psi) = 1$ for all $\psi \in \Gamma''$. This is impossible since $\Gamma'' \vdash \bot$.
Hence $\Gamma' \models \varphi$. □

This lemma may not seem very impressive, but it enables us to show that some propositions are not theorems, simply by showing that they are not tautologies. Without this lemma that would have been a very awkward task. We would have to show that there is no derivation (without hypotheses) of the given proposition. In general this requires insight in the nature of derivations, something which is beyond us at the moment.

Example: $\nvdash p_0$, $\nvdash (\varphi \to \psi) \to \varphi \wedge \psi$.

In the first example take the constant 0 valuation. $v(p_0) = 0$, so $\not\models p_0$ and hence $\nvdash p_0$.

In the second example we are faced with a meta proposition (a *schema*); strictly speaking it cannot be derivable (only *real* propositions can be). By $\vdash (\varphi \to \psi) \to \varphi \wedge \psi$ we mean that all propositions of that form (obtained by substituting real propositions for φ and ψ, if you like) are derivable. To refute it we need only one instance which is not derivable. Take $\varphi = \psi = p_0$.

In order to prove the converse of lemma 1.6.1 we need a few new notions. The first one has an impressive history; it is the notion of *freedom from contradiction* or *consistency*. It was made the cornerstone of the foundations of mathematics by Hilbert.

1.6.2. Definition. A set Γ of propositions is *consistent* if $\Gamma \nvdash \bot$.

In words: one cannot derive a contradiction from Γ.

The consistency of Γ can be expressed in various other forms:

1.6.3. Lemma. The following three conditions are equivalent:

(*i*) Γ is consistent,

(*ii*) For no φ $\Gamma \vdash \varphi$ and $\Gamma \vdash \neg \varphi$,

(*iii*) There is at least one φ such that $\Gamma \nvdash \varphi$.

Proof. Let us call Γ *inconsistent* if $\Gamma \vdash \bot$, then we can just as well prove the equivalence of

(*iv*) Γ is inconsistent,

(*v*) There is a φ such that $\Gamma \vdash \varphi$ and $\Gamma \vdash \neg \varphi$, (*vi*) For all φ $\Gamma \vdash \varphi$,

(*iv*) ⇒ (*vi*) Let $\Gamma \vdash \bot$, i.e. there is a derivation D with conclusion $\bot$ and hypotheses in Γ. By ($\bot$) we can add one inference, $\bot \vdash \varphi$, to D, so that $\Gamma \vdash \varphi$. This holds for all φ.

(*vi*) ⇒ (*v*) Trivial.

(*v*) ⇒ (*iv*) Let $\Gamma \vdash \varphi$ and $\Gamma \vdash \neg\varphi$. From the two associated derivations one obtains a derivation for $\Gamma \vdash \bot$ by ($\rightarrow$ E). □

Clause (*vi*) shows us why inconsistent sets (theories) are devoid of mathematical interest. For, if everything is derivable, we cannot distinguish between "good" and "bad" propositions. Mathematics tries to find distinctions, not to blur them.

In mathematical practice one tries to establish consistency by exhibiting a model (think of the consistency of the negation of Euclid's fifth postulate and the non-euclidean geometries). In the context of propositional logic this means looking for a suitable valuation.

1.6.4. Lemma. Γ is consistent if there is a valuation v such that $v(\psi) = 1$ for all $\psi \in \Gamma$.

Proof. Suppose $\Gamma \vdash \bot$, then by lemma 1.6.1 $\Gamma \models \bot$, so for any valuation v $v(\psi) = 1$ for all $\psi \in \Gamma \Rightarrow v(\bot) = 1$. Since $v(\bot) = 0$ for all v, there is no v with $v(\psi) = 1$ for all $\psi \in \Gamma$. Contradiction.
Hence Γ is consistent. □

Examples.

1. $\{p_0, \neg p_1, p_1 \rightarrow p_0\}$ is consistent. A suitable v is one satisfying $v(p_0) = 1$, $v(p_1) = 0$.
2. $\{p_0, p_1, \ldots\}$ is consistent. Choose v the constant 1 valuation.

Clause (*v*) of lemma 1.6.3 tells us that $\Gamma \cup \{\varphi, \neg\varphi\}$ is inconsistent. Now, how could $\Gamma \cup \{\neg\varphi\}$ be inconsistent? It seems plausible to blame this on the derivability of φ. The following confirms this.

1.6.5. Lemma. (*i*) $\Gamma \cup \{\neg\varphi\}$ is inconsistent $\Rightarrow \Gamma \vdash \varphi$,
(*ii*) $\Gamma \cup \{\varphi\}$ is inconsistent $\Rightarrow \Gamma \vdash \neg\varphi$.

Proof. The assumptions of (*i*) and (*ii*) yield two derivations

$$(i)\quad \dfrac{\begin{matrix}\cancel{\neg\varphi}\\ D\\ \bot\end{matrix}}{\varphi}\,RAA \qquad\qquad (ii)\quad \dfrac{\begin{matrix}\cancel{\varphi}\\ D'\\ \bot\end{matrix}}{\neg\varphi}\rightarrow I$$

with conclusion $\bot$. By applying (RAA), and $\rightarrow I$, we obtain derivations, with hypotheses in Γ, of φ, resp. $\neg\varphi$.

1.6.6. Definition. A set Γ is *maximally consistent* iff

(*i*) Γ is consistent,

(*ii*) $\Gamma \subseteq \Gamma'$ and Γ' consistent $\Rightarrow \Gamma = \Gamma'$.

Remark: one could replace (*ii*) by (*ii'*): If Γ is a proper subset of Γ', then Γ' is inconsistent.

Maximally consistent sets play an important role in logic. We will show that there are lots of them.

Here is one example: $\Gamma = \{\varphi \mid v(\varphi) = 1\}$ for a fixed v.
By lemma 1.6.4 Γ is consistent. Consider a consistent set Γ' such that $\Gamma \subseteq \Gamma'$. Now let $\psi \in \Gamma'$ and suppose $v(\psi) = 0$, then $v(\neg\psi) = 1$, and so $\neg\psi \in \Gamma$. But since $\Gamma \subseteq \Gamma'$ this implies that Γ' is inconsistent. Contradiction. Therefore $v(\psi) = 1$ for all $\psi \in \Gamma'$, so by definition $\Gamma = \Gamma'$.

The following fundamental lemma is proved directly. The reader may recognize in it an analogue of the maximal ideal existence lemma from ring theory (or the Boolean prime ideal theorem), which is usually proved by an application of Zorn's lemma.

1.6.7. Lemma. Each consistent set Γ is contained in a maximally consistent set Γ^*.

Proof. There are countably many propositions, so suppose we have a list $\varphi_0, \varphi_1, \varphi_2, \ldots$ of all propositions (cf. exercise 5). We define a non-decreasing sequence of sets Γ_i such that the union is maximally consistent.

$$\Gamma_0 = \Gamma,$$

$$\Gamma_{n+1} = \begin{cases} \Gamma_n \cup \{\varphi_n\} & \text{if } \Gamma_n \cup \{\varphi_n\} \text{ is consistent,} \\ \Gamma_n & \text{else.} \end{cases}$$

$$\Gamma^* = \cup\{\Gamma_n \mid n \in N\}.$$

(*a*) Γ_n is consistent for all n.
Immediate, by induction on n.

(*b*) Γ^* is consistent.

Suppose $\Gamma^* \vdash \bot$, then, by the definition of $\vdash$ there is derivation D of $\bot$ with hypotheses in Γ^*. D has finitely many hypotheses $\psi_0,\ldots,\psi_k$. Since $\Gamma^* = \cup\{\Gamma_n | n \in N\}$, we have for each $i \leq k$ $\psi_i \in \Gamma_{n_i}$ for some n_i. Let n be $\max_{i\leq k}(n_i)$, then $\psi_0,\ldots,\psi_k \in \Gamma_n$ and hence $\Gamma_n \vdash \bot$. But Γ_n is consistent. Contradiction.

(c) Γ^* is maximally consistent.

Let $\Gamma^* \subseteq \Delta$ and Δ consistent. If $\psi \in \Delta$, then $\psi = \varphi_m$ for some m. Since $\Gamma_m \subseteq \Gamma^* \subseteq \Delta$ and Δ consistent, $\Gamma_m \cup \{\varphi_m\}$ is consistent. Therefore $\Gamma_{m+1} = \Gamma_m \cup \{\varphi_m\}$, i.e. $\varphi_m \in \Gamma_{m+1} \subseteq \Gamma^*$. This shows $\Gamma^* = \Delta$. □

1.6.8. Lemma. If Γ is maximally consistent, then Γ is closed under derivability (i.e. $\Gamma \vdash \varphi \Rightarrow \varphi \in \Gamma$).

Proof. Let $\Gamma \vdash \varphi$ and suppose $\varphi \notin \Gamma$. Then $\Gamma \cup \{\varphi\}$ must be inconsistent. Hence $\Gamma \vdash \neg\varphi$, so Γ is inconsistent. Contradiction. □

1.6.9. Lemma. Let Γ be maximally consistent; then

(i) for all φ either $\varphi \in \Gamma$, or $\neg\varphi \in \Gamma$,

(ii) for all φ,ψ $\quad \varphi \rightarrow \psi \in \Gamma \Leftrightarrow (\varphi \in \Gamma \Rightarrow \psi \in \Gamma)$.

Proof. *(i)* We know that not both φ and $\neg\varphi$ can belong to Γ. Consider $\Gamma' = \Gamma \cup \{\varphi\}$. If Γ' is inconsistent, then, by 1.6.5, 1.6.8, $\neg\varphi \in \Gamma$. If Γ' is consistent, then $\varphi \in \Gamma$ by the maximality of Γ.

(ii) Let $\varphi \rightarrow \psi \in \Gamma$ and $\varphi \in \Gamma$. To show: $\psi \in \Gamma$. Since $\varphi, \varphi \rightarrow \psi \in \Gamma$ and since Γ is closed under derivability (lemma 1.6.8), we get $\psi \in \Gamma$ by $\rightarrow$E. Conversely: let $\varphi \in \Gamma \Rightarrow \psi \in \Gamma$ be given. We want to show $\varphi \rightarrow \psi \in \Gamma$. Suppose $\varphi \rightarrow \psi \notin \Gamma$. Now, using *(i)* and the provable equivalence $\neg(\varphi \rightarrow \psi) \leftrightarrow (\varphi \wedge \neg\psi)$ (cf. section 1.5, exercise 1), we get $\varphi \wedge \neg\psi \in \Gamma$. Since $\varphi \wedge \neg\psi \vdash \varphi$ and $\varphi \wedge \neg\psi \vdash \neg\psi$, we get $\varphi \in \Gamma$ and $\neg\psi \in \Gamma$, or $\psi \notin \Gamma$. Contradiction. □

Note that we automatically have the following.

Corollary: If Γ is maximally consistent, then

$$\varphi \in \Gamma \;\Leftrightarrow\; \neg\varphi \notin \Gamma,$$
$$\neg\varphi \in \Gamma \;\Leftrightarrow\; \varphi \notin \Gamma.$$

1.6.10. Lemma. If Γ is consistent, then there exists a valuation v such that $v(\psi) = 1$ for all $\psi \in \Gamma$.

Proof. *(a)* By 1.6.7, Γ is contained in a maximally consistent Γ^*.

(b) Define $v(p_i) = \begin{cases} 1 & \text{if } p_i \in \Gamma^* \\ 0 & \text{else.} \end{cases}$

and extend v to PROP.

Claim: $v(\varphi) = 1 \Leftrightarrow \varphi \in \Gamma^*$. Use induction on φ.

1. For atomic φ the claim holds by definition.

2. $\varphi = \psi \wedge \sigma$.

$v(\varphi) = 1 \Leftrightarrow v(\psi) = v(\sigma) = 1 \Leftrightarrow$ (induction hypothesis) $\psi, \sigma \in \Gamma^*$. Apply lemma 1.6.8: $\psi \wedge \sigma \in \Gamma^*$. Conversely $\psi \wedge \sigma \in \Gamma^* \Leftrightarrow \psi, \sigma \in \Gamma^*$ (1.6.8). The rest follows from the induction hypothesis.

3. $\varphi = \psi \rightarrow \sigma$.

$v(\psi \rightarrow \sigma) = 0 \Leftrightarrow v(\psi) = 1$ and $v(\sigma) = 0 \Leftrightarrow$ (induction hypothesis) $\psi \in \Gamma^*$ and $\sigma \notin \Gamma^* \Leftrightarrow \psi \rightarrow \sigma \notin \Gamma^*$ (by 1.6.9).

(c) Since $\Gamma \subseteq \Gamma^*$ we have $v(\psi) = 1$ for all $\psi \in \Gamma$. $\square$

1.6.11. Corollary. $\Gamma \nvdash \varphi \Leftrightarrow$ there is a valuation v such that $v(\psi) = 1$ for all $\psi \in \Gamma$ and $v(\varphi) = 0$.

Proof. $\Gamma \nvdash \varphi \Leftrightarrow \Gamma \cup \{\neg \varphi\}$ consistent $\Leftrightarrow$ there is v such that $v(\psi) = 1$ for all $\psi \in \Gamma \cup \{\neg \varphi\}$, or $v(\psi) = 1$ for all $\psi \in \Gamma$ and $v(\varphi) = 0$. $\square$

1.6.12. Completeness theorem. $\Gamma \vdash \varphi \Leftrightarrow \Gamma \models \varphi$.

Proof. $\Gamma \nvdash \varphi \Rightarrow \Gamma \not\models \varphi$ by 1.6.11. The converse holds by 1.6.1.

In particular we have $\vdash \varphi \Leftrightarrow \models \varphi$, so the set of theorems is exactly the set of tautologies.

The completeness theorem tells us that the tedious task of making derivations can be replaced by the (equally tedious, but automatic) task of checking tautologies. This simplifies the search for theorems considerably; for derivations one has to be (moderately) clever, for truth tables one has to possess perseverance.

For logical theories one sometimes considers another notion of completeness: a set Γ is called *complete* if for each φ, either $\Gamma \vdash \varphi$, or $\Gamma \vdash \neg \varphi$. This notion is closely related to "maximally consistent". From exercise 6 it follows that $\mathrm{Cons}(\Gamma) = \{\sigma \mid \Gamma \vdash \sigma\}$ (*the set of consequences of* Γ) is maximally consistent if Γ

is a complete set. The converse also holds (cf. exercise 10).
Propositional logic is not complete in this sense, e.g. $\nvdash p_0$ and $\nvdash \neg p_0$.

There is another important notion which is traditionally considered in logic: that of *decidability*. Propositional logic is decidable in the following sense: there is an effective procedure to check the derivability of propositions φ. Put otherwise: there is an algorithm that for each φ tests if $\vdash \varphi$.

The algorithm is simple: write down the complete truth table for φ and check if the last column contains only 1's. If so, then $\models \varphi$ and, by the completeness theorem, $\vdash \varphi$. If not, then $\not\models \varphi$ and hence $\nvdash \varphi$. This is certainly not the best possible algorithm, one can find more economical ones. There are also algorithms that give more information, e.g. they not only test $\vdash \varphi$, but also yield a derivation, if one exists. Such algorithms require, however, a deeper analysis of derivations. This falls outside the scope of the present book.

There is one aspect of the completeness theorem that we want to discuss now. It does not come as a surprise that truth follows from derivability. After all we start with a combinatorial notion, defined inductively, and we end up with 'being true for all valuations'.
A simple inductive proof does the trick. For the converse the situation is totally different. By definition $\Gamma \models \varphi$ means that $v(\varphi) = 1$ for all valuations v that make all propositions of Γ true. So we know something about the behaviour of *all* valuations with respect to Γ and φ. Can we hope to extract from such infinitely many set theoretical facts the finite, concrete information needed to build a derivation for $\Gamma \vdash \varphi$? Evidently the available facts do not give us much to go on. Let us therefore simplify matters a bit by cutting down the Γ; after all we use only finitely many formulas of Γ in a derivation, so let us suppose that those formulas $\psi_1,\dots,\psi_n$ are given. Now we can hope for more success, since only finitely many atoms are involved, and hence we can consider a finite "part" of the infinitely many valuations that play a role.
That is to say only the restrictions of the valuations to the set of atoms occurring in $\psi_1,\dots,\psi_n,\varphi$ are relevant. Let us simplify the problem one more step. We know that $\psi_1,\dots,\psi_n \vdash \varphi$ $(\psi_1,\dots,\psi_n \models \varphi)$ can be replaced by $\vdash \psi_1 \wedge \dots \wedge \psi_n \to \varphi$ $(\models \psi_1 \wedge \dots \wedge \psi_n \to \varphi)$, on the ground of the implication rules (the definition of valuation). So we ask ourselves: given the truth table for a tautology σ, can we effectively find a derivation for σ?

This question is not answered by the completeness theorem, since our proof of it is not effective (at least not prima facie so). It has been answered positively, e.g. by Post, Bernays and Kalmar (cf. *Kleene* IV, §29) and it is easily treated by means of Gentzen techniques, or semantic tableaux. We will just sketch a method of proof. We can effectively find a conjunctive normal form σ^* for σ such that $\vdash \sigma \leftrightarrow \sigma^*$ and $\models \sigma \leftrightarrow \sigma^*$. It is easily shown that σ is a tautology iff each conjunct contains an atom and its negation, or $\neg \bot$. So all we have to do is to provide derivations for $p_i \vee \neg p_i$ and $\neg \bot$, and glue it all together to obtain a derivation of σ^*, which immediately yields a derivation of σ.

EXERCISES.

1. Check which of the following sets are consistent.
   (*a*) $\{\neg p_1 \wedge p_2 \to p_0, p_1 \to (\neg p_0 \to p_2), p_0 \leftrightarrow \neg p_2\}$,
   (*b*) $\{p_0 \to p_1, p_1 \to p_2, p_2 \to p_3, p_3 \to \neg p_0\}$,
   (*c*) $\{p_0 \to p_1, p_0 \wedge p_2 \to p_1 \wedge p_3, p_0 \wedge p_2 \wedge p_4 \to p_1 \wedge p_3 \wedge p_5, \ldots\}$.

2. Show that the following are equivalent.
   (*a*) $\{\varphi_1, \ldots, \varphi_n\}$ is consistent,
   (*b*) $\nvdash \neg(\varphi_1 \wedge \varphi_2 \wedge \ldots \wedge \varphi_n)$,
   (*c*) $\nvdash \varphi_1 \wedge \varphi_2 \wedge \ldots \wedge \varphi_{n-1} \to \neg \varphi_n$.

3. φ is *independent* from Γ if $\Gamma \nvdash \varphi$ and $\Gamma \nvdash \neg \varphi$.
   Show that: $p_1 \to p_2$ is independent from $\{p_1 \leftrightarrow p_0 \wedge \neg p_2, p_2 \to p_0\}$.

4. A set Γ is *independent* if for each $\varphi \in \Gamma$ $\quad \Gamma - \{\varphi\} \nvdash \varphi$.
   (*a*) Show that each finite set Γ has an independent subset Δ such that $\Delta \vdash \varphi$ for all $\varphi \in \Gamma$.
   (*b*) Let $\Gamma = \{\varphi_0, \varphi_1, \varphi_2, \ldots\}$. Find an equivalent set $\Gamma' = \{\psi_0, \psi_1, \ldots\}$ (i.e. $\Gamma \vdash \psi_i$ and $\Gamma' \vdash \varphi_i$ for all *i*) such that $\vdash \psi_{n+1} \to \psi_n$, but $\nvdash \psi_n \to \psi_{n+1}$. Note that Γ' may be finite.
   (*c*) Consider an infinite Γ' as in (*b*). Define $\sigma_0 = \psi_0$, $\sigma_{n+1} = \psi_n \to \psi_{n+1}$. Show that $\Delta = \{\sigma_0, \sigma_1, \sigma_2, \ldots\}$ is equivalent to Γ' and independent.
   (*d*) Show that each set Γ is equivalent to an independent set Δ.
   (*e*) Show that Δ need not be a subset of Γ (consider $\{p_0, p_0 \wedge p_1, p_0 \wedge p_1 \wedge p_2, \ldots\}$).

5. Find an effective way of enumerating all propositions (hint: consider sets Γ_n of all propositions of rank $\leqslant n$ with atoms from $p_0, \ldots, p_n$).

6. Show that Γ is maximally consistent if either $\varphi \in \Gamma$ or $\neg \varphi \in \Gamma$ for all φ.

7. Show that $\{p_0, p_1, p_2, \ldots p_n, \ldots\}$ is complete.

8. (*Compactness theorem*). Show that: there is v such that $v(\psi) = 1$ for all $\psi \in \Gamma \Leftrightarrow$ for each finite subset $\Delta \subseteq \Gamma$ there is a v such that $v(\sigma) = 1$ for all $\sigma \in \Delta$.
Formulated in terms of exercise 13 of 1.3: $[\![\Gamma]\!] \neq \emptyset$ if $[\![\Delta]\!] \neq \emptyset$ for all finite $\Delta \subseteq \Gamma$.

9. Consider an infinite set $\{\varphi_1, \varphi_2, \varphi_3, \ldots\}$.
If for each v there is an n such that $v(\varphi_n) = 1$, then there is an m such that $\vdash \varphi_1 \vee \ldots \vee \varphi_m$. (hint: consider the negations $\neg \varphi_1, \neg \varphi_2 \ldots$ and apply exercise 8).

10. Show: $Cons(\Gamma) = \{\sigma \mid \Gamma \vdash \sigma\}$ is maximally consistent $\Leftrightarrow$ Γ is complete.

11. Show that: Γ is maximally consistent $\Leftrightarrow$ there is a unique v such that $v(\psi) = 1$ for all $\psi \in \Gamma$, where Γ is a theory.

12. Let φ be a proposition containing the atom p.
For convenience we write $\varphi(\sigma)$ for $\varphi[\sigma/p]$.
We abbreviate $\neg \bot$ by $\top$.
(*i*) Show: $\varphi(\top) \vdash \varphi(\top) \leftrightarrow \top$ and
$\varphi(\top) \vdash \varphi(\varphi(\top))$.
(*ii*) Show: $\neg \varphi(\top) \vdash \varphi(\top) \leftrightarrow \bot$,
$\varphi(p), \neg \varphi(\top) \vdash p \leftrightarrow \bot$,
$\varphi(p), \neg \varphi(\top) \vdash \varphi(\varphi(\top))$.
(*iii*) Show: $\varphi(p) \vdash \varphi\,\varphi(\top)$.

13. If the atoms p and q do not occur in ψ and φ respectively, then
$\models \varphi(p) \to \psi \Rightarrow \models \varphi(\sigma) \to \psi$ for all σ,
$\models \varphi \to \psi(q) \Rightarrow \models \varphi \to \psi(\sigma)$ for all σ.

14. Let $\vdash \varphi \to \psi$. We call σ an *interpolant* if $\vdash \varphi \to \sigma$ and $\vdash \sigma \to \psi$, and moreover σ contains only atoms common to φ and ψ.
Consider $\varphi(p,r)$, $\psi(r,q)$ with all atoms displayed.
Show that $\varphi(\varphi(\top,r),r)$ is an interpolant (use exercise 12, 13).

15. Prove the general *Interpolation Theorem* (Craig):
For any φ, ψ with $\vdash \varphi \to \psi$ there exists an interpolant (iterate the procedure of exercise 14).

1.7. THE MISSING CONNECTIVES

The language of section 1.5. contained only the connectives $\wedge$, $\rightarrow$ and $\perp$. We already know that, from the semantical point of view, this language is sufficiently rich i.e. the missing connectives can be defined. As a matter of fact we have already used the negation and the equivalence in the preceding sections.

It is a matter of sound mathematical practice to introduce new notions if their use simplifies our labour, and if they codify informal existing practice. This, clearly, is a reason for introducing $\neg$, $\leftrightarrow$ and $\vee$.

Now there are two ways to proceed: one can introduce the new connectives as abbreviations (of complicated propositions), or one can enrich the language by actually adding the connectives to the alphabet, and providing rules of derivation. The first procedure was adopted above, it is completely harmless, e.g. each time one reads $\varphi \leftrightarrow \psi$, one has to replace this by $(\varphi \rightarrow \psi) \wedge (\psi \rightarrow \varphi)$. So it represents nothing but a shorthand, introduced for convenience. The second procedure is of a more theoretical nature. The language is enriched and the set of derivations is enlarged. As a consequence one has to review the theoretical results (such as the completeness theorem) obtained for the simpler language.

We will adopt the first procedure and also outline the second approach.

1.7.1. <u>Definition</u>.

$$\varphi \vee \psi \;:=\; \neg(\neg\varphi \wedge \neg\psi),$$
$$\neg\varphi \;:=\; \varphi \rightarrow \perp,$$
$$\varphi \leftrightarrow \psi \;:=\; (\varphi \rightarrow \psi) \wedge (\psi \rightarrow \varphi).$$

N.B. this means that the above expressions are *not* part of the language, but abbreviations for certain propositions.

The properties of $\vee$, $\neg$ and $\leftrightarrow$ are given in the following.

1.7.2. <u>Lemma</u>.
(*i*) $\varphi \vdash \varphi \vee \psi$, $\quad \psi \vdash \varphi \vee \psi$,
(*ii*) $\Gamma,\varphi \vdash \sigma$ and $\Gamma,\psi \vdash \sigma \Rightarrow \Gamma,\varphi \vee \psi \vdash \sigma$,
(*iii*) $\varphi, \neg\varphi \vdash \perp$,
(*iv*) $\Gamma,\varphi \vdash \perp \Rightarrow \Gamma \vdash \neg\varphi$,
(*v*) $\varphi \leftrightarrow \psi, \varphi \vdash \psi$, $\quad \varphi \leftrightarrow \psi, \psi \vdash \varphi$,
(*vi*) $\Gamma,\varphi \vdash \psi$ and $\Gamma,\psi \vdash \varphi \Rightarrow \Gamma \vdash \varphi \leftrightarrow \psi$.

Proof. The only non-trivial part is (*ii*). We exhibit a derivation of σ from Γ and $\varphi \vee \psi$ (i.e. $\neg(\neg\varphi \wedge \neg\psi)$), given derivations D_1 and D_2 of $\Gamma,\varphi \vdash \sigma$ and $\Gamma,\psi \vdash \sigma$.

$$\cfrac{\cfrac{\cfrac{\cfrac{\cfrac{\begin{matrix}[\varphi]^{1}\\ D_1\\ \sigma\end{matrix} \quad [\neg\sigma]^{3}}{\bot}}{\neg\varphi}\,{\scriptstyle (1)} \qquad \cfrac{\cfrac{\begin{matrix}[\psi]^{2}\\ D_2\\ \sigma\end{matrix} \quad [\neg\sigma]^{3}}{\bot}}{\neg\psi}\,{\scriptstyle (2)}}{\neg\varphi\wedge\neg\psi} \qquad \neg(\neg\varphi\wedge\neg\psi)}{\bot}}{\sigma}\,{\scriptstyle (3)}\ \text{RAA}$$

The remaining cases are left to the reader. □

Note that (*i*) and (*ii*) read as introduction and elimination rules for $\vee$, (*iii*) and (*iv*) as ditto for $\neg$, (*vi*) and (*v*) as ditto for $\leftrightarrow$. They legalize the following shortcuts in derivations:

$$\vee I: \quad \frac{\varphi}{\varphi\vee\psi} \qquad \frac{\psi}{\varphi\vee\psi} \qquad\qquad \vee E: \quad \frac{\varphi\vee\psi \quad \begin{matrix}[\varphi]\\ \vdots\\ \sigma\end{matrix} \quad \begin{matrix}[\psi]\\ \vdots\\ \sigma\end{matrix}}{\sigma}$$

$$\neg I: \quad \frac{\begin{matrix}[\varphi]\\ \vdots\\ \bot\end{matrix}}{\neg\varphi} \qquad\qquad \neg E: \quad \frac{\varphi \qquad \neg\varphi}{\bot}$$

$$\leftrightarrow I: \quad \frac{\begin{matrix}[\varphi]\\ \vdots\\ \psi\end{matrix} \quad \begin{matrix}[\psi]\\ \vdots\\ \varphi\end{matrix}}{\varphi\leftrightarrow\psi} \qquad\qquad \leftrightarrow E: \quad \frac{\varphi \quad \varphi\leftrightarrow\psi}{\psi} \qquad \frac{\psi \quad \varphi\leftrightarrow\psi}{\varphi}$$

Consider for example an application of $\vee E$:

$$\frac{\begin{matrix}D_0\\ \varphi\vee\psi\end{matrix} \quad \begin{matrix}[\varphi]\\ D_1\\ \sigma\end{matrix} \quad \begin{matrix}[\psi]\\ D_2\\ \sigma\end{matrix}}{\sigma}$$

this is a mere shorthand for

$$\dfrac{\dfrac{\begin{matrix}\mathcal{D}_0\\ \neg(\neg\varphi\wedge\neg\psi)\end{matrix}\qquad \dfrac{\dfrac{\dfrac{\begin{matrix}[\varphi]^1\\ \mathcal{D}_1\\ \sigma\end{matrix}\quad [\neg\sigma]^2}{\bot}}{\neg\varphi}\qquad \dfrac{\dfrac{\begin{matrix}[\psi]^1\\ \mathcal{D}_2\\ \sigma\end{matrix}\quad [\neg\sigma]^2}{\bot}}{\neg\psi}}{\neg\varphi\wedge\neg\psi}}{\bot}\,(1)}{\sigma}\,(2)$$

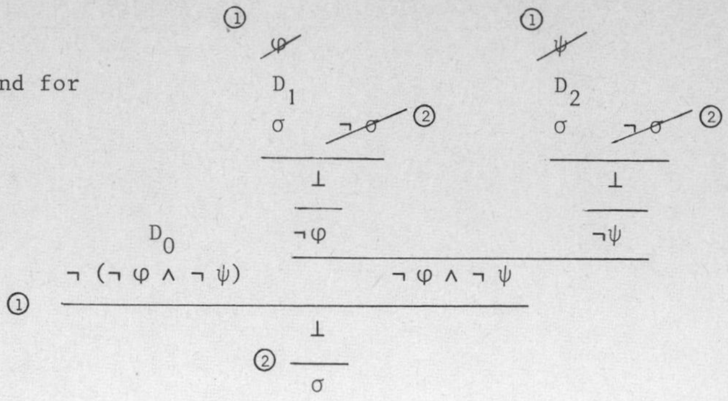

The reader is urged to use the above shortcuts in actual derivations, whenever convenient. As a rule, only $\vee$I and $\vee$E are of importance, the reader has of course recognized the rules for $\neg$ and $\leftrightarrow$ as slightly eccentric applications of familiar rules.

Examples. $\vdash (\varphi\wedge\psi)\vee\sigma \leftrightarrow (\varphi\vee\sigma)\wedge(\psi\vee\sigma)$.

(1)

$$\dfrac{\dfrac{(\varphi\wedge\psi)\vee\sigma\qquad \dfrac{\dfrac{[\varphi\wedge\psi]^1}{\varphi}}{\varphi\vee\sigma}\qquad \dfrac{[\sigma]^1}{\varphi\vee\sigma}}{\varphi\vee\sigma}\,(1)\qquad \dfrac{(\varphi\wedge\psi)\vee\sigma\qquad \dfrac{\dfrac{[\varphi\wedge\psi]^2}{\psi}}{\psi\vee\sigma}\qquad \dfrac{[\sigma]^2}{\psi\vee\sigma}}{\psi\vee\sigma}\,(2)}{(\varphi\vee\sigma)\wedge(\psi\vee\sigma)}$$

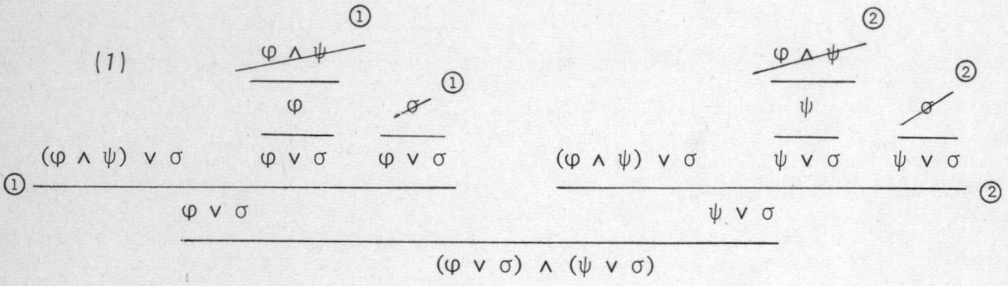

Conversely

(2)

$$\dfrac{\dfrac{(\varphi\vee\sigma)\wedge(\psi\vee\sigma)}{\varphi\vee\sigma}\qquad \dfrac{\dfrac{(\varphi\vee\sigma)\wedge(\psi\vee\sigma)}{\psi\vee\sigma}\qquad \dfrac{\dfrac{[\varphi]^2\quad[\psi]^1}{\varphi\wedge\psi}}{(\varphi\wedge\psi)\vee\sigma}\qquad \dfrac{[\sigma]^1}{(\varphi\wedge\psi)\vee\sigma}}{(\varphi\wedge\psi)\vee\sigma}\,(1)\qquad \dfrac{[\sigma]^2}{(\varphi\wedge\psi)\vee\sigma}}{(\varphi\wedge\psi)\vee\sigma}\,(2)$$

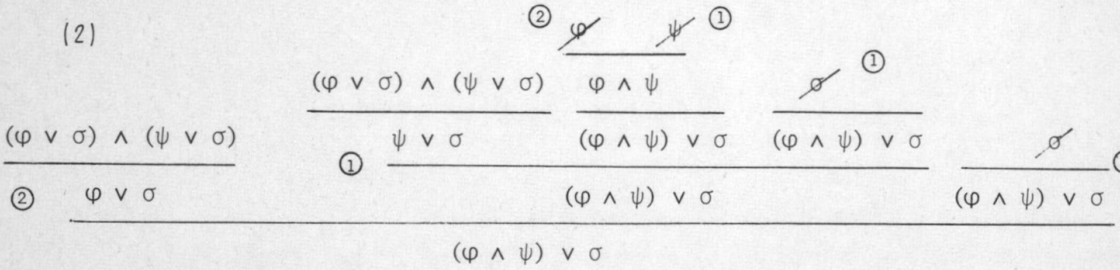

Combining (1) and (2) we get one derivation

$$\dfrac{\begin{matrix}\cancel{(\varphi\wedge\psi)\vee\sigma}\\ \mathcal{D}\\ (\varphi\vee\sigma)\wedge(\psi\vee\sigma)\end{matrix}\qquad\qquad \begin{matrix}\cancel{(\varphi\vee\sigma)\wedge(\psi\vee\sigma)}\\ \mathcal{D}'\\ (\varphi\wedge\psi)\vee\sigma\end{matrix}}{(\varphi\wedge\psi)\vee\sigma\leftrightarrow(\varphi\vee\sigma)\wedge(\psi\vee\sigma).}\ \leftrightarrow I$$

$\vdash\varphi\vee\neg\varphi$

$$\dfrac{\dfrac{\dfrac{\overset{①}{\cancel{\varphi}}}{\varphi\vee\neg\varphi}\vee I\qquad \overset{③}{\cancel{\neg(\varphi\vee\neg\varphi)}}}{\dfrac{\bot}{\neg\varphi}\,①}\qquad\qquad \dfrac{\dfrac{\overset{②}{\cancel{\neg\varphi}}}{\varphi\vee\neg\varphi}\qquad \overset{③}{\cancel{\neg(\varphi\vee\neg\varphi)}}}{\dfrac{\bot}{\neg\neg\varphi}\,②}}{③\,\dfrac{\bot}{\varphi\vee\neg\varphi}\,\text{RAA}}$$

$\vdash(\varphi\wedge\psi)\to\neg\varphi\vee\neg\psi$

$$\dfrac{\cancel{\neg(\varphi\wedge\psi)}\qquad \dfrac{\dfrac{\cancel{\neg(\neg\varphi\vee\neg\psi)}\qquad \dfrac{\cancel{\neg\varphi}}{\neg\varphi\vee\neg\psi}}{\dfrac{\bot}{\varphi}}\qquad \dfrac{\cancel{\neg(\neg\varphi\vee\neg\psi)}\qquad \dfrac{\cancel{\neg\psi}}{\neg\varphi\vee\neg\psi}}{\dfrac{\bot}{\psi}}}{\varphi\wedge\psi}}{\dfrac{\dfrac{\bot}{\neg\varphi\vee\neg\psi}}{\neg(\varphi\wedge\psi)\to\neg\varphi\vee\neg\psi}}$$

We now give a sketch of the second procedure.
We add $\vee$, $\neg$ and $\leftrightarrow$ to the language, and extend the set of propositions correspondingly.
Next we adopt the rules for $\vee$, $\neg$ and $\leftrightarrow$ listed above.

We now have the following:

1.7.3. <u>Theorem</u>. $\vdash \varphi \vee \psi \leftrightarrow \neg(\neg\varphi \wedge \neg\psi)$,

$\vdash \neg\varphi \leftrightarrow (\varphi \to \bot)$,

$\vdash (\varphi \leftrightarrow \psi) \leftrightarrow (\varphi \to \psi) \wedge (\psi \to \varphi)$.

Proof. Observe that by lemma 1.7.2. the left-hand sides and the right-hand sides obey exactly the same derivability relations (derivation rules, if you wish). This leads immediately to the desired result. We give one example.

$\varphi \vdash \neg(\neg\varphi \wedge \neg\psi)$ and $\psi \vdash \neg(\neg\varphi \wedge \neg\psi)$ (1.7.2.(i)), by $\vee E$

$$\varphi \vee \psi \vdash \neg(\neg\varphi \wedge \neg\psi) \quad \ldots\ldots \quad (1)$$

Conversely $\varphi \vdash \varphi \vee \psi$ and $\psi \vdash \varphi \vee \psi$ (by $\vee I$), by 1.7.2(ii)

$$\neg(\neg\varphi \wedge \neg\psi) \vdash \varphi \vee \psi \ldots\ldots \quad (2)$$

Apply $\leftrightarrow I$, to (1) and (2), then $\vdash \varphi \vee \psi \leftrightarrow \neg(\neg\varphi \wedge \neg\psi)$.
The rest is left to the reader. □

For more results the reader is directed to the exercises.

The rules for $\vee$, $\leftrightarrow$, and $\neg$ capture indeed the intuitive meaning of those connectives. Let us consider disjunction:
($\vee I$) - If we know φ then we certainly know $\varphi \vee \psi$ (we even know exactly which one).
($\vee E$) - Suppose we know $\varphi \vee \psi$, and from both φ and ψ we can derive σ, then we can also derive σ from $\varphi \vee \psi$. We may point out that here a constructive element has crept into the system: if we know $\varphi \vee \psi$, then this is based on the knowledge of φ or of ψ (and we know which one). Take that particular proposition and carry out the appropriate derivation. Matters of constructiveness play a role in demarcating the borderline between classical (two-valued) logic and intuitionistic (effective) logic.

EXERCISES.

1. Show $\vdash \varphi \vee \psi \to \varphi \vee \psi$, $\vdash \varphi \vee \varphi \leftrightarrow \varphi$.

2. Consider the full language L with the connectives $\wedge$, $\to$, $\bot$, $\leftrightarrow$, $\vee$, and the restricted languale L' with connectives $\wedge$, $\to$, $\bot$.
   Using the appropriate derivation rules we get the derivability notions $\vdash$ and $\vdash'$.

We define an obvious translation from L into L':

$$\begin{aligned}
\varphi^{+} &:= \varphi \text{ for atomic } \varphi, \\
(\varphi \Box \psi)^{+} &:= \varphi^{+} \Box \psi^{+} \quad \text{for } \Box = \wedge, \rightarrow, \\
(\varphi \vee \psi)^{+} &:= \neg(\neg \varphi^{+} \wedge \neg \psi^{+}), \\
(\varphi \leftrightarrow \psi)^{+} &:= (\varphi^{+} \rightarrow \psi^{+}) \wedge (\psi^{+} \rightarrow \psi^{+}), \\
(\neg \varphi)^{+} &:= \varphi^{+} \rightarrow \bot.
\end{aligned}$$

Show (*i*) $\vdash \varphi \leftrightarrow \varphi^{+}$,

(*ii*) $\vdash \varphi \Leftrightarrow \vdash' \varphi^{+}$,

(*iii*) $\varphi^{+} = \varphi$ for $\varphi \in L'$.

(*iv*) Show that the full logic, is *conservative* over the restricted logic, i.e. for $\varphi \in L'$ $\vdash \varphi \Leftrightarrow \vdash' \varphi$.

3. Show that the completeness theorem holds for the full logic.
   Hint: use exercise 2.

4. Show (*a*) $\vdash \top \vee \bot$,
   (*b*) $\vdash (\varphi \leftrightarrow \top) \vee (\varphi \leftrightarrow \bot)$.

5. Show $\vdash (\varphi \vee \psi) \leftrightarrow ((\varphi \rightarrow \psi) \rightarrow \psi)$.

6. Show (*a*) Γ is complete $\Leftrightarrow$ ($\Gamma \vdash \varphi \vee \psi \Leftrightarrow \Gamma \vdash \varphi$ or $\Gamma \vdash \psi$, for all φ, ψ)
   (*b*) Γ is maximally consistent $\Leftrightarrow$ Γ is consistent and for all φ, ψ ($\varphi \vee \psi \in \Gamma \Leftrightarrow \varphi \in \Gamma$ or $\psi \in \Gamma$).

2. Predicate Logic

2.1. QUANTIFIERS

In propositional logic we used large chuncks of mathematical language, namely those parts that can have a truth value. Unfortunately this use of language is patently insufficient for mathematical practice. A simple argument, such as "all squares are positive, 9 is a square, therefore 9 is positive" cannot be dealt with. From the propositional point of view the above sentence is of the form $\varphi \wedge \psi \rightarrow \sigma$, and there is no reason why this sentence should be true, although we obviously accept it as true. The moral is that we have to extend the language, in such a way as to be able to discuss objects and relations. In particular we wish to introduce means to talk about *all* objects of the domain of discourse, e.g. we want to allow statements of the form "all even numbers are a sum of two odd primes". Dually, we want a means of expressing "there exists an object such that ....", e.g. in "there exists a real number whose square is 2".

Experience has taught us that the basic mathematical statements are of the form "a has the property P" or "a and b are in the relation R", etc. Examples are: "n is even", "f is differentiable", "3 = 5", "7 < 12", "B is between A and C"
Therefore we build our language from symbols for *properties*, *relations* and *objects*. Furthermore we add *variables* to range over objects (so called individual variables), and the usual logical connectives now including the *quantifiers* $\forall$ and $\exists$ (for "for all" and "there exists").
We first give a few examples, without paying much attention to the formal details.

$\exists x P(x)$ - there is an x with property P,
$\forall y P(y)$ - for all y P holds (all y have the property P),
$\forall x \exists y (x = 2y)$ - for all x there is a y such that x is two times y,
$\forall \epsilon (\epsilon > 0 \rightarrow \exists n (\frac{1}{n} < \epsilon))$ - for all positive ϵ there is an n such that $\frac{1}{n} < \epsilon$,
$x < y \rightarrow \exists z (x < z \wedge z < y)$ - if $x < y$, then there is a z such that $x < z$ and $z < y$,
$\forall x \exists y (x \cdot y = 1)$ - for each x there exists an inverse y.

We know from elementary set theory that functions are a special kind of relations. It would, however, be in flagrant conflict with mathematical practice to avoid functions (or mappings). Moreover, it would be extremely cumbersome. So we will incorporate functions in our language.

Roughly speaking the language deals with two categories of syntactical entities: one for objects - the *terms*, one for statements - the *formulas*. Examples of terms are: 17, x, (2+5) - 7, x^{3y+1}.

What is the subject of predicate logic with a given language? Or, to put it differently, what are terms and formulas about? The answer is: formulas can express properties concerning a given set of relations and functions on a fixed domain of discourse. We have already met such situations in mathematics; we talked about *structures*, e.g. groups, rings, modules, ordered sets (see any algebra text). We will make structures our point of departure and we will get to the logic later.

In our logic we will speak about "all numbers", or "all elements", but not about "all ideals" or "all subsets", etc. Loosely speaking, our variables will vary over elements of a given universe (e.g. the n×n matrices over the reals), but not over properties or relations, or properties of properties, etc. For this reason the predicate logic of this book is called *first-order logic*, or also *elementary logic*. In everyday mathematics, e.g. analysis, one uses higher order logic. In a way it is a surprise that first-order logic can do so much for mathematics, as we will see.
A short introduction to second-order logic will be presented in chapter 4.

2.2. STRUCTURES

A group is a (non-empty) set equipped with two operations - a binary one and a unary one - and a neutral element (satisfying certain laws).
A partially ordered set is a set, equipped with a binary relation (satisfying certain laws).
We generalize this as follows:

2.1.1. Definition. A *structure* is an ordered sequence
$\langle A, R_1,\ldots,R_n, F_1,\ldots,F_m, \{c_i \mid i \in I\}\rangle$,
where: A is a non-empty set,
$R_1,\ldots,R_n$ are *relations* on A,
$F_1,\ldots,F_m$ are *functions* on A,
the c_i $(i \in I)$ are elements of A (*constants*).

Examples. $\langle \mathbb{R},+,\cdot,-,^{-1},0,1 \rangle$ - the field of real numbers,

$\langle \mathbb{N},< \rangle$ - the ordered set of natural numbers.

We denote structures by Gothic capitals: $\mathfrak{A}, \mathfrak{B}, \mathfrak{C}, \mathfrak{D}, \ldots$..

If we overlook for a moment the special properties of the relations and operations (e.g. commutativity of addition on the reals), then what remains is the *type* of a structure, which is given by the number of relations, functions (or operations), and their respective arguments, plus the number (cardinality) of constants.

2.2.2. Definition. The *similarity type* of a structure $\mathfrak{A} = \langle A, R_1,\ldots,R_n, F_1,\ldots,F_m, \{c_i \mid i \in I\}\rangle$ is a sequence, $\langle r_1,\ldots,r_n; a_1,\ldots,a_m; \kappa\rangle$, where $R_i \subseteq A^{r_i}$, $F_j : A^{a_j} \to A$, $\kappa = |\{c_i \mid i \in I\}|$ (cardinality of I).

The two structures in our example have (similarity) type $\langle -; 2,2,1,1; 2 \rangle$ and $\langle 2; - ; 0\rangle$. The absence of relations, functions is indicated by - . There is no objection to extending the notion of structure to contain arbitrarily many relations or functions, but the most common structures have finite types (including finitely many constants).

If $R \subseteq A$, then we call R a property (or *unary relation*), if $R \subseteq A^2$, then we call R a *binary relation*, if $R \subseteq A^n$, then we call R an *n-ary relation*.

The set A is called the *universe* of $\mathfrak{A}$. Notation $A = |\mathfrak{A}|$. $\mathfrak{A}$ is called (in)finite if its universe is (in)finite.

Among the relations one finds in structures, there is a very special one: the *identity* (or *equality*) *relation*.
Since mathematical structures, as a rule, are equipped with the identity relation, we do not list the relation separately. It does, therefore, not occur in the similarity type. We henceforth assume all structures to possess an identity relation. For purely logical investigations it makes, of course, perfect sense to consider a logic without identity, but the present book caters for mathematical readers.

One might (and some authors do) consider "limiting cases" of relations, i.e. 0-ary relations and functions. A 0-ary relation would be a subset of $A^{\emptyset}$. Since $A^{\emptyset} = \{\emptyset\}$, there are two such relations: $\emptyset$ and $\{\emptyset\}$ (considered as ordinals: 0 and 1). A 0-ary function is a mapping from $A^{\emptyset}$ into A, i.e. a mapping from $\{\emptyset\}$ into A. Since the mapping has a singleton as domain, we can identify it with its range.

In this way 0-ary functions can play the role of constants.
The advantage of the procedure is, however, negligable in the present context, so we will keep our constants.

EXERCISES.

1. Write down the similarity type for the following structures:
   (*i*) $\langle \mathbb{Q}, <, 0 \rangle$,
   (*ii*) $\langle \mathbb{N}, +, \cdot, S, 0, 1, 2, 3, 4, \ldots, n, \ldots \rangle$, where $S(x) = x + 1$,
   (*iii*) $\langle \mathcal{P}(\mathbb{N}), \subseteq, \cup, \cap, ^c, \emptyset \rangle$,
   (*iv*) $\langle \mathbb{Z}/(5), +, \cdot, -, ^{-1}, 0, 1, 2, 3, 4 \rangle$,
   (*v*) $\langle \{0,1\}, \wedge, \vee, \rightarrow, \neg, 0, 1 \rangle$ where $\wedge, \vee, \rightarrow, \neg$ operate according to the ordinary truth tables,
   (*vi*) $\langle \mathbb{R}, 1 \rangle$,
   (*vii*) $\langle \mathbb{R} \rangle$,
   (*viii*) $\langle \mathbb{R}, \mathbb{N}, <, T, ^2, |\ |, - \rangle$, where $T(a,b,c)$ is the relation 'b is between a and c', ^{2} is the square function, and $|\ |$ the absolute value.

2. Give structures with types $\langle 1, 1; - ; 3 \rangle$, $\langle 4; - ; 0 \rangle$.

2.3. THE LANGUAGE OF A SIMILARITY TYPE

The considerations of this section are generalizations of those in section 1.1. Since the arguments are rather similar, we will leave a number of details to the reader. For convenience we fix the similarity type in this section: $\langle r_1, \ldots, r_n ; a_1, \ldots, a_m ; \kappa \rangle$.

The alphabet consists of the following symbols:

1. *Predicate symbols*: $P_1, \ldots, P_n$, $=$
2. *Function symbols*: $f_1, \ldots, f_m$
3. *Constant symbols*: $\bar{c}_i$ for $i \in I$
4. *Variables*: $x_0, x_1, x_2, \ldots$ (countably many)
5. *Connectives*: $\vee, \wedge, \rightarrow, \neg, \leftrightarrow, \bot, \forall, \exists$
6. *Auxilliary symbols*: (,), , .

$\forall$ and $\exists$ are called the *universal* and *existential quantifier*.

Next we define the two syntactical categories.

2.3.1. Definition. TERM is the smallest set X with the properties

(*i*) $\bar{c}_i \in X$ $(i \in I)$ and $x_i \in X$ $(i \in N)$,

(*ii*) $t_1,\ldots,t_{a_i} \in X \rightarrow f_i(t_1,\ldots,t_{a_i}) \in X$, for $1 \leqslant i \leqslant m$.

TERM is out *set of terms*.

2.3.2. Definition. FORM is the smallest set X with the properties:

(*i*) $\bot \in X$, $t_1,\ldots,t_{r_i} \in \text{TERM} \Rightarrow P_i(t_1,\ldots,t_{r_i}) \in X$

$t_1,t_2 \in \text{TERM} \Rightarrow t_1 = t_2 \in X$,

(*ii*) $\varphi,\psi \in X \Rightarrow (\varphi \,\square\, \psi) \in X$, where $\square \in \{\wedge,\vee,\rightarrow,\leftrightarrow\}$,

(*iii*) $\varphi \in X \Rightarrow (\neg\, \varphi) \in X$,

(*iv*) $\varphi \in X \Rightarrow (\forall x_i)\varphi,\ (\exists x_i)\varphi \in X$.

FORM is our set of formulas. We have introduced $t_1 = t_2$ separately, but we could have subsumed it under the first clause. If convenient, we will not treat equality separately.
The formulas introduced in (*i*) are called *atoms*.

Some authors consider also 0-ary predicate symbols, or *proposition symbols*. A proposition symbol should be interpreted as a 0-ary relation, i.e. as 0 or 1 (cf. 2.2.2). This is in accordance with the practice of propositional logic to interpret propositions as true or false.

For our present purpose propositions are an expendable luxury. In dealing with concrete mathematical situations (e.g. groups or posets) one has no reason to introduce propositions (things with a fixed truth value). However, propositions are convenient (and even important) in the context of Boolean-valued logic or Heyting-valued logic.

We will essentially allow one proposition: $\bot$, the symbol for the false proposition (cf. 1.2).
It is ,however, convenient to have an extra proposition available to simplify the substitution procedures in predicate logic (cf. 2.5.6). For full generality we should allow arbitrarily many proposition symbols (e.g. to handle repeated substitution or simultaneous substitution). The reader can easily supplement our treatment of proposition symbols if he wishes to do so.

If the alphabet contains proposition symbols we have to adapt various definitions, e.g. in definition 2.3.2 we have to add to clause (*i*): if \$ is a propositional symbol, then \$ $\in$ X.

One has to make similar changes in a number of definitions, lemmas, theorems etc., in particular in those cases where inductive techniques are used. We leave the adaption to the reader.

Just as in the case of PROP, we have induction principles for TERM and FORM.

2.3.3. Lemma. Let $A(t)$ be a property of terms.
If $A(t)$ holds for t a variable or a constant, and if
$A(t_1), A(t_2), \ldots, A(t_n) \Rightarrow A(f(t_1,\ldots,t_n))$, for all function symbols f,
then $A(t)$ holds for all $t \in$ TERM.

Proof. cf. 1.1.3. □

2.3.4. Lemma. Let $A(\varphi)$ be a property of formulas.
If *(i)* $A(\varphi)$ for atomic φ,
(ii) $A(\varphi), A(\psi) \Rightarrow A((\varphi \,\square\, \psi))$,
(iii) $A(\varphi) \Rightarrow A((\neg\varphi))$,
(iv) $A(\varphi) \Rightarrow A((\forall x_i)\varphi)$, $A((\exists x_i)\varphi)$ for all i, then $A(\varphi)$ holds for all $\varphi \in$ FORM.

Proof. cf. 1.1.3. □

We will straight away introduce a number of abbreviations.
In the first place we adopt the bracket conventions of propositional logic. Furthermore we delete the brackets round $\forall x$ and $\exists x$, whenever possible. We agree that quantifiers bind more strongly than binary connectives.
Furthermore we join strings of quantifiers, e.g. $\forall x_1 x_2 \exists x_3 x_4 \varphi$ stands for $\forall x_1 \forall x_2 \exists x_3 \exists x_4 \varphi$. We will also assume that n in $f(t_1,\ldots,t_n)$, $P(t_1,\ldots,t_n)$ always indicates the correct number of arguments.

A word of warning: the use of = might confuse a careless reader.
The symbol '=' is used in the language L, where it is a proper syntactic object. It occurs in formulas such as $x_0 = x_7$, but it also occurs in the meta-language, e.g., in the form $x = y$, which must be read "x and y are both the same variable". However, the identity symbol in $x = y$ can just as well be the legitimate symbol from the alphabet, i.e. $x = y$ is a meta-atom, which can be converted into a proper atom by substituting genuine variable symbols for x and y.

One way out of this confusion is to have two notations: $\doteq$ in the alphabet, = in the meta-language (actually, there is in addition := for definitional equality). The above examples, written accordingly, are: $x_0 \doteq x_7$; $x = y$; $x \doteq y$.

We will use $\doteq$ a few times, but we prefer to stick to a simple "=" trusting to the alertness of the reader.

2.3.5. Example of a language of type $\langle 2;\ 2,1;\ 1 \rangle$.

predicate symbols: $L, \doteq$
function symbols: p, i
constant symbol: $\bar{e}$
Some terms: $t_1 := x_0;\ t_2 := p(x_1, x_2);\ t_3 := p(\bar{e}, \bar{e});\ t_4 := i(x_7);$
$t_5 := p(i(p(x_2, \bar{e})), i(x_1))$.

Some formulas: $\varphi_1 := x_0 \doteq x_2;$
$\varphi_2 := t_3 \doteq t_4;$
$\varphi_3 := L(i(x_5), \bar{e});$
$\varphi_4 := (x_0 \doteq x_1 \rightarrow x_1 \doteq x_0);$
$\varphi_5 := (\forall x_0)(\forall x_1)(x_0 \doteq x_1 \rightarrow \neg L(x_0, x_1));$
$\varphi_6 := (\forall x_0)(\exists x_1)(p(x_0, x_1) \doteq \bar{e});$
$\varphi_7 := (\exists x_1)(\neg x_1 \doteq \bar{e} \wedge p(x_1, x_1) \doteq e)$.

(We have chosen a suggestive notation; think of the language of ordered groups: L for "less than", p,i for "product" and "inverse").
Note that the order in which the various symbols are listed is important. In our example p has 2 arguments and i has 1.

In mathematics there are a number of *variable binding operations*, such as summation, integration, abstraction: e.g. consider integration, in $\int_0^1 \sin x dx$ the variable plays an unusual role for a variable. For x cannot "vary"; we cannot (without writing nonsense) substitute any number we like for x. In the integral the variable x is reduced to a tag. We say that the variable x is bound by the integration symbol.

Analogously we distinguish in logic between *free* and *bound* variables.

In defining various syntactical notions we again freely use the principle of *definition by recursion* (cf. 1.1 and Appendix).

Definition by recursion on TERM:

Let H_0: Var ∪ Const $\rightarrow$ A (H_0 is defined on variables and constants),
$H_i: A^{a_i} \rightarrow A$, then there is a unique mapping H: TERM $\rightarrow$ A such that

$$\begin{cases} H(t) = H_0(t) \text{ a variable or a constant,} \\ H(f_i(t_1, \ldots, t_{a_i})) = H_i(H(t_1), \ldots, H(t_{a_i})). \end{cases}$$

Definition by recursion on FORM:

Let $H_{at} : At \to A$, (H_{at} is defined on atoms)

$H_{\square} : A^2 \to A$, $\square \in \{\vee,\wedge,\to,\leftrightarrow\}$

$H_{\neg} : A \to A$,

$H_{\forall} : A \times N \to A$,

$H_{\exists} : A \times N \to A$, then there is a unique mapping H: FORM $\to$ A such that

$H(\varphi) = H_{at}(\varphi)$ for atomic φ,

$H(\varphi \square \psi) = H_{\square}(H(\varphi), H(\psi))$,

$H(\neg \varphi) = H_{\neg}(H(\varphi))$,

$H(\forall x_i \varphi) = H_{\forall}(H(\varphi), i)$,

$H(\exists x_i \varphi) = H_{\exists}(H(\varphi), i)$.

The justification is immediate: the value of a term (formula) is uniquely determined by the values of its parts. This allows us to find the value of $H(\varphi)$ in finitely many steps.

2.3.6. Definition. The set FV(t) of free variables of t is defined by

(i) $FV(x_i) := \{x_i\}$,

$FV(\bar{c}_i) := \emptyset$.

(ii) $FV(f(t_1,\ldots,t_n)) := FV(t_1) \cup \ldots \cup FV(t_n)$.

Remark: To avoid messy notation of indices, etc., we write an f (or P) with the correct number of arguments. The reader can easily provide the correct details, should he wish to do so.

2.3.7. Definition. The set $FV(\varphi)$ of free variables of φ is defined by

(i) $FV(P(t_1,\ldots,t_p)) := FV(t_1) \cup \ldots \cup FV(t_p)$,

$FV(t_1 = t_2) := FV(t_1) \cup FV(t_2)$, $FV(\perp) := \emptyset$,

(ii) $FV(\varphi \square \psi) := FV(\varphi) \cup FV(\psi)$,

$FV(\neg \varphi) := FV(\varphi)$,

(iii) $FV(\forall x_i \varphi) := FV(\exists x_i \varphi) := FV(\varphi) - \{x_i\}$.

2.3.8. Definition. t or φ is called *closed* if $FV(t) = \emptyset$, resp. $FV(\varphi) = \emptyset$. A closed formula is also called a *sentence*. A formula without quantifiers is called *open*. $TERM_c$ denotes the set of closed terms; SENT denotes the the set of sentences.

It is left to the reader to define the set $BV(\varphi)$ of *bound variables* of φ.

Continuation of example 2.3.5.

$FV(t_2) = \{x_1,x_2\}$; $FV(t_3) = \emptyset$; $FV(\varphi_2) = FV(t_3) \cup FV(t_4) = \{x_7\}$;

$FV(\varphi_7) = \emptyset$; $BV(\varphi_4) = \emptyset$; $BV(\varphi_6) = \{x_0,x_1\}$. $\varphi_5,\varphi_6,\varphi_7$ are sentences.

Warning. $FV(\varphi) \cap BV(\varphi)$ need not be empty, in other words, the same variable may occur free *and* bound. To handle such situations one can consider free (resp. bound) *occurrences* of variables. When necessary we will make informally use of occurrences of variables.

Example: $\forall x_1(x_1 = x_2) \to P(x_1)$ contains x_1 both free and bound.

The substitution operator for formulas can be copied from section 1.2 if we exercise due care. Recall that in propositional calculus we substituted propositions for atoms. In order to use the same technique here we introduce an auxilliary atom \$.
For there is only one atomic proposition in our language, i.e. $\bot$. If we were to use only $\bot$, then in a substitution we would have to replace all occurrences of $\bot$ simultaneously. So the result of a substitution would always be $\bot$-free. This is not so serious in the presence of $\neg$, but it would be disastrous in more restricted languages.

We therefore define a substitution operator $\varphi[\psi/\$]$ similar to the substitution operator for propositional logic, introduced in section 1.2 (the details are left to the reader as an exercise).
Since we are interested in formulas in the original language we will tacitly assume that \$ does not occur in ψ, whenever convenient. There is no difficulty in introducing a substitution operator in the general case, where we allow arbitrarily many propositional symbols. The reader should try to write down a definition of a simultaneous substitution operator. Our motivation for considering substitution of formulas for propositional symbols is that thus we avoid difficulties involving variables.

In predicate calculus we also have a substitution operator for terms.

2.3.9. Definition. Let s and t be terms, then $s[t/x]$ is defined by

(*i*) $y[t/x] := \begin{cases} y & \text{if } y \neq x \\ t & \text{if } y = x \end{cases}$

$c[t/x] := c$

(*ii*) $f(t_1,\dots,t_p)[t/x] := f(t_1[t/x],\dots,t_p[t/x])$.

Note that in the clause (i) the equality symbol occurs in the meta-language, $y = x$ means "x and y are the same variables".

2.3.10. Definition. $\varphi[t/x]$ is defined by

(i) $\bot[t/x] := \bot$,

$P(t_1,\dots,t_p)[t/x] := P(t_1[t/x],\dots,t_p[t/x])$,

$(t_1 = t_2)[t/x] := t_1[t/x] = t_2[t/x]$,

(ii) $(\varphi \square \psi)[t/x] := \varphi[t/x] \square \psi[t/x]$,

$(\neg\varphi)[t/x] := \neg\varphi[t/x]$,

(iii) $(\forall y\varphi)[t/x] := \begin{cases} \forall y\varphi[t/x] \text{ if } x \neq y \\ \forall y\varphi \text{ if } x = y, \end{cases}$

$(\exists y\varphi)[t/x]$ - idem.

Continuation of example 2.3.5.

$$t_4[t_2/x_1] = i(x_7);\ t_4[t_2/x_7] = i(p(x_1,x_2));$$

$$t_5[x_2/x_1] = p(i(p(x_2,\bar{e})),i(x_2)),$$

$$\varphi_1[t_3/x_0] = p(\bar{e},\bar{e}) \doteq x_2\ ;\ \varphi_5[t_3/x_0] = \varphi_5.$$

We will sometimes make *simultaneous substitutions*, the definition is a slight modification of definitions 2.3.9 and 2.3.10. The reader is asked to write down the formal definitions. We denote the result of a simultaneous substitution of $t_1,\dots,t_n$ for $y_1,\dots,y_n$ in t by $t[t_1,\dots,t_n/y_n,\dots,y_n]$ (similarly for φ).

Note that a simultaneous substitution is not the same as its corresponding repeated substitution.

Example: $(x_0 \doteq x_1)[x_1,x_0/x_0,x_1] = (x_1 \doteq x_0)$,

but $(x_0 \doteq x_1)[x_1/x_0])[x_0/x_1] = (x_1 \doteq x_1)[x_0/x_1] = (x_0 \doteq x_0)$.

The quantifier clause in definition 2.3.10 forbids substitution for bound variables. There is, however, one more case we want to forbid: a substitution, in which some variable after the substitution becomes bound. We will give an example of such a substitution; the reason why we forbid it is that it can change the truth value in an absurd way. At this moment we do not have a truth definition, so the argument is purely heuristic.

Example: $\exists x(y < x)[x/y] = \exists x(x < x)$.

Note that the right-hand side is false in an ordered structure, whereas $\exists x(y < x)$ may very well be true.
We make our restriction precise:

2.3.11. Definition. t is *free for* x *in* φ if

(*i*) φ is atomic,

(*ii*) $\varphi := \varphi_1 \square \varphi_2$ (or $\varphi := \neg \varphi_1$) and t is free for x in φ_1 and φ_2 (resp. φ_1),

(*iii*) $\varphi := \exists y\psi$, or $\varphi := \forall y\psi$, and $x \notin FV(\forall y\psi)$, or $y \notin FV(t)$ and t is free for x in ψ.

Examples: (1) x_2 is free for x_0 in $\exists x_3 P(x_0,x_3)$,

(2) $f(x_0,x_1)$ is not free for x_0 in $\exists x_1 P(x_0,x_3)$,

(3) x_5 is free for x_1 in $P(x_1,x_3) \to \exists x_1 Q(x_1,x_2)$.

From now on we tacitly suppose that all our substitutions satisfy our condition of 2.3.11.

For convenience we introduce an informal notation that simplifies reading and writing.

Notation: In order to simplify the substitution notation and to confirm to an ancient suggestive tradition we will write down (meta-) expressions like $\varphi(x,y,z)$, $\psi(x,x)$, etc.
This neither means that the listed variables occur free nor that no other ones occur free. It is merely a convenient way to handle substitution informally: $\varphi(t)$ is the result of replacing x by t in $\varphi(x) \cdot \varphi(t)$ is called a (*substitution*) *instance* of $\varphi(x)$.

We use the languages introduced above to describe structures, or classes of structures of a given type. The predicate symbols, function symbols and constant symbols act as names for various relations, operations and constants. In describing a structure it is a great help to be able to refer to all elements of $|\mathfrak{A}|$ individually, i.e. to have *names* for all elements (if only as an auxilliary device). Therefore we introduce

2.3.12. Definition. The *extended language*, $L(\mathfrak{A})$, of $\mathfrak{A}$ is obtained from the language L, of the type of $\mathfrak{A}$, by adding constant symbols for all elements of $|\mathfrak{A}|$. We denote the constant symbol, belonging to $a \in |\mathfrak{A}|$, by $\bar{a}$.

Example. Consider the language L of groups; then $L(\mathfrak{A})$, for $\mathfrak{A}$ the additive group of integers, has (extra) constant symbols $\overline{0},\overline{1},\overline{2},\ldots,\overline{-1},\overline{-2},\overline{-3},\ldots$ •

EXERCISES

1. Write down an alphabet for the languages of the types given in exercise 1 of section 2.2.

2. Write down five terms of the language belonging to exercise 1, *(iii)* *(viii)*, Write down two atomic formulas of the language belonging to exercise 1, *(vii)* and two closed atoms for exercise 1, *(iii)*, *(vi)*.

3. Write down an alphabet for languages of types $\langle 3;1,1,2;0\rangle$, $\langle -;2;0\rangle$; $\langle 1;-;3\rangle$.

4. Check which terms are free in the following cases, and carry out the substitution.
   - *(a)* x for x in $x = x$,
   - *(b)* y for x in $x = x$,
   - *(c)* $x + y$ for y in $z = \overline{0}$,
   - *(d)* $\overline{0} + y$ for y in $\exists x(y - x)$,
   - *(e)* $x + y$ for z in $\exists w(w + x = \overline{0})$,
   - *(f)* $x + w$ for z in $\forall w(x + z = 0)$,
   - *(g)* $x + y$ for z in $\forall w(x + z = \overline{0}) \wedge \exists y(z = x)$,
   - *(h)* $x + y$ for z in $\forall u(u = v) \rightarrow \forall z(z = y)$.

2.4. SEMANTICS

The art of interpreting (mathematical) statements presupposes a strict separation between "language" and the mathematical "universe" of entities. The objects of language are symbols, or strings of symbols, the entities of mathematics are numbers, sets, functions, triangles, etc. It is a matter for the philosophy of mathematics to reflect on the universe of mathematics; here we will simply accept it as given to us. Our requirements concerning the mathematical universe are, at present, fairly modest. For example, ordinary set theory will do very well for us. Likewise our desiderata with respect to language are modest. We just suppose that there is an unlimited supply of symbols.

The idea behind the semantics of predicate logic is very simple. Following Tarski, we assume that a statement σ is true in a structure, if it is actually the case that σ applies (the sentence "Snow is white" is true if snow actually is white). A mathematical example: "$\overline{2} + \overline{2} = \overline{4}$" is true in the structure

of natural numbers (with addition) if 2 + 2 = 4 (i.e. if addition of the *numbers* 2 and 2 yields the *number* 4).
Interpretation is the art of relating syntactic objects (strings of symbols) and states of affairs "in reality".

We will start by giving an example of an interpretation in a simple case. We consider the structure $\mathfrak{A} = \langle \mathbb{Z}, <, +, -, 0 \rangle$, i.e. the ordered group of integers. The language has in its alphabet

predicate symbols: $\doteq, L$

function symbols: P, M

constant symbol: $\bar{0}$.

$L(\mathfrak{A})$ has, in addition to all that, constant symbols $\bar{m}$ for all $m \in \mathbb{Z}$.
We first interpret the closed terms of $L(\mathfrak{A})$; the interpretation $t^{\mathfrak{A}}$ of a term t is an element of $\mathbb{Z}$.

t	$t^{\mathfrak{A}}$
$\bar{m}$	m
$P(t_1, t_2)$	$t_1^{\mathfrak{A}} + t_2^{\mathfrak{A}}$
$M(t)$	$-t^{\mathfrak{A}}$

Roughly speaking, we interpret $\bar{m}$ as "its number", P as *plus*, M as *minus*. Note that we interpret only closed terms. This stands to reason, how should one assign a definite integer to x?

Next we interpret *sentences* of $L(\mathfrak{A})$ by assigning one of the truth values 0 or 1. As far as the propositional connectives are concerned, we follow the semantics for propositional logic.

$$v(\bot) = 0,$$

$$v(t = s) = \begin{cases} 1 \text{ if } t^{\mathfrak{A}} = s^{\mathfrak{A}} \\ 0 \text{ else,} \end{cases}$$

$$v(L(t,s)) = \begin{cases} 1 \text{ if } t^{\mathfrak{A}} < s^{\mathfrak{A}} \\ 0 \text{ else,} \end{cases}$$

$$\left.\begin{array}{l} v(\varphi \square \psi) \\ v(\neg \varphi) \end{array}\right\} \text{ as in 1.2.1,}$$

$$v(\forall x \varphi) = \min\{v(\varphi[\bar{n}/x]) \mid n \in \mathbb{Z}\},$$

$$v(\exists x \varphi) = \max\{v(\varphi[\bar{n}/x]) \mid n \in \mathbb{Z}\}.$$

A few explanations are in order.

1. In fact we have defined a function v by recursion on φ.
2. The valuation of a universally quantified formula is obtained by taking the minimum of all valuations of the individual instances, i.e. the value is 1 (true) iff all instances have the value 1. In this respect $\forall$ is a generalisation of $\wedge$. Likewise $\exists$ is a generalisation of $\vee$.
3. v is uniquely determined by $\mathfrak{A}$, hence $v_{\mathfrak{A}}$ would be a more appropriate notation. For convenience we will, however, stick to just v.

Examples.

1. $(P(P(\bar{2},\bar{3}),M(\bar{7})))^{\mathfrak{A}} = P(\bar{2},\bar{3})^{\mathfrak{A}} + M(\bar{7})^{\mathfrak{A}} = (\bar{2}^{\mathfrak{A}} + \bar{3}^{\mathfrak{A}}) + (-\bar{7}^{\mathfrak{A}}) = 2+3+(-7) = -2$,
2. $v(\bar{2} \doteq \overline{-1}) = 0$, since $2 \neq -1$,
3. $v(\bar{0} \doteq \bar{1} \to L(\overline{25},\overline{10})) = 1$, since $v(\bar{0} = \bar{1}) = 0$ and $v(L(\overline{25},\overline{10})) = 0$; by the interpretation of the implication the value is 1,
4. $v(\forall x \exists y (L(x,y))) = \min_n(\max_m v(L(\bar{n},\bar{m})))$

   $v(L(\bar{n},\bar{m})) = 1$ for $m > n$, so for fixed n, $\max_m v(L(\bar{n},\bar{m})) = 1$, and hence

   $\min_n \max_m v(L(\bar{n},\bar{m})) = 1$.

Let us now present a definition of interpretation for the general case. Consider $\mathfrak{A} = \langle A, R_1,\dots,R_n, F_1,\dots,F_m, \{c_i \mid i \in I\}\rangle$ of a given similarity type $\langle r_1,\dots,r_n; a_1,\dots,a_m, |I|\rangle$.
The corresponding language has predicate symbols $\bar{R}_1,\dots,\bar{R}_n$, function symbols $\bar{F}_1,\dots,\bar{F}_m$ and constant symbols $\bar{c}_i$.
$L(\mathfrak{A})$ has moreover constant symbols $\bar{a}$ for all $a \in |\mathfrak{A}|$.

2.4.1. Definition. $t^{\mathfrak{A}}$, the interpretation of a closed term of $L(\mathfrak{A})$ in $\mathfrak{A}$, is a mapping from $TERM_c \to |\mathfrak{A}|$ satisfying

(i) $\bar{c}_i^{\mathfrak{A}} = c_i$; $\bar{a}^{\mathfrak{A}} = a$,

(ii) $(\bar{F}_i(t_1,\dots,t_p))^{\mathfrak{A}} = F_i(t_1^{\mathfrak{A}},\dots,t_p^{\mathfrak{A}})$.

2.4.2. Definition. $v^{\mathfrak{A}}(\varphi)$, the interpretation of a sentence φ of $L(\mathfrak{A})$ in $\mathfrak{A}$, is a mapping from the sentences of $L(\mathfrak{A})$ to $\{0,1\}$, satisfying

(i) $v^{\mathfrak{A}}(\bot) := 0$,

(ii) $v^{\mathfrak{A}}(\bar{P}_i(t_1,\dots,t_p)) := \begin{cases} 1 \text{ if } \langle t_1^{\mathfrak{A}},\dots,t_p^{\mathfrak{A}}\rangle \in P_i \\ 0 \text{ else,} \end{cases}$

$$v^{\mathfrak{A}}(t_1 = t_2) := \begin{cases} 1 \text{ if } t_1^{\mathfrak{A}} = t_2^{\mathfrak{A}} \\ 0 \text{ else,} \end{cases}$$

(iii) $v^{\mathfrak{A}}(\varphi \wedge \psi) := \min(v^{\mathfrak{A}}(\varphi), v^{\mathfrak{A}}(\psi))$,

$v^{\mathfrak{A}}(\varphi \vee \psi) := \max(v^{\mathfrak{A}}(\varphi), v^{\mathfrak{A}}(\psi))$,

$v^{\mathfrak{A}}(\varphi \rightarrow \psi) := \max(1 - v^{\mathfrak{A}}(\varphi), v^{\mathfrak{A}}(\psi))$,

$v^{\mathfrak{A}}(\varphi \leftrightarrow \psi) := 1 - |v^{\mathfrak{A}}(\varphi) - v^{\mathfrak{A}}(\psi)|$,

$v^{\mathfrak{A}}(\neg \varphi) := 1 - v^{\mathfrak{A}}(\varphi)$,

(iv) $v^{\mathfrak{A}}(\forall x \varphi) := \min\{v^{\mathfrak{A}}(\varphi[\bar{a}/x]) \mid a \in |\mathfrak{A}|\}$,

$v^{\mathfrak{A}}(\exists x \varphi) := \max\{v^{\mathfrak{A}}(\varphi[\bar{a}/x]) \mid a \in |\mathfrak{A}|\}$.

In predicate logic the valuation-notation is not very convenient, therefore we introduce the following.

Notation: $\mathfrak{A} \models \varphi$ stands for $v^{\mathfrak{A}}(\varphi) = 1$.
We say that "φ is true, valid, in $\mathfrak{A}$" if $\mathfrak{A} \models \varphi$.
The relation $\models$ is called the *satisfaction relation.*

So far we have only defined truth for sentences of $L(\mathfrak{A})$. In order to extend $\models$ to arbitrary formulas we introduce a new notation.

2.4.3. Definition. Let $FV(\varphi) = \{z_1, \ldots, z_k\}$, then $Cl(\varphi) := \forall z_1 z_2 \ldots z_k \varphi$ is the *universal closure* of φ (we assume the order of variables z_i to be fixed in some way).

2.4.4. Definition.

(i) $\mathfrak{A} \models \varphi$ iff $\mathfrak{A} \models Cl(\varphi)$,

(ii) $\models \varphi$ iff $\mathfrak{A} \models \varphi$ for all $\mathfrak{A}$ (of the appropriate type),

(iii) $\Gamma \models \varphi$ iff $((\mathfrak{A} \models \psi$ for all $\psi \in \Gamma) \Rightarrow \mathfrak{A} \models \varphi)$, where $\Gamma \cup \{\varphi\}$ consists of sentences.

If $\mathfrak{A} \models \sigma$, we call $\mathfrak{A}$ a *model* of σ. In general: if $\mathfrak{A} \models \sigma$ for all $\sigma \in \Gamma$, we call $\mathfrak{A}$ a *model* of Γ.
We say that φ is *true* if $\models \varphi$. φ is a *semantic consequence* of Γ if $\Gamma \models \varphi$, i.e. φ holds in each model of Γ. Note that this is all a straight-forward generalisation of 1.2.4.

If φ is a formula with free variables, say $FV(\varphi) = \{z_1, \ldots, z_k\}$, then we say that φ is *satisfied by* $a_1, \ldots, a_k \in |\mathfrak{A}|$ if $\mathfrak{A} \models \varphi[\bar{a}_1, \ldots, \bar{a}_k / z_1, \ldots, z_k]$, φ is called *satisfiable in* $\mathfrak{A}$ if there are $a_1, \ldots, a_k$ such that φ is satisfied by

$a_1,\ldots,a_k$. φ is called *satisfiable* if it is satisfiable in some $\mathfrak{A}$.
Note that that φ is satisfiable in $\mathfrak{A}$ if $\mathfrak{A} \models \exists z_1 \ldots z_k \varphi$.

The properties of the satisfaction relation are in understandable and convenient correspondence with the intuitive meaning of the connectives.

2.4.5. Lemma. If we restrict ourselves to sentences, then

(*i*) $\mathfrak{A} \models \varphi \wedge \psi \Leftrightarrow \mathfrak{A} \models \varphi$ *and* $\mathfrak{A} \models \psi$,

(*ii*) $\mathfrak{A} \models \varphi \vee \psi \Leftrightarrow \mathfrak{A} \models \varphi$ *or* $\mathfrak{A} \models \psi$,

(*iii*) $\mathfrak{A} \models \neg\varphi \Leftrightarrow \mathfrak{A} \not\models \varphi$,

(*iv*) $\mathfrak{A} \models \varphi \to \psi \Leftrightarrow (\mathfrak{A} \models \varphi \Rightarrow \mathfrak{A} \models \psi)$,

(*v*) $\mathfrak{A} \models \varphi \leftrightarrow \psi \Leftrightarrow (\mathfrak{A} \models \varphi \Leftrightarrow \mathfrak{A} \models \psi)$,

(*vi*) $\mathfrak{A} \models \forall x\, \varphi \Leftrightarrow \mathfrak{A} \models \varphi[\bar{a}/x]$, for all $a \in |\mathfrak{A}|$,

(*vii*) $\mathfrak{A} \models \exists x\, \varphi \Leftrightarrow \mathfrak{A} \models \varphi[\bar{a}/x]$, for some $a \in |\mathfrak{A}|$.

Proof. Immediate from definition 2.4.2. We will do two cases.

(*iv*) $\mathfrak{A} \models \varphi \to \psi \Leftrightarrow v^{\mathfrak{A}}(\varphi \to \psi) = \max(1 - v^{\mathfrak{A}}(\varphi), v^{\mathfrak{A}}(\psi)) = 1$.
Suppose $\mathfrak{A} \models \varphi$, i.e. $v^{\mathfrak{A}}(\varphi) = 1$, then clearly $v^{\mathfrak{A}}(\psi) = 1$, or $\mathfrak{A} \models \psi$.
Conversely, let $\mathfrak{A} \models \varphi \to \mathfrak{A} \models \psi$, and suppose $\mathfrak{A} \not\models \varphi \to \psi$, then
$v^{\mathfrak{A}}(\varphi \to \psi) = \max(1 - v^{\mathfrak{A}}(\varphi), v^{\mathfrak{A}}(\psi)) = 0$. Hence $v^{\mathfrak{A}}(\psi) = 0$ and therefore
$v^{\mathfrak{A}}(\varphi) = 1$. Contradiction.

(*vii*) $\mathfrak{A} \models \exists x \varphi(x) \Leftrightarrow \max\{v^{\mathfrak{A}}(\varphi(\bar{a})) \mid a \in |\mathfrak{A}|\} = 1 \Leftrightarrow$ there is an $a \in |\mathfrak{A}|$
such that $v^{\mathfrak{A}}\varphi(\bar{a}) = 1 \Leftrightarrow$ there is an $a \in |\mathfrak{A}|$ such that $\mathfrak{A} \models \varphi(\bar{a})$.

Lemma 2.4.5 tells us that the interpretation of sentences in $\mathfrak{A}$ runs parallel to the construction of the sentences by means of the connectives. In other words, we replace the connectives by their analogues in the meta-language and interpret the atoms by checking the relations in the structure.

E.g. take our example of the ordered additive group of integers.
$\mathfrak{A} \models \neg \forall x \exists y\ (x \doteq P(y,y)) \Leftrightarrow$ It is not the case that for each number n there exists an m such that $n = 2m \Leftrightarrow$ not every number can be halved in $\mathfrak{A}$. This clearly is correct, take for instance $n = 1$.

For completeness sake we indicate how to interprete propositions in the present setting. Recall that a 0-ary relation is one of the sets $\emptyset$ or $\{\emptyset\}$. Let the proposition symbol P have an interpretation $P^{\mathfrak{A}}$ in $\mathfrak{A}$. We put $v(P) = 1$ if $P^{\mathfrak{A}} = \{\emptyset\}$ and $v(P) = 0$ if $P^{\mathfrak{A}} = \emptyset$.
There is a good motivation for this definition: an n-ary predicate symbol P is

interpreted by a subset $P^{\mathfrak{A}}$ of A^n, and $\mathfrak{A} \models \exists x_1 \ldots x_n \; P(x_1,\ldots,x_n)$ iff $P^{\mathfrak{A}} \neq \emptyset$. Consider the special case $n = 0$, then $P^{\mathfrak{A}}$ is a subset of $A^{\emptyset} = \{\emptyset\}$ and P, preceded by a string of zero existential quantifiers, (i.e. P itself) holds in $\mathfrak{A}$ iff $P^{\mathfrak{A}} \neq \emptyset$, so $P^{\mathfrak{A}} = \{\emptyset\}$.

We can now augment definition 2.4.2 so that interpretations of propositions are included.

EXERCISES

1. Let $\mathfrak{N} = \langle N,+,\cdot,S,0\rangle$, and L a language of type $\langle -;2,2,1;1\rangle$.
   - *(i)* Give two distinct terms t in L such that $t^{\mathfrak{N}} = 5$,
   - *(ii)* Show that for each natural number $n \in N$ there is a term t such that $t^{\mathfrak{N}} = n$,
   - *(iii)* Show that for each $n \in N$ there are infinitely many terms t such that $t^{\mathfrak{N}} = n$.

2. Let $\mathfrak{A}$ be the structure of exercise 1 *(v)* of section 2.2.
   Evaluate $((\overline{1} \rightarrow \overline{0}) \leftrightarrow \neg\, \overline{0})^{\mathfrak{A}}$, $(\overline{1} \rightarrow \neg\, (\neg\, \overline{0} \vee \overline{1}))^{\mathfrak{A}}$.

3. Let $\mathfrak{A}$ be the structure of exercise 1 *(viii)*.
   Evaluate $(|(\overline{\sqrt{3}})^2 + \overline{-5}|)^{\mathfrak{A}}$, $(\overline{1} + (\overline{-2}) + -(\overline{-2}))^{\mathfrak{A}}$.

4. Show that in lemma 2.4.5 the restriction to sentences is necessary.

5. For sentences σ we have $\mathfrak{A} \models \sigma$ or $\mathfrak{A} \models \neg\,\sigma$.
   Show that this does not hold for φ with $FV(\varphi) \neq \emptyset$.
   Show that not even for sentences does $\models \sigma$ or $\models \neg\,\sigma$ hold.

6. Show, by induction on φ, $\mathfrak{A} \models \varphi(t) \Leftrightarrow \mathfrak{A} \models \varphi(\overline{t^{\mathfrak{A}}})$ for closed terms t (in $L(\mathfrak{A})$).

7. Show that $\mathfrak{A} \models \varphi \Rightarrow \mathfrak{A} \models \psi$ for all $\mathfrak{A}$, implies $\models \varphi \Rightarrow \models \psi$, but not vice versa.

2.5. SIMPLE PROPERTIES OF PREDICATE LOGIC

Our definition of validity (truth) was a straightforward extension of the valuation-definition of propositional logic. As a consequence formulas, which are instances of tautologies, are true in all structures $\mathfrak{A}$ (exercise 1). So we can copy many results from sections 1.2 and 1.3. We will use these results with a simple reference to propositional logic.

The specific properties concerning quantifiers will be treated in this section. First we consider the generalizations of De Morgan's laws.

2.5.1. Theorem. (*i*) $\models \neg \forall x\varphi \leftrightarrow \exists x \neg \varphi$,

(*ii*) $\models \neg \exists x\varphi \leftrightarrow \forall x \neg \varphi$,

(*iii*) $\models \forall x\varphi \leftrightarrow \neg\exists x \neg \varphi$,

(*iv*) $\models \exists x\varphi \leftrightarrow \neg\forall x \neg \varphi$.

Proof. If there are no free variables involved, then the above equivalences are almost trivial. We will do one general case.

(*i*) Let $FV(\forall x\varphi) = \{z_1,\ldots,z_k\}$, then we must show
$\mathfrak{A} \models \forall z_1,\ldots,z_k(\neg \forall x\varphi(x,z_1,\ldots,z_k) \leftrightarrow \exists x \neg \varphi(x,z_1,\ldots,z_k))$, for all $\mathfrak{A}$.
So we have to show $\mathfrak{A} \models \neg \forall x\varphi(x,\bar{a}_1,\ldots,\bar{a}_k) \leftrightarrow \exists x \neg \varphi(x,\bar{a}_1,\ldots,\bar{a}_k)$ for arbitrary $a_1,\ldots,a_k \in |\mathfrak{A}|$. We apply lemma 2.4.5:
$\mathfrak{A} \models \neg \forall x\varphi(x,\bar{a}_1,\ldots,\bar{a}_k) \Leftrightarrow \mathfrak{A} \not\models \forall x\varphi(x,\bar{a}_1,\ldots,\bar{a}_k) \Leftrightarrow$ not for all $b \in |\mathfrak{A}|$
$\mathfrak{A} \models \varphi(\bar{b},\bar{a}_1,\ldots,\bar{a}_k) \Leftrightarrow$ there is a $b \subset |\mathfrak{A}|$ such that $\mathfrak{A} \not\models \varphi(\bar{b},\bar{a}_1,\ldots,\bar{a}_k)$
$\Leftrightarrow$ there is a $b \in |\mathfrak{A}|$ such that $\mathfrak{A} \models \neg\varphi(\bar{b},\bar{a}_1,\ldots,\bar{a}_k) \Leftrightarrow$
$\mathfrak{A} \models \exists x \neg\varphi(x,\bar{a}_1,\ldots,\bar{a}_n)$,

(*ii*) is similarly dealt with,
(*iii*) and (*iv*) can be obtained from (*i*), (*ii*). □

The order of quantifiers of the same sort is irrelevant, and quantification over a variable that does not occur can be deleted.

2.5.2. Theorem. (*i*) $\models \forall x\forall y\varphi \leftrightarrow \forall y\forall x\varphi$,

(*ii*) $\models \exists x\exists y\varphi \leftrightarrow \exists y\exists x\varphi$,

(*iii*) $\models \forall x\varphi \leftrightarrow \varphi$ if $x \notin FV(\varphi)$,

(*iv*) $\models \exists x\varphi \leftrightarrow \varphi$ if $x \notin FV(\varphi)$.

Proof. Left to the reader. □

We have already observed that $\forall$ and $\exists$ are, in a way, generalizations of $\wedge$ and $\vee$. Therefore it is not surprising that $\forall$ (and $\exists$) distributes over $\wedge$ (resp. $\vee$). $\forall$ (and $\exists$) distributes over $\vee$ (resp. $\wedge$) only if a certain condition is met.

2.5.3. Theorem. (*i*) $\models \forall x(\varphi \wedge \psi) \leftrightarrow \forall x\varphi \wedge \forall x\psi$,

(*ii*) $\models \exists x(\varphi \vee \psi) \leftrightarrow \exists x\varphi \vee \exists x\psi$,

(*iii*) $\models \forall x(\varphi(x) \vee \psi) \leftrightarrow \forall x\varphi(x) \vee \psi$ if $x \notin FV(\psi)$,

(*iv*) $\models \exists x(\varphi(x) \wedge \psi) \leftrightarrow \exists x\varphi(x) \wedge \psi$ if $x \notin FV(\psi)$.

Proof. (*i*) and (*ii*) are immediate.

(*iii*) Let $FV(\forall x(\varphi(x) \vee \psi)) = \{z_1,\dots,z_k\}$. We must show that $\mathfrak{A} \models \forall z_1,\dots,z_k[\forall x(\varphi(x) \vee \psi) \leftrightarrow \forall x\varphi(x) \vee \psi]$ for all $\mathfrak{A}$, so we show, using lemma 2.4.5, that $\mathfrak{A} \models \forall x(\varphi(x,\bar{a}_1,\dots,\bar{a}_k)) \vee \psi(\bar{a}_1,\dots,\bar{a}_k)) \Leftrightarrow$ $\mathfrak{A} \models \forall x\varphi(x,\bar{a}_1,\dots,\bar{a}_k) \vee \psi(\bar{a}_1,\dots,\bar{a}_k)$ for all $\mathfrak{A}$ and all $a_1,\dots,a_k \in |\mathfrak{A}|$.

$\Leftarrow$: $\mathfrak{A} \models \forall x\varphi(x,\text{——}) \vee \psi(\text{——}) \Leftrightarrow \mathfrak{A} \models \forall x\varphi(x,\text{——})$ or $\mathfrak{A} \models \psi(\text{——}) \Leftrightarrow$ for all $b \in |\mathfrak{A}|$ $\mathfrak{A} \models \varphi(\bar{b},\text{——})$ or $\mathfrak{A} \models \psi(\text{——})$.
If $\mathfrak{A} \models \psi(\text{——})$, then also $\mathfrak{A} \models \varphi(\bar{b},\text{——}) \vee \psi(\text{——})$ for all b, so $\mathfrak{A} \models \forall x(\varphi(x,\text{——}) \vee \psi(\text{——}))$. If $\mathfrak{A} \models \varphi(\bar{b},\text{——})$ for all b, then $\mathfrak{A} \models \varphi(\bar{b},\text{——}) \vee \psi(\text{——})$ for all b, so $\mathfrak{A} \models \forall x(\varphi(x,\text{——}) \vee \psi(\text{——}))$. In both cases we get the desired result.

$\Rightarrow$: We know that for each $b \in |\mathfrak{A}|$ $\mathfrak{A} \models \varphi(\bar{b},\text{——}) \vee \psi(\text{——})$. If $\mathfrak{A} \models \psi(\text{——})$, then also $\mathfrak{A} \models \forall x\varphi(x,\text{——}) \vee \psi(\text{——})$, so we are done.
If $\mathfrak{A} \not\models \psi(\text{——})$ then necessarily $\mathfrak{A} \models \varphi(\bar{b},\text{——})$ for all b, so $\mathfrak{A} \models \forall x\varphi(x,\text{——})$ and hence $\mathfrak{A} \models \forall x\varphi(x,\text{——}) \vee \psi(\text{——})$. □

(*iv*) is similar.

WARNING. $\forall x(\varphi(x) \vee \psi(x)) \rightarrow \forall x\varphi(x) \vee \forall x\psi(x)$, and

$\exists x\varphi(x) \wedge \exists x\psi(x) \rightarrow \exists x(\varphi(x) \wedge \psi(x))$ are *not* true.

All the same it is possible to manoevre the quantifiers of a formula to the front. The trick is well known from analysis. We know that we can change the variable in an integral in a suitable way: $\int xydy = \int xzdz$ and $x\int xdx = x\int ydy = \int xydy$. For quantifiers we have an analogous law.

2.5.4. Theorem. (*change of bound variables*)
If z does not occur in φ, then $\models \exists x\varphi(x) \leftrightarrow \exists z\varphi(z)$,

$$\models \forall x\varphi(x) \leftrightarrow \forall z\varphi(z).$$

(A more symmetric formulation is: $\models \exists x\varphi[x/y] \leftrightarrow \exists z\varphi[z/y]$ and $\models \forall x\varphi[x/y] \leftrightarrow \forall z\varphi[z/y]$, where $x,z \notin FV(\varphi)$).

For the proof of the theorem we need a lemma on substitutions:

2.5.5. Lemma. (*i*) If $z \notin FV(t)$, then $t[\bar{a}/x] = (t[z/x])[\bar{a}/z]$,

(*ii*) If z does not occur in φ, then $\varphi[\bar{a}/x] = (\varphi[z/x])[\bar{a}/z]$,

(*iii*) Let t be free for x in φ and ψ, then
$(\varphi[\psi/\$])[t/x] = (\varphi[t/x])[\psi[t/x]/\$]$.

Proof. (*i*) A simple induction on t,

(*ii*) Induction on φ.

For atomic φ (*ii*) follows directly from (*i*).
The case of the propositional connectives is left to the reader.
Let $\varphi = \forall y \psi(y)$.

There are two cases to be considered.

1. $x = y$, then $\varphi[\bar{a}/x] = \varphi$, and $\varphi[z/x] = \varphi$.
   Since z does not occur in φ, $\varphi[\bar{a}/z] = \varphi$. This proves case 1.
2. $x \neq y$, then $\varphi[\bar{a}/x] = \forall y \psi[\bar{a}/x]$ and $(\varphi[z/x])[\bar{a}/z] = (\forall y \psi[z/x])[\bar{a}/z]$.
   Since z does not occur in φ, $z \neq y$, so
   $(\forall y \psi[z/x])[\bar{a}/z] = \forall y((\psi[z/x])[\bar{a}/z]) = \forall y \psi[\bar{a}/x]$, by the induction hypothesis.
   This finishes case 2.

The case $\varphi = \exists y \psi$ is similar.

(*iii*) Induction on φ. An exercise for the reader. □

Proof of theorem 2.5.4. It is no restriction to suppose $FV(\varphi) = \{x\}$, because in the presence of extra variables we introduce constants in the extended language, cf. the proof of 2.5.3. We show that $\mathfrak{A} \models \exists x \varphi \Leftrightarrow \mathfrak{A} \models \exists z \varphi[z/x]$.

$\mathfrak{A} \models \exists x \varphi(x) \Leftrightarrow \mathfrak{A} \models \varphi(\bar{a})$ for some $a \in |\mathfrak{A}|$,

$\Leftrightarrow \mathfrak{A} \models (\varphi[z/x])[\bar{a}/z]$ for some $a \in |\mathfrak{A}|$,

$\Leftrightarrow \mathfrak{A} \models \exists z \varphi[z/x]$.

Give a similar proof for the universal quantifier case. □

We now can pull out quantifiers:

$\forall x \varphi(x) \vee \forall x \psi(x) \leftrightarrow \forall x \varphi(x) \vee \forall y \psi(y)$ and

$\forall x \varphi(x) \vee \forall y \psi(y) \leftrightarrow \forall xy(\varphi(x) \vee \psi(y))$, for a suitable y.

In order to handle predicate logic in an algebraic way we need the technique of substituting equivalents for equivalents.

2.5.6. Substitution theorem.

(*i*) $\mathfrak{A} \models \varphi \leftrightarrow \psi \Rightarrow \mathfrak{A} \models \sigma[\varphi/\$] \leftrightarrow \sigma[\psi/\$]$,

$(ii)\quad \mathfrak{A} \models t = s \;\Rightarrow\; \mathfrak{A} \models \sigma[t/x] \leftrightarrow \sigma[s/x]$,

$(iii)\quad \models \varphi \leftrightarrow \psi \;\Rightarrow\; \models \sigma[\varphi/\$] \leftrightarrow \sigma[\psi/\$]$,

$(iv)\quad \models t = s \;\Rightarrow\; \models \sigma[t/x] \leftrightarrow \sigma[s/x]$.

Proof. The symbol '\$' is used here only as a place holder.
For (ii) we need the fact that $\mathfrak{A} \models t = s \Rightarrow t^{\mathfrak{A}} = s^{\mathfrak{A}}$ for closed t and s in $L(\mathfrak{A})$. This is easily shown by induction.
Consider (ii). Let $FV(\sigma) \cup FV(t) \cup FV(s) = \{z_1,\dots,z_k\}$. We must show

$$\mathfrak{A} \models \forall z_1,\dots,z_k(\sigma[t/x] \leftrightarrow \sigma[s/x]),$$

or $\mathfrak{A} \models (\sigma[t/x] \leftrightarrow \sigma[s/x])[\bar{a}_1,\dots,\bar{a}_k/z_1,\dots,z_k]$, for all $a_1,\dots,a_k$.
We will simplify the notation a bit, let σ be $\sigma(x,z_1,\dots,z_k)$ and
$t = t(z_1,\dots,z_k)$, $s = s(z_1,\dots,z_k)$.
Then $\sigma(t(z_1,\dots,z_k),z_1,\dots,z_k)[\bar{a}_1,\dots,\bar{a}_k/z_1,\dots,z_k] =$

$\sigma(t(\bar{a}_1,\dots,\bar{a}_k),\bar{a}_1,\dots,\bar{a}_k)$, similarly for s.

Now one shows $v(\sigma(t(-),-)) = v(\sigma(s(-),-))$, where we use the $-$ notation to indicate the $\bar{a}_i$'s. This follows directly from the fact that $t^{\mathfrak{A}}(-) = s^{\mathfrak{A}}(-)$.
The details are left to the reader.

To show (i) we use a similar convention on the variables:
$FV(\sigma) \cup FV(\varphi) \cup FV(\psi) \subseteq \{z_1,\dots,z_k\}$.
We are given that $v(\varphi(\bar{a}_1,\dots,a_k)) = v(\psi(\bar{a}_1,\dots,\bar{a}_k))$, for all $a_i \in |\mathfrak{A}|$ and we want to show $v((\sigma[\varphi/\$])[\bar{a}_1,\dots,\bar{a}_k/z_1,\dots,z_k]) = v((\sigma[\psi/\$])[\bar{a}_1,\dots,\bar{a}_k/z_1,\dots,z_k])$.
Use induction on σ.

1. σ is atomic. If $\sigma \neq \$$, then the identity is trivial.
   If $\sigma = \$$, it is trivial too.

2. If $\sigma = \sigma_1 \,\square\, \sigma_2$, or $\sigma = \neg\sigma_1$, then the result follows immediately from the induction hypothesis, since the value of σ is a function of the values of its parts.

3. $\sigma = \forall x\cdot\tau$. This case is slightly more involved, since φ or ψ may contain x free.
   Let us suppose that $x = z_1$.
   $v((\sigma[\varphi/\$])[\bar{a}_1,\dots,\bar{a}_k/z_1,\dots,z_k]) =$
   $v((\forall z_1\cdot\tau[\varphi/\$])[\bar{a}_1,\dots,\bar{a}_k/z_1,\dots,z_k]) =$
   $v(\forall z_1\cdot(\tau[\bar{a}_2,\dots,a_k/z_2,\dots,z_k])(\varphi[\bar{a}_2,\dots,\bar{a}_k/z_2,\dots,z_k]/\$]) =$
   $\min_b v((\tau[\bar{b},\bar{a}_1,\dots,\bar{a}_k/z_1,\dots,z_k])(\varphi[\bar{b},\bar{a}_1,\dots,\bar{a}_k/z_1,\dots,z_k]/\$) =$
   $\min_b v((\tau[\varphi/\$])[\bar{b},\bar{a}_1,\dots,\bar{a}_k/z_1,\dots,z_k]) = j$.

We now apply the induction hypothesis:

$v((\tau[\varphi/\$])[\bar{b},\bar{a}_1,\ldots,\bar{a}_k/z_1,\ldots,z_k]) = v((\tau[\psi/\$])[\bar{b},\bar{a}_1,\ldots,\bar{a}_k/z_1,\ldots,z_k])$

for all $b,a_1,\ldots,a_k \in |\mathfrak{A}|$. Hence by a computation, as above, we obtain

$j = v((\forall z_1.\tau[\psi/\$])[\bar{a}_1,\ldots,\bar{a}_k/z_1,\ldots,z_k])$.

This establishes the required identity.

The proof for $\exists x\cdot\tau$ is completely similar.

(iii) and *(iv)* are immediate corollaries of *(i)* and *(ii)*. □

Proofs involving detailed analysis of substitution are rather dreary but, unfortunately, unavoidable. The reader may simplify the above and other proofs by supposing the formulas involved to be closed. There is no real loss in generality, since we only introduce a number of constants from $L(\mathfrak{A})$ and check that the result is valid for all choices of constants.

We now really can manipulate formulae in an algebraic way. Again, write φ eq ψ for $\models \varphi \leftrightarrow \psi$.

Examples.

1. $\forall x\varphi(x) \rightarrow \psi$ eq $\neg\forall x\varphi(x) \vee \psi$ eq $\exists x(\neg\varphi(x) \vee \psi)$ eq $\exists x(\neg\varphi(x) \vee \psi)$ eq $\exists x(\varphi(x) \rightarrow \psi)$, where $x \notin FV(\psi)$.

2. $\forall x\varphi(x) \rightarrow \exists x\varphi(x)$ eq $\neg\forall x\varphi(x) \vee \exists x\varphi(x)$ eq $\exists x(\neg\varphi(x) \vee \varphi(x))$. The formula in the scope of the quantifier is true (already by propositional logic), so the formula itself is true.

2.5.7. Definition. A formula φ is in *prenex (normal) form* if φ consists of a (possibly empty) string of quantifiers followed by an open formula. We also say that φ is a prenex formula.

Examples. $\exists x\forall y\exists z\exists v\,(x = z \vee y = z \rightarrow v < y)$,

$\forall x\forall y\exists z(P(x,y) \wedge Q(y,x) \rightarrow P(z,z))$.

By pulling out quantifiers we can reduce each formula to a formula in prenex form.

2.5.8. Theorem. For each φ there is a prenex formula ψ such that $\models \varphi \leftrightarrow \psi$.

Proof. First eliminate $\rightarrow$ and $\leftrightarrow$. Use induction on the resulting formula φ'.

For atomic φ' the theorem is trivial.
If $\varphi' = \varphi_1 \vee \varphi_2$ and φ_1, φ_2 are equivalent to prenex ψ_1, ψ_2 then
$\psi_1 = (Q_1 y_1)\ldots(Q_n y_n)\psi^1$.
$\psi_2 = (Q'_1 z_1)\ldots(Q'_m z_m)\psi^2$, where Q_i, Q'_j are quantifiers and ψ^1, ψ^2 open. By theorem 2.5.4 we can choose all bound variables distinct, taking care that no variable is both free and bound. Applying theorem 2.5.3 we find

$\models \varphi' \leftrightarrow (Q_1 y_1)\ldots(Q_n y_n)(Q'_1 z_1)\ldots(Q'_m z_m)(\psi^1 \vee \psi^2)$, so we are done.

The remaining cases are left to the reader. □

2.5.9. Relativization.

In ordinary mathematics it is usually taken for granted that the benevolent reader can guess the intentions of the author, not only the explicit ones, but also the ones that are tacitly handed down generations of mathematicians. Take for example the definition of convergence of a sequence:
$\forall \varepsilon > 0 \quad \exists n \forall m \; (|a_n - a_{n+m}| < \varepsilon)$. In order to make sense out of this expression one has to add: the variables n,m range over natural numbers. Unfortunately our syntax does not allow for variables of different sorts. So how do we incorporate expressions of the above kind? The answer is simple: we add predicates of the desired sort and indicate inside the formula the "nature" of the variable.

Example. Let $\mathfrak{A} = \langle \mathbb{R}, \mathbb{Q}, < \rangle$ be the structure of the reals with the set of rational numbers singled out, provided with the natural order. The sentence
$\sigma := \forall xy(x < y \rightarrow \exists z(Q(z) \wedge x < z \wedge z < y))$ can be interpreted in $\mathfrak{A}$: $\mathfrak{A} \models \sigma$, and it tells us that the rationals are dense in the reals (in the natural ordering).

We find this mode of expression, however, rather cumbersome. Therefore we introduce the notation *relativized quantifiers*. Since it does not matter whether we express informally "x is rational" by $x \in \mathbb{Q}$ or $Q(x)$, we will suit ourselves and any time choose the notation which is most convenient.

We use $(\exists x \in Q)$ and $(\forall x \in Q)$ as informal notation for "there exists an x in $\mathbb{Q}$" and "for all x in $\mathbb{Q}$".
Now we can write σ as $\forall xy(x < y \rightarrow \exists z \in Q(x < z \wedge z < y))$.
Note that we do *not* write $(\forall xy \in R)(\text{——})$, since:

(1) there is no relation $\mathbb{R}$ in $\mathfrak{A}$,
(2) variables automatically range over $|\mathfrak{A}| = \mathbb{R}$.

Let us now define the relativization of a quantifier properly:

If P is a unary predicate symbol, then

$(\forall x \in P)\varphi := (\forall x)(P(x) \rightarrow \varphi)$,

$(\exists x \in P)\varphi := (\exists x)(P(x) \wedge \varphi)$.

This notation has the intended meaning, as appears from

$\mathfrak{A} \models (\forall x \in P)\varphi \Leftrightarrow$ for all $a \in P^{\mathfrak{A}}$ $\mathfrak{A} \models \varphi[\bar{a}/x]$,

$\mathfrak{A} \models (\exists x \in P)\varphi \Leftrightarrow$ there exists an $a \in P^{\mathfrak{A}}$ such that $\mathfrak{A} \models \varphi[\bar{a}/x]$.

Proof. Immediate. □

We will often use informal notations, such as $(\forall x > 0)$ or $(\exists y \neq 1)$, which can be cast into the above form. The meaning of such notations will always be evident.

One can restrict *all* quantifiers to the same set (predicate), this amounts to passing to a restricted universe (cf. exercise 10).

EXERCISES

1. Let $x \notin FV(\psi)$.
   Show (*i*) $\models (\forall x\varphi \rightarrow \psi) \leftrightarrow \exists x(\varphi \rightarrow \psi)$,
   (*ii*) $\models (\exists x\varphi \rightarrow \psi) \leftrightarrow \forall x(\varphi \rightarrow \psi)$,
   (*iii*) $\models (\psi \rightarrow \exists x\varphi) \leftrightarrow \exists x(\psi \rightarrow \varphi)$,
   (*iv*) $\models (\psi \rightarrow \forall x\varphi) \leftrightarrow \forall x(\psi \rightarrow \varphi)$.

2. Show that the condition on $FV(\psi)$ in exercise 1 is necessary.

3. Show $\not\models \forall x\exists y\varphi \leftrightarrow \exists y\forall x\varphi$.

4. Show $\models \varphi \Rightarrow \models \forall x\varphi$ and $\models \exists x\varphi$.

5. Show $\not\models \exists x\varphi \rightarrow \forall x\varphi$.

6. Show $\not\models \exists x\varphi \wedge \exists x\psi \rightarrow \exists x(\varphi \wedge \psi)$.

7. Show that the condition on z in Theorem 2.5.4 is necessary.

8. Show (*i*) $\models \forall x(\varphi \rightarrow \psi) \rightarrow (\forall x\varphi \rightarrow \forall x\psi)$,
   (*ii*) $\models \exists x(\varphi \rightarrow \psi) \rightarrow (\exists x\varphi \rightarrow \exists x\psi)$,
   (*iii*) $\models \forall x(\varphi \leftrightarrow \psi) \rightarrow (\forall x\varphi \leftrightarrow \forall x\psi)$,
   (*iv*) $\models \exists x(\varphi \leftrightarrow \psi) \rightarrow (\exists x\varphi \leftrightarrow \exists x\psi)$,

(v) $\models (\forall x\varphi \to \exists x\psi) \leftrightarrow \exists x(\varphi \to \psi)$,

(vi) $\models (\exists x\varphi \to \forall x\psi) \leftrightarrow \forall x(\varphi \to \psi)$.

9. Show that the converses of exercise 8 (i) - (iv) do not hold.

10. Let L have a unary predicate P. Define the relativization σ^P of σ by

$$\begin{aligned} \varphi^P &:= \varphi \text{ for atomic } \varphi, \\ (\varphi \square \psi)^P &:= \varphi^P \square \psi^P, \\ (\neg \varphi)^P &:= \neg \varphi^P \\ (\forall x\varphi)^P &:= \forall x(P(x) \to \varphi), \\ (\exists x\varphi)^P &:= \exists x(P(x) \wedge \varphi). \end{aligned}$$

Let $\mathfrak{A}$ be a structure without functions and constants. Consider the structure $\mathfrak{B}$ with universe $P^{\mathfrak{A}}$ and relations which are restrictions of the relations of $\mathfrak{A}$.

Show $\mathfrak{A} \models \sigma^P \Leftrightarrow \mathfrak{B} \models \sigma$ for sentences σ.

Why are only relations allowed in $\mathfrak{B}$?

11. Let S be a binary predicate symbol.
Show $\models \neg \exists y \forall x(S(y,x) \leftrightarrow \neg S(x,x))$.
(Think of "y shaves x" and recall Russell's barber's paradox).

2.6. IDENTITY

We have limited ourselves in this book to the consideration of structures with identity, and hence of languages with identity. Therefore we classified '=' as a logical symbol, rather than a mathematical one. We can, however, not treat = as just some binary predicate, since identity satisfies a number of characteristic axioms, listed below.

I_1 $\forall x(x = x)$,

I_2 $\forall xy(x = y \to y = x)$,

I_3 $\forall xyz(x = y \wedge y = z \to x = z)$,

I_4 $\forall x_1 \ldots x_n y_1 \ldots y_n (\bigwedge\!\!\!\bigwedge_{i \leq n} x_i = y_i \to t(x_1,\ldots,x_n) = t(y_1,\ldots,y_n))$,

$\forall x_1 \ldots x_n y_1 \ldots y_n (\bigwedge\!\!\!\bigwedge_{i \leq n} x_i = y_i \to (\varphi(x_1,\ldots,x_n) \to (\varphi(y_1,\ldots,y_n)))$.

One simply checks that I_1, I_2, I_3 are true, in all structures . For I_4, observe that we can suppose the formulas to be closed. Otherwise we add quantifiers for the remaining variables and add dummy identities, e.g.

$$\forall z_1 \ldots z_k x_1 \ldots x_n y_1 \ldots y_n \left(\bigwedge_{i \leq n} x_i = y_i \wedge \bigwedge_{i \leq k} z_k = z_k \rightarrow t(x_1, \ldots, x_n) = t(y_1, \ldots, y_n) \right).$$

Now $(t(\bar{a}_1, \ldots, \bar{a}_n))^{\mathfrak{A}}$ defines a function on $|\mathfrak{A}|^n$, hence

$a_i = b_i \quad (i \leq n) \Rightarrow (t(\bar{a}_1, \ldots, \bar{a}_n))^{\mathfrak{A}} = (t(\bar{b}_1, \ldots, \bar{b}_n))^{\mathfrak{A}}$. This establishes the first part of I_4.

The second part is proved by induction on φ (using the first part): e.g. consider the universal quantifier case and let $a_i = b_i$ for all $i \leq n$.

$\mathfrak{A} \models \forall u \varphi(u, \bar{a}_1, \ldots, \bar{a}_n) \Leftrightarrow$,

$\mathfrak{A} \models \varphi(\bar{c}, \bar{a}_1, \ldots, \bar{a}_n)$ for all c $\Leftrightarrow$ (induction hypothesis),

$\mathfrak{A} \models \varphi(\bar{c}, \bar{b}_1, \ldots, \bar{b}_n)$ for all c $\Leftrightarrow$ $\mathfrak{A} \models \forall u \varphi(u, \bar{b}_1, \ldots, \bar{b}_n)$.

So $\mathfrak{A} \models \bigwedge_{i \leq n} \bar{a}_i = \bar{b}_i \Rightarrow \mathfrak{A} \models \forall u \varphi(u, \bar{a}_1, \ldots, \bar{a}_n) \rightarrow \forall u \varphi(u, \bar{b}_1, \ldots, \bar{b}_n))$ for all $a_1, \ldots, a_n$, $b_1, \ldots, b_n$, hence

$$\mathfrak{A} \models \forall x_1 \ldots x_n y_1 \ldots y_n \left(\bigwedge_{i \leq n} x_i = y_i \rightarrow (\forall u \varphi(u, x_1, \ldots, x_n) \rightarrow \forall u \varphi(u, y_1, \ldots, y_n)\right).$$

Note that φ (respectively t), in I_4 can be any formula (respectively term), so I_4 stands for infinitely many axioms.
We call such an "instant axiom" an *axiom schema*.

The first three axioms state that identity is an equivalence relation. I_4 states that identity is a congruence with respect to all (definable) relations.

It is important to realize that from the axioms alone, we cannot determine the precise nature of the interpreting relation. We explicitly adopt the convention that '=' will always be interpreted by real equality.

EXERCISES

1. Show $\models \forall x \exists y (x = y)$.

2. Show $\models \forall x (\varphi(x) \rightarrow \exists y (x = y \wedge \varphi(y)))$,
   $\models \forall x (\varphi(x) \leftrightarrow \forall y (x = y \rightarrow \varphi(y)))$,
   if y does not occur in $\varphi(x)$.

3. Show that $\models \varphi(t) \leftrightarrow \forall x (x = t \rightarrow \varphi(x))$ if $x \notin FV(t)$.

4. Show that the conditions in exercises 2 and 3 are necessary.

5. Consider $\sigma_1 = \forall x(x \sim x)$,

   $\sigma_2 = \forall xy(x \sim y \rightarrow y \sim x)$,

   $\sigma_3 = \forall xyz(x \sim y \wedge y \sim z \rightarrow x \sim z)$.

   Show that if $\mathfrak{A} \models \sigma_1 \wedge \sigma_2 \wedge \sigma_3$, where $\mathfrak{A} = \langle A,R \rangle$, then R is an equivalence relation. N.B. $x \sim y$ is a suggestive notation for an atom $P(x,y)$.

6. Let $\sigma_4 = \forall xyz(x \sim y \wedge x \sim z \rightarrow y \sim z)$.

   Show that $\sigma_1, \sigma_4 \models \sigma_2 \wedge \sigma_3$.

7. Consider the schema σ_5: $x \sim y \rightarrow (\varphi[x/z] \rightarrow \varphi[y/z])$.

   Show that $\sigma_1, \sigma_5 \models \sigma_2 \wedge \sigma_3$.

   N.B. if σ is a schema, then $\Delta \cup \sigma \models \varphi$ stands for $\Delta \cup \Gamma \models \varphi$, where Γ consists of all instances of σ.

2.7. EXAMPLES

We will consider languages for some familiar kinds of structures. Since all languages are built in the same way, we shall not list the logical symbols. All structures are supposed to satisfy the identity axioms $I_1 - I_4$.

For a refinement see lemma 2.10.2.

1. *The language of identity.* Type $\langle -;-;0 \rangle$

Alphabet.

Predicate symbol: =

The structures of this type are of the form $\mathfrak{A} = \langle A \rangle$, and satisfy I_1, I_2, I_3. (In this language I_4 follows from I_1, I_2, I_3, cf. 2.10 exercise 5).

In an identity structure there is so little "structure", that all one can virtually do is look for the number of elements (cardinality).
There are sentences λ_n and μ_n saying that there are at least (or at most) n elements (exercise 3, section 3.1)

$$\lambda_n := \exists y_1 \ldots y_n \bigwedge_{i \neq j} y_i \neq y_j, \qquad (n > 1),$$

$$\mu_n := \forall y_0 \ldots y_n \bigvee_{i \neq j} y_i = y_j.$$

So $\mathfrak{A} \models \lambda_n \wedge \mu_n$ iff $|\mathfrak{A}|$ has exactly n elements.
Since universes are not empty $\models \exists x(x = x)$.

We can also formulate "*there exists a unique* x *such that...*".

Definition. $\exists! x\varphi(x) := \exists x(\varphi(x) \wedge \forall y(\varphi(y) \rightarrow x = y))$, where y does not occur in $\varphi(x)$.

Note that $\exists! x\varphi(x)$ is an (informal) abbreviation.

2. *The language of partial order.* Type $\langle 2;-;0\rangle$

Alphabet.

Predicate symbol: $=, \leqslant$

$\mathfrak{A}$ is a *partially ordered set (poset)* if $\mathfrak{A}$ is a model of

$\forall xyz(x \leqslant y \wedge y \leqslant z \rightarrow x \leqslant z)$

$\forall xy\ (x \leqslant y \wedge y \leqslant x \leftrightarrow x = y)$

The notation may be misleading, since one usually introduces the relation $\leqslant$ (e.g. on the reals) as a disjunction: $x < y$ or $x = y$. In our alphabet the relation is primitive, another symbol might have been preferable, but we chose to observe the tradition. Note that the relation is reflexive: $x \leqslant x$.

Partially ordered sets are very basic in mathematics, they appear in many guises.

It is often convenient to visualize posets by means of diagrams, where $a \leqslant b$ is represented as equal or above (respectively to the right).
One of the traditions in logic is to keep objects and their names apart. Thus we speak of function symbols which are interpreted by functions, etc. However, in practice this is a bit cumbersome. We prefer to use the same notation for the syntactic objects and their interpretations, e.g. if $\mathfrak{R} = \langle R, \leqslant\rangle$ is the partially ordered set of reals, then $\mathfrak{R} \models \forall x \exists y(x \leqslant y)$.
The '$\leqslant$' in $\mathfrak{R}$ stands for the actual relation and the '$\leqslant$' in the sentence stands for the predicate symbol. The reader is urged to distinguish symbols in their various guises.

We show some diagrams of posets.

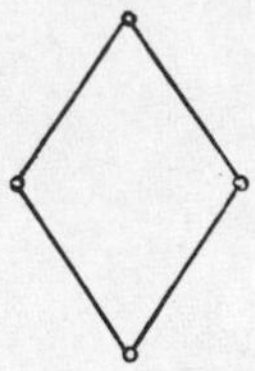

figure 1

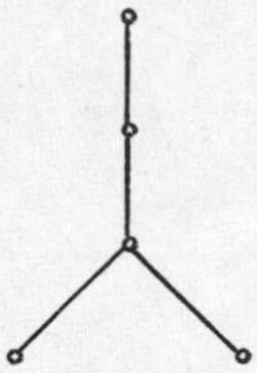

figure 2

figure 3

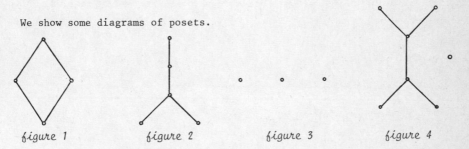

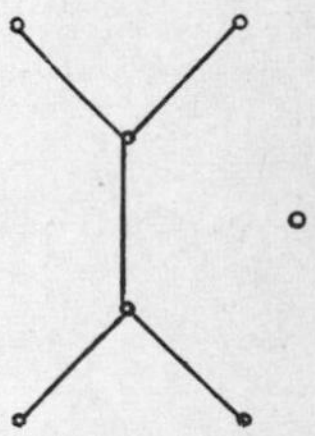

figure 4

From the diagrams we can easily read a number of properties.
E.g. $\mathfrak{A}_1 \models \exists x \forall y (x \leqslant y)$ ($\mathfrak{A}_i$ is the structure with the diagram of figure i), i.e. $\mathfrak{A}_1$ has a least element (a *minimum*).
$\mathfrak{A}_3 \models \forall x \neg \exists y (x \leqslant y \wedge \neg x = y)$. i.e. in $\mathfrak{A}_3$ no element is properly less than another element.

We introduce the following abbreviations:

$x \neq y := \neg x = y$ and $x < y := x \leqslant y \wedge x \neq y$.

Definition.

(*i*) $\mathfrak{A}$ is a (*linearly* or *totally*) ordered set if
$\mathfrak{A} \models \forall xy (x \leqslant y \vee y \leqslant x)$ (each two elements are comparable)

(*ii*) $\mathfrak{A}$ is *densely ordered* if
$\mathfrak{A} \models \forall xy (x < y \rightarrow \exists z (x < z \wedge z < y))$ (between any two elements there is a third one).

It is an amusing exercise to find sentences that distinguish between structures and vice versa.
E.g. We can distinguish $\mathfrak{A}_3$ and $\mathfrak{A}_4$ (from the diagrams above) as follows: in $\mathfrak{A}_4$ there is precisely *one* element that is incomparable with all other elements, in $\mathfrak{A}_3$ there are more such elements. Put $\sigma(x) := \forall y (y \neq x \rightarrow \neg y \leqslant x \wedge \neg x \leqslant y)$.
Then

$\mathfrak{A}_4 \models \forall xx' (\sigma(x) \wedge \sigma(x') \rightarrow x = x')$, but
$\mathfrak{A}_3 \models \neg \forall xx' (\sigma(x) \wedge \sigma(x') \rightarrow x = x')$.

3. *The language of groups.* Type $\langle -;2,1;1 \rangle$

Alphabet.

Predicate symbol: =
Function symbols: $\cdot$, $^{-1}$
Constant symbol: e

Notation: In order to conform with practice we write $t \cdot s$ and t^{-1} instead of $\cdot(t,s)$ and $^{-1}(t)$.

$\mathfrak{A}$ is a *group* if it is a model of

$\forall xyz ((x \cdot y) \cdot z = x \cdot (y \cdot z))$,
$\forall x (x \cdot e = x \wedge e \cdot x = x)$,
$\forall x (x \cdot x^{-1} = e \wedge x^{-1} \cdot x = e)$.

When convenient, we will write ts for t.s, and we will adopt the bracket conventions from algebra.

A group $\mathfrak{A}$ is *commutative* or *abelian* if $\mathfrak{A} \models \forall xy(xy = yx)$.

Commutative groups are often described in the language of *additive* groups, which have the following

alphabet: Predicate symbol: =

Function symbol: +,-

Constant symbol: 0

4. The language of plane projective geometry. Type ⟨2;-;0⟩

The structures one considers are projective planes, which are usually taken to consist of *points* and *lines* with an *incidence relation*. In this approach the type would be ⟨1,1,2;-;0⟩. We can, however, use a more simple type, since a point can be defined as something that is incident with a line, and a line as something for which we can find a point which is incident with it. Of course this requires a non-symmetric incidence relation.

We will now list the axioms, which deviate somewhat from the traditional set. It is a simple exercise to show that the system is equivalent to the standard sets.

Alphabet.

Predicate symbols: I,= .

We introduce the following abbreviations:

$\Pi(x) := \exists y(xIy)$,

$\Lambda(y) := \exists x(xIy)$.

$\mathfrak{A}$ is a *projective plane* it satisfies

$\gamma_0 : \forall x(\Pi(x) \leftrightarrow \neg \Lambda(x))$,

$\gamma_1 : \forall xy(\Pi(x) \wedge \Pi(y) \rightarrow \exists z(xIz \wedge yIz))$,

$\gamma_2 : \forall uv(\Lambda(u) \wedge \Lambda(v) \rightarrow \exists x(xIu \wedge xIv))$,

$\gamma_3 : \forall xyuv(xIu \wedge yIu \wedge xIv \wedge yIv \rightarrow x = y \vee u = v)$,

$\gamma_4 : \exists x_0x_1x_2u_0u_1u_2(\bigwedge\limits_{i\leqslant 2} x_iIu_i \wedge \bigwedge\limits_{\substack{i\neq j\\ i,j\leqslant 2}} \neg x_iIu_j \wedge \neg \exists v \bigwedge\limits_{i\leqslant 2} x_iIv \wedge \neg \exists y \bigwedge\limits_{i\leqslant 2} yIu_i)$.

γ_0 tells us that in a projective plane everything is either a point, or a line. γ_1 and γ_2 tell us that "any two lines intersect in a point" and "any two points can be joined by a line", by γ_3 this point (or line) is unique if the given lines (or points) are distinct. Finally γ_4 makes projective planes non-trivial, in the sense that there are enough points and lines.

$\Pi^{\mathfrak{A}} = \{a \in |\mathfrak{A}| \mid \mathfrak{A} \models \Pi(\bar{a})\}$ and $\Lambda^{\mathfrak{A}} = \{b \in |\mathfrak{A}| \mid \mathfrak{A} \models \Lambda(\bar{b})\}$ are the sets of *points* and *lines* of $\mathfrak{A}$. $I^{\mathfrak{A}}$ is the *incidence relation* on $\mathfrak{A}$.

The above formalization is rather awkward. One usually employs a two-sorted formalism, with P,Q,R,... varying over points and ℓ,m,n,... varying over lines. The first axiom is then suppressed by convention.

The remaining axioms become

γ_1': $\forall PQ\exists\ell(PI\ell \wedge QI\ell)$,

γ_2': $\forall\ell m\exists P(PI\ell \wedge PIm)$,

γ_3': $\forall PQ\ell m(PI\ell \wedge QI\ell \wedge PIm \wedge QIm \rightarrow P = Q \vee \ell = m)$,

γ_4': $\exists P_0P_1P_2\ell_1\ell_2\ell_3(\bigwedge_{i\leqslant 2} P_iI\ell_i \wedge \bigwedge_{\substack{i\neq j\\ i,j\leqslant 2}} \neg P_iI\ell_j \wedge \neg\exists\ell \bigwedge_{i\leqslant 2} P_iI\ell \wedge \neg\exists P \bigwedge_{i\leqslant 2} PI\ell_i)$.

The translation from one language to the other presents no difficulty. The above axioms are different from the ones usually given in the course in projective geometry. We have chosen these particular axioms because they are easy to formulate and also because the so-called *Duality principle* follows immediately. (cf. 2.10, exercise 6).

5. *The language of rings with unity.* Type ⟨ -;2,2,1;2⟩

Alphabet.

Predicate symbol: =

Function symbols: +,·,-

Constant symbols: 0,1

$\mathfrak{A}$ is a *ring* (with unity) if it is a model of

$\forall xyz((x+y) + z = x + (y+z))$,

$\forall xy(x+y = y+x)$,

$\forall xyz((xy)z = x(yz))$,

$\forall xyz(x(y+z) = xy+xz)$,

$\forall x(x+0 = x)$,

$\forall x(x + (-x) = 0)$,

$\forall x(1\cdot x = x \wedge x\cdot 1 = x)$,

$0 \neq 1$.

A ring $\mathfrak{A}$ is *commutative* if $\mathfrak{A} \models \forall xy(xy = yx)$.

A ring $\mathfrak{A}$ is a *division ring* if $\mathfrak{A} \models \forall x(x \neq 0 \rightarrow \exists y(xy = 1))$.

A commutative division ring is called a *field*.

Actually it is more convenient to have an inverse-function symbol available in the language of fields, which therefore has type $\langle -;2,2,1,1;2\rangle$.

We add to the above list the sentence

$\forall x(x \neq 0 \rightarrow x \cdot x^{-1} = 1 \wedge x^{-1} \cdot x = 1)$

and $0^{-1} = 1$.

Note that we must somehow "fix the value of 0^{-1}", the reason will appear in 2.10, exercise 2.

6. *The language of arithmetic.* Type $\langle -;2,2,1;1\rangle$

Alphabet.

Predicate symbol: $=$

Function symbols: $+, \cdot, S$

Constant symbol: 0

(S stands for the successor function $n \rightarrow n+1$).

Historically, the language of arithmetic was introduced by Peano with the intention to describe the natural numbers with plus, times and successor up to an isomorphism. This in contrast to, e.g. the theory of groups, in which one tries to capture a large class of non-isomorphic structures. It has turned out, however, that Peano's axioms characterize a large class of structures, which we will call (lacking a current term) *Peano structures*.

A *Peano structure* $\mathfrak{A}$ is a model of

$\forall x(0 \neq S(x))$,

$\forall xy(S(x) = S(y) \rightarrow x = y)$,

$\forall x(x+0 = x)$,

$\forall xy(x + S(y) = S(x+y))$,

$\forall x(x \cdot 0 = 0)$,

$\forall xy(x \cdot S(y) = x \cdot y + x)$,

$\varphi(0) \wedge \forall x(\varphi(x) \rightarrow \varphi(S(x))) \rightarrow \forall x\varphi(x)$.

The last axiom schema is called the *induction schema* or the *principle of mathematical induction*.

It will prove handy to have a few notations. We define

$\bar{1} := S(\bar{0})$, $\bar{2} := S(\bar{1})$ and in general $\overline{n+1} := S(\bar{n})$,
$x < y := \exists z(x+Sz = y)$,
$x \leqslant y := x < y \vee x = y$.

There is one Peano structure which is the intended model of arithmetic, namely the structure of the ordinary natural numbers, with the ordinary addition, multiplication and successor (e.g. the finite ordinals in set theory). We call this Peano structure the *standard model* $\mathfrak{N}$, and the ordinary natural numbers are called the *standard numbers*.

One easily checks that $\bar{n}^{\mathfrak{N}} = n$ and $\mathfrak{N} \models \bar{n} < \bar{m} \Leftrightarrow n < m$: by definition of interpretation we have $\bar{0}^{\mathfrak{N}} = 0$. Assume $\bar{n}^{\mathfrak{N}} = n$, $\overline{n+1}^{\mathfrak{N}} = (S(\bar{n}))^{\mathfrak{N}} = \bar{n}^{\mathfrak{N}} + 1 = n + 1$. We now apply mathematical induction in the meta-language, and obtain $\bar{n}^{\mathfrak{N}} = n$ for all n.
For the second claim see exercise 13.

In $\mathfrak{N}$ we can define all kinds of sets, relations and numbers. To be precise, we say that a k-ary relation R in $\mathfrak{N}$ is defined by φ if
$\langle a_1,\ldots,a_k\rangle \in R \Leftrightarrow \mathfrak{N} \models \varphi(\bar{a}_1,\ldots,\bar{a}_k)$.
An element $a \in |\mathfrak{N}|$ is defined in $\mathfrak{N}$ by φ if
$\mathfrak{N} \models \varphi(\bar{b}) \Leftrightarrow b = a$, or $\mathfrak{N} \models \forall x(\varphi(x) \leftrightarrow x = \bar{a})$.

Examples.

1. The set of even numbers is defined by
$$E(x) := \exists y(x = y+y).$$

2. The divisibility relation is defined by
$$x|y := \exists z(xz = y).$$

3. The set of prime numbers is defined by
$$P(x) := \forall yz(x = yz \rightarrow y = 1 \vee z = 1).$$

We can say that we have introduced predicates E, | and P by (explicit) definition.

7. *The language of graphs.*

We usually think of graphs as geometric figures consisting of vertices and edges connecting certain of the vertices. A suitable language for the theory of graphs is obtained by introducing a predicate R which expresses the fact that two vertices are connected by an edge. Hence, we don't need variables or constants for edges.

Alphabet.

Predicate symbols: R, = .

A *graph* is a structure $\mathfrak{A} = \langle A,R \rangle$ satisfying the following axioms:

$$\forall xy(R(x,y) \rightarrow R(y,x))$$
$$\forall x \neg R(x,x)$$

This definition is in accordance with the geometric tradition. There are elements, called vertices, of which some are connected by edges. Note that two vertices are connected by at most one edge.

Examples:

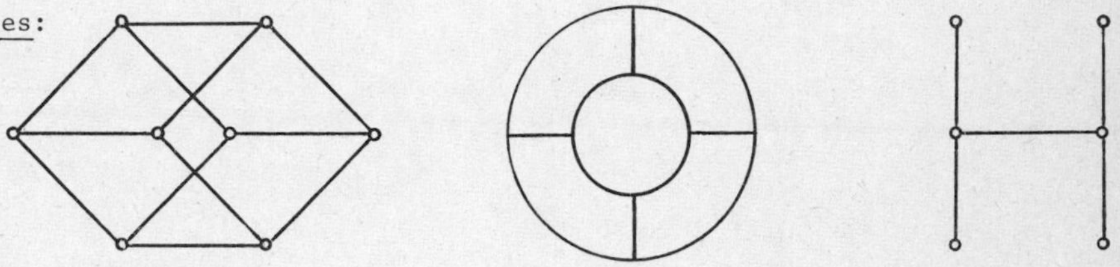

We can also consider graphs in which the edges are directed. A *directed graph* $\mathfrak{A} = \langle A,R \rangle$ satisfies $\forall x \neg R(x,x)$.

Examples:

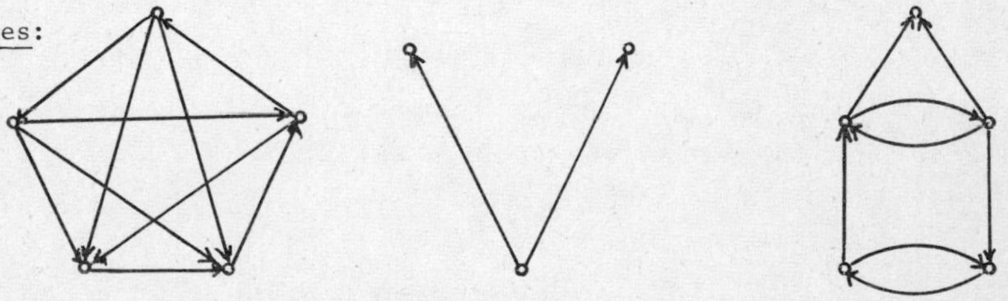

If we drop the condition of irreflexivity then a "graph" is just a set with a binary relation. We can generalize the notion even further, so that more edges may connect a pair of vertices.

In order to treat those generalized graphs we consider a language with two unary predicates V, E and one ternary predicate C.

Think of $V(x)$ as "x is a vertex". $E(x)$ as "x is an edge", and $C(x,y,z)$ as "z connects x and y".

A *multigraph* is a structure $\mathfrak{A} = \langle A,V,E,C \rangle$ satisfying the following axioms:

$$\forall x(V(x) \rightarrow \neg E(x)),$$
$$\forall xyz(C(x,y,z) \rightarrow V(x) \wedge V(y) \wedge E(z)),$$
$$\forall xz \neg C(x,x,z),$$
$$\forall xyz(C(x,y,z) \rightarrow C(y,x,z)).$$

Examples

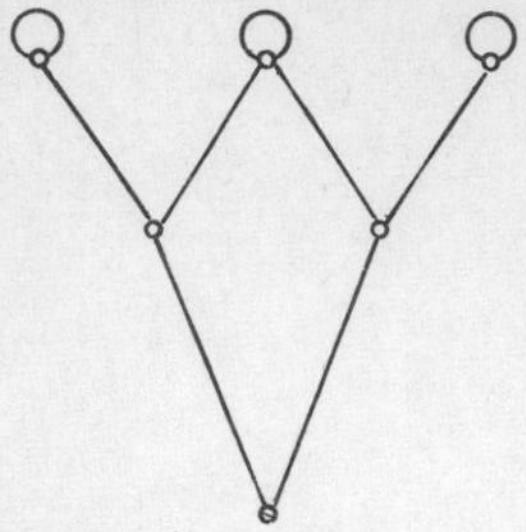

A pseudograph is a structure satisfying all axioms of the multigraph except possibly the irreflexivity axiom $\forall xz \neg C(x,x,z)$.

Remark: The nomenclature in graph theory is not very uniform. We have chosen our formal framework such that it lends itself to treatment in first-order logic.

For the purpose of describing multigraphs a two-sorted language (cf. geometry) is well-suited. The reformulation is left to the reader.

EXERCISES.

1. Consider the language of partial order. Define predicates for (*a*) x is the *maximum*; (*b*) x is *maximal*; (*c*) there is no element between x and y; (*d*) x is an *immediate successor* (respectively *predecessor*) of y; (*e*) z is the *infimum* of x and y.

2. Give a sentence σ such that $\mathfrak{A}_2 \models \sigma$ and $\mathfrak{A}_4 \models \neg\sigma$ (for $\mathfrak{A}_i$ associated to the diagrams of p. 85).

3. Let $\mathfrak{N} = \langle N, \leqslant \rangle$ and $\mathfrak{A} = \langle Z, \leqslant \rangle$ be the ordered sets of natural, respectively integer, numbers. Give a sentence σ such that $\mathfrak{N} \models \sigma$ and $\mathfrak{B} \models \neg\sigma$. Do the same for $\mathfrak{A}$ and $\mathfrak{B} = \langle Q, \leqslant \rangle$ (the ordered set of rationals). N.B. σ is to be in the language of posets.

4. Let $\sigma = \exists x \forall y (x \leqslant y \vee y \leqslant x)$
   Find posets $\mathfrak{A}$ and $\mathfrak{B}$ such that $\mathfrak{A} \models \sigma$ and $\mathfrak{B} \models \neg\sigma$.

5. Do the same for $\sigma = \forall xy \exists z[(x \leqslant z \wedge y \leqslant z) \vee (z \leqslant x \vee z \leqslant y)]$.

6. Using the language of identity structures give an (infinite) set Γ such that

$\mathfrak{A}$ is a model of Γ iff $\mathfrak{A}$ is infinite.

7. Consider the language of groups.
Define the properties: (*a*) x is idempotent; (*b*) x belongs to the center.

8. Let $\mathfrak{A}$ be a ring, give a sentence σ such that $\mathfrak{A} \models \sigma \Leftrightarrow \mathfrak{A}$ is an integral domain (has no divisors of zero).

9. Give a formula $\varphi(x)$ in the language of rings such that $\mathfrak{A} \models \varphi(\bar{a}) \Leftrightarrow$ the principal ideal (*a*) is prime (in $\mathfrak{A}$).

10. Define in the language of arithmetic: (*a*) x and y are relatively prime; (*b*) x is the smallest prime greater than y; (*c*) x is the greatest number with $2x < y$.

11. $\sigma := \forall x_1 \ldots x_n \exists y_1 \ldots y_m \psi$ and $\tau := \exists y_1 \ldots y_m \psi$ are sentences in a language without function symbols and constants, where φ and ψ are quantifier free.
Show: $\vdash \sigma \Leftrightarrow \sigma$ holds in all structures with n elements.
$\vdash \tau \Leftrightarrow \tau$ holds in all structures with 1 element.

12. *Monadic predicate calculus* has only unary predicate symbols (no identity).
Consider $\mathfrak{A} = \langle A, R_1, \ldots, R_n \rangle$ where all R_i are sets. Define
$a \sim b := a \in R_i \Leftrightarrow b \in R_i$ for all $i \leqslant n$.
Show that $\sim$ is an equivalence relation and that $\sim$ has at most 2^n equivalence classes. The equivalence class of a is denoted by $[a]$. Define $B = A/\sim$ and $[a] \in S_i \Leftrightarrow a \in R_i$, $\mathfrak{B} = \langle B, S_1, \ldots, S_n \rangle$.
Show $\mathfrak{A} \models \sigma \Leftrightarrow \mathfrak{B} \models \sigma$ for all σ containing only the predicate symbols $P_1, \ldots, P_n$. For such σ show $\models \sigma \Leftrightarrow \mathfrak{A} \models \sigma$ for all $\mathfrak{A}$ with at most 2^n elements. Using this fact, outline a decision procedure for truth in monadic predicate calculus.

13. Let $\mathfrak{N}$ be the standard model of arithmetic.
Show $\mathfrak{N} \models \bar{n} < \bar{m} \Leftrightarrow n < m$.

14. Let $\mathfrak{A} = \langle N, < \rangle$ and $\mathfrak{B} = \langle N, \Delta \rangle$, where $n \Delta m$ iff (*i*) $n < m$ and n, m both even or both odd, or (*ii*) if n is even and m odd.
Give a sentence σ such that $\mathfrak{A} \models \sigma$ and $\mathfrak{B} \models \neg \sigma$.

15. If $\langle A, R \rangle$ is a projective plane, then $\langle A, \breve{R} \rangle$ is also a projective plane (*the dual plane*), where $\breve{R}$ is the converse of the relation R.

Formulated in the two sorted language: if $\langle A_p, A_\ell, I \rangle$ is a projective plane, then so is $\langle A_\ell, A_p, \breve{I} \rangle$.

2.8 NATURAL DEDUCTION

We extend the system of section 1.5 to predicate logic. For reasons similar to the ones mentioned in section 1.5 we consider a language with connectives $\wedge$, $\rightarrow$, $\perp$ and $\forall$. The existential quantifier is left out, but will be considered later.

We adopt all the rules of propositional logic and we add

$$\forall I \ \frac{\varphi(x)}{\forall x\, \varphi(x)} \qquad\qquad \forall E \ \frac{\forall x\, \varphi(x)}{\varphi(t)}$$

where in $\forall I$ the variable x may not occur free in any hypothesis on which $\varphi(x)$ depends, i.e. an uncancelled hypothesis in the derivation of $\varphi(x)$. In $\forall E$ we, of course, require t to be free for x.

We will demonstrate the necessity of the above restrictions, keeping in mind that the system at least has to be *sound*, i.e. that derivable statements should be true.

Restriction in $\forall I$:

$$\cfrac{\cfrac{\cfrac{\cfrac{\cancel{x = 0}}{\forall x(x = 0)}\ \forall I \text{ applied wrongly}}{x = 0 \rightarrow \forall x(x = 0)}}{\forall x((x = 0) \rightarrow \forall x(x = 0))}}{0 = 0 \rightarrow \forall x(x = 0)}$$

So $\vdash 0 = 0 \rightarrow \forall x(x = 0)$, but clearly $\not\models 0 = 0 \rightarrow \forall x(x = 0)$ (take any structure containing more than just 0).

Restriction in $\forall E$:

$$\cfrac{\cfrac{\cancel{\forall x \neg \forall y(x = y)}}{\neg \forall y(y = y)}\ \forall E \text{ applied wrongly}}{\forall x \neg \forall y(x = y) \rightarrow \neg \forall y(y = y)}$$

Note that y is not free for x in $\neg \forall y(x = y)$. The derived sentence is clearly not true in structures with at least two elements.

We now give some examples of derivations.
We assume that the reader has by now enough experience in cancelling hypotheses, so that we will no longer indicate the cancellations by encircled numbers.

$$\dfrac{\dfrac{\dfrac{\dfrac{\dfrac{\cancel{\forall x\, \forall y\, \varphi(x,y)}}{\forall y\, \varphi(x,y)}\,\forall E}{\varphi(x,y)}\,\forall E}{\forall x\, \varphi(x,y)}\,\forall I}{\forall y\, \forall x\, \varphi(x,y)}\,\forall I}{\forall x\, \forall y\, \varphi(x,y) \to \forall y\, \forall x\, \varphi(x,y)}\,\to I$$

$$\dfrac{\dfrac{\dfrac{\dfrac{\dfrac{\cancel{\forall x(\varphi(x) \wedge \psi(x))}}{\varphi(x) \wedge \psi(x)}}{\varphi(x)}}{\forall x\, \varphi(x)} \qquad \dfrac{\dfrac{\dfrac{\cancel{\forall x(\varphi(x) \wedge \psi(x))}}{\varphi(x) \wedge \psi(x)}}{\psi(x)}}{\forall x\, \psi(x)}}{\forall x\, \varphi(x) \wedge \forall x\, \psi(x)}}{\forall x(\varphi \wedge \psi) \to \forall x\, \varphi \wedge \forall x\, \psi}$$

Let $x \notin FV(\varphi)$

$$\dfrac{\dfrac{\dfrac{\dfrac{\dfrac{\cancel{\forall x(\varphi \to \psi(x))}}{\varphi \to \psi(x)}\,\forall E \quad \cancel{\varphi}}{\psi(x)}\,\to E}{\forall x\, \psi(x)}\,\forall I}{\varphi \to \forall x\, \psi(x)}\,\to I}{\forall x(\varphi \to \psi(x)) \to (\varphi \to \forall x\, \psi(x))}$$

$$\dfrac{\dfrac{\cancel{\varphi}}{\forall x\, \varphi}\,\forall I \qquad \dfrac{\cancel{\forall x\, \varphi}}{\varphi}\,\forall E}{\varphi \leftrightarrow \forall x\, \varphi}$$

$\forall I$ is allowed, since $x \notin FV(\varphi)$, and $\forall E$ is applicable.

Note that $\forall I$ in the bottom left derivation is allowed because $x \notin FV(\varphi)$, for at that stage φ is still (part of) a hypothesis.

The reader will have grasped the technique behind the quantifier rules: reduce a $\forall x\, \varphi$ to φ and reintroduce $\forall$ later, if necessary. Intuitively, one makes the following step: to show "for all x ... x ..." it suffices to show "... x ..." for an arbitrary x. The latter statement is easier to handle. Without going into fine philosophical distinctions, we note that the distinction "for all x...x..." - "for an arbitrary x...x...", is embodied in our system by the distinction "quantified statement" - "free variable statement".

The reader will also have observed that, roughly speaking, elimination precedes introduction. There is a sound explanation for this phenomenon, but the proper treatment belongs to *proof theory*, where *normal derivations* (derivations without superfluous steps) are considered. See D.Prawitz, *Natural Deduction*. For the moment the reader may accept the above mentioned fact as a convenient rule of thumb.

We can formulate the derivability properties of the universal quantifier in terms of the relation $\vdash$:

$$\Gamma \vdash \varphi(x) \Rightarrow \Gamma \vdash \forall x\varphi(x) \quad \text{if } x \notin FV(\psi) \text{ for all } \psi \in \Gamma$$
$$\Gamma \vdash \forall x\varphi(x) \Rightarrow \Gamma \vdash \varphi(t) \quad \text{if } t \text{ free for } x \text{ in } \varphi.$$

The above implications follow directly from ($\forall$I) and ($\forall$E).

Our next goal is the correctness of the system of natural deduction for predicate logic. We first extend the definition of $\models$.

2.8.1. Definition. Let Γ be a set of formulae and let $\{x_{i_1}, x_{i_2}, \ldots\} = \cup\{FV(\psi) \mid \psi \in \Gamma \cup \{\sigma\}\}$. If $\underset{\sim}{a}$ is a sequence $(a_1, a_2, \ldots)$ of elements (repetitions allowed) of $|\mathfrak{A}|$, then $\Gamma(\underset{\sim}{a})$ is obtained from Γ by replacing simultaneously in all formulas of Γ the x_{i_j} by $\overline{a}_j$ $(j \geq 1)$ (for $\Gamma = \{\psi\}$ we write $\psi(\underset{\sim}{a})$).

We now define

(*i*) $\mathfrak{A} \models \Gamma(\underset{\sim}{a})$ if $\mathfrak{A} \models \psi$ for all $\psi \in \Gamma(\underset{\sim}{a})$
(*ii*) $\Gamma \models \sigma$ if $\mathfrak{A} \models \Gamma(\underset{\sim}{a}) \Rightarrow \mathfrak{A} \models \sigma(\underset{\sim}{a})$ for all $\mathfrak{A}, \underset{\sim}{a}$.

In case only sentences are involved, the definition can be simplified: $\Gamma \models \sigma$ if $\mathfrak{A} \models \Gamma \Rightarrow \mathfrak{A} \models \sigma$ for all $\mathfrak{A}$.
If $\Gamma = \emptyset$, we write $\models \sigma$.

We can paraphrase this definition as : $\Gamma \models \sigma$, if for all structures $\mathfrak{A}$ and all choices of $\underset{\sim}{a}$, $\sigma(\underset{\sim}{a})$ is true in $\mathfrak{A}$ if all hypotheses of $\Gamma(\underset{\sim}{a})$ are true in $\mathfrak{A}$.

Now we can formulate

2.8.2. Lemma (Soundness) $\Gamma \vdash \sigma \Rightarrow \Gamma \models \sigma$.

Proof. By definition of $\Gamma \vdash \sigma$ it suffices to show that for each derivation D with hypothesis set Γ and conclusion σ $\Gamma \models \sigma$. We use induction on D (cf. 1.6.1 and exercise 2).

Since we have cast our definition of satisfaction in terms of valuations, which evidently contains the propositional logic as a special case, we can copy the cases of (1) the one element derivation, (2) the derivations with a propositional rule as last step, from lemma 1.6.1 (please check this claim).

So we have to treat derivations with ($\forall$I) or ($\forall$E) as the final step.

(∀I) $\dfrac{\begin{matrix}D\\ \varphi(x)\end{matrix}}{\forall x\, \varphi(x)}$ D has its hypotheses in Γ and x is not free in Γ. Induction hypothesis: $\Gamma \models \varphi(x)$, or $\mathfrak{A} \models \Gamma(\underset{\sim}{a}) \Rightarrow \mathfrak{A} \models (\varphi(x))(\underset{\sim}{a})$

for all $\mathfrak{A}$ and all $\underset{\sim}{a}$. It is no restriction to suppose that x is the first of the free variables involved (why?). So we can substitute $\overline{a}_1$ for x in φ. Therefore we have:

for all a_1 and $\underset{\sim}{a}' = (a_2,\ldots)$

$$\mathfrak{A} \models \Gamma(\underset{\sim}{a}') \Rightarrow \mathfrak{A} \models (\varphi(\overline{a}_1))(\underset{\sim}{a}'), \text{ or}$$

for all $\underset{\sim}{a}'$ $\quad \mathfrak{A} \models \Gamma(\underset{\sim}{a}') \Rightarrow (\mathfrak{A} \models (\varphi(\overline{a}_1))(\underset{\sim}{a}')$ for all a_1 , or

for all $\underset{\sim}{a}'$ $\quad \mathfrak{A} \models \Gamma(\underset{\sim}{a}') \Rightarrow \mathfrak{A} \models (\forall x\, \varphi(x))(\underset{\sim}{a}')$.

This shows $\Gamma \models \forall x\, \varphi(x)$.

(Note that in this proof we have used $\forall x\,(\sigma \to \tau(x)) \to (\sigma \to \forall x\, \tau(x))$, where $x \notin FV(\sigma)$, in the metalanguage. Of course we may use sound principles on the metalevel).

(∀E) $\dfrac{\begin{matrix}D\\ \forall x\, \varphi(x)\end{matrix}}{\varphi(t)}$ Induction hypothesis: $\Gamma \models \forall x\, \varphi(x)$, i.e. $\mathfrak{A} \models \Gamma(\underset{\sim}{a}) \Rightarrow \mathfrak{A} \models (\forall x\, \varphi(x))(\underset{\sim}{a})$, for all $\underset{\sim}{a}$ and $\mathfrak{A}$.

So let $\mathfrak{A} \models \Gamma(\underset{\sim}{a})$, then $\mathfrak{A} \models (\varphi(\overline{b}))(\underset{\sim}{a})$ for all $b \in |\mathfrak{A}|$. In particular we may take $t_1^{\mathfrak{A}}$ for b, where $t_1 = t(\underset{\sim}{a})$ (i.e. t with the variables replaced by the corresponding $\overline{a}_i$'s.) So $\mathfrak{A} \models (\varphi(\overline{t_1^{\mathfrak{A}}}))(\underset{\sim}{a})$. As we will show below, $v(\varphi(\overline{t_1^{\mathfrak{A}}})(\underset{\sim}{a})) = v(\varphi(t))(\underset{\sim}{a}))$, hence $\mathfrak{A} \models (\varphi(t))(\underset{\sim}{a})$. □

We now prove the required fact about the substitution of t.

2.8.3 <u>Lemma</u>. Let t be free for x in φ and $FV(\varphi) \cup FV(t) = \{z_1,\ldots,z_k\}$, then

$$v(\varphi(\overline{(t[\overline{a}_1,\ldots,\overline{a}_k/z_1,\ldots,z_k])^{\mathfrak{A}}})[\overline{a}_1,\ldots,\overline{a}_k/z_1,\ldots,z_k]) =$$
$$v(\varphi(t)[\overline{a}_1,\ldots,\overline{a}_k/z_1,\ldots,z_k]).$$

In words: the values of "first substituting t and then substituting the constants $\overline{a}_i$" and "first evaluating t in $\mathfrak{A}$ with the a_i's, substituting the result in φ and then substituting the a_i's" are identical.

Proof. Induction on φ.

1. φ atomic. Consider $\varphi = P(s_1,\ldots,s_n)$.
   $\varphi(x) = P(s_1(x),\ldots,s_n(x))$ and $\varphi(t) = P(s_1(t),\ldots,s_n(t))$.

$v(P(s_1(t),\dots)[\bar{a}_1,\dots,\bar{a}_k/z_1,\dots,z_k] = 1 \Leftrightarrow$
$\langle (s_1(t)[-/\sim])^{\mathfrak{A}},\dots,(s_n(t)[-/\sim])^{\mathfrak{A}}\rangle \in P^{\mathfrak{A}}$.

We now use the fact that in general

$$(s(t)[-/\sim])^{\mathfrak{A}} = (s[-/\sim](\overline{(t[-/\sim])^{\mathfrak{A}}}))^{\mathfrak{A}} \quad \text{(exercise 3).}$$

So we have

$$\langle (s_1[-/\sim](\overline{(t[-/\sim])^{\mathfrak{A}}}))^{\mathfrak{A}},\dots \rangle \in P^{\mathfrak{A}}, \text{ or },$$

$$v(P(s_1[-/\sim](\overline{(t[-/\sim])^{\mathfrak{A}}}),\dots)) = 1, \text{ or},$$

$$v(P(s_1(t'),\dots,s_n(t'))[-/\sim]) = 1, \text{ where } t' = \overline{(t[-/\sim])^{\mathfrak{A}}}.$$

2. The case of the propositional connectives is trivial, as $v(\varphi \square \psi) = f_\square(v(\varphi),v(\psi))$ for given $f_\square$. So the induction hypothesis leads immediately to the result (similarly for $\neg$).

3. $\forall x\, \varphi(x,t)[-/\sim]$

$v(\forall x\, (\varphi(x,t)[-/\sim])) = \min_b v(\varphi(\bar{b},t)[-/\sim])$ (this step is correct because x does not occur among the $z_1,\dots,z_k$)

$= \min_b v(\varphi(\bar{b},\overline{(t[-/\sim])^{\mathfrak{A}}})[-/\sim])$ (induction hypothesis)

$= v(\forall x\cdot\varphi(x,t')[-/\sim])$, where $t' = \overline{(t[-/\sim])^{\mathfrak{A}}}$.

This finishes the case of $\forall$. For $\exists$ replace min by max. □

Having established the soundness of our system, we can easily get non-derivability results.

Examples. 1. $\nvdash \forall x\, \exists y\, \varphi \to \exists y\, \forall x\, \varphi$.

Take $\mathfrak{A} = \langle \{0,1\}, \{\langle 0,1\rangle, \langle 1,0\rangle\}\rangle$ (type $\langle 2;-;0\rangle$) and consider

$\varphi := P(x,y)$, the predicate interpreted in $\mathfrak{A}$.

$\mathfrak{A} \models \forall x\exists y P(x,y)$, since for 0 we have $\langle 0,1\rangle \in P$ and for 1 we have $\langle 1,0\rangle \in P$.

But, $\mathfrak{A} \models \exists y\forall x P(x,y)$, since for 0 we have $\langle 0,0\rangle \notin P$ and for 1 we have $\langle 1,1\rangle \notin P$.

2. $\forall x\varphi(x,x), \forall xy\, (\varphi(x,y) \to \varphi(x,y)) \nvdash \forall xyz\, (\varphi(x,y) \wedge \varphi(y,z) \to \varphi(x,z))$.

Consider $\mathfrak{L} = \langle \mathbb{R},P\rangle$ with $P = \{\langle a,b\rangle \mid |a-b| \leq 1\}$.

The following result, although not very surprising, is often quite helpful.

2.8.3 Theorem. If c does not occur in Γ and $\Gamma \vdash \varphi(c) \Rightarrow \Gamma \vdash \forall x\varphi(x)$.

Proof. Use induction on the derivation. □

EXERCISES.

1. Show (*i*) $\vdash \forall x\ (\varphi(x) \to \psi(x)) \to (\forall x\ \varphi(x) \to \forall x\ \psi(x))$

   (*ii*) $\vdash \forall x\ \varphi(x) \to \neg \forall x\ \neg \varphi(x)$

   (*iii*) $\vdash \forall x\ \varphi(x) \to \forall z\ \varphi(z)$ if z does not occur in $\varphi(x)$.

2. Extend the definition of derivation to the present system (cf. 1.5.1).

3. Show $(s(t)[\overline{a}/x])^{\mathfrak{A}} = (s(\overline{(t[\overline{a}/x])^{\mathfrak{A}}})[\overline{a}/x])^{\mathfrak{A}}$ by induction on s.

4. Let $\Gamma \vdash \varphi$, then $\Gamma[y/c] \vdash \varphi[y/c]$ where y is a variable that does not occur in Γ or φ (take Γ finite). The modified substitution is self-evident. Use induction on the derivation.

5. Assign to each atom $P(t_1,\ldots,t_n)$ a proposition symbol, denoted by P. Now define a translation † from the language of predicate logic into the language of propositional logic by $(P(t_1,\ldots,t_n))^\dagger := P$ and $\bot^\dagger := \bot$

   $(\varphi \square \psi)^\dagger := \varphi^\dagger \square \psi^\dagger$

   $(\neg \varphi)^\dagger := \neg \varphi^\dagger$

   $(\forall x\ \varphi)^\dagger := \varphi^\dagger$

   Show $\Gamma \vdash \varphi \Rightarrow \Gamma^\dagger \vdash^\dagger \varphi^\dagger$, where $\vdash^\dagger$ stands for "derivable without using ($\forall$I) or ($\forall$E)" (does the converse hold?)

   Conclude the consistency of predicate logic.

   Show that predicate logic is conservative over propositional logic (cf. definition 3.1.3).

2.9 ADDING THE EXISTENTIAL QUANTIFIER

Let us introduce $\exists x\varphi$ as an abbreviation for $\neg \forall x \neg \varphi$ (theorem 2.5.1 tells us that there is a good reason for doing so). We can prove the following

2.9.1 <u>Lemma</u>. (*i*) $\varphi(t) \vdash \exists x\ \varphi(x)$ (t free for x in φ)

(*ii*) $\Gamma, \varphi(x) \vdash \psi \Rightarrow \Gamma, \exists x\ \varphi(x) \vdash \psi$

if x is not free in ψ or any formula of Γ.

Proof. (*i*)

$$\dfrac{\dfrac{\dfrac{[\forall x\ \neg\varphi(x)]}{\neg\varphi(t)}\ \forall E \qquad \varphi(t)}{\bot}\ \to E}{\neg \forall x\ \neg \varphi(x)}\ \to I$$

so $\varphi(t) \vdash \exists x\ \varphi(x)$

(*ii*)

$$\dfrac{\dfrac{\neg\forall x\,\neg\varphi(x) \qquad \dfrac{\dfrac{\dfrac{\begin{array}{c}\cancel{\varphi(x)}\\ D\\ \psi\end{array} \qquad \neg\psi}{\bot}\,\to E}{\neg\varphi(x)}\,\to I}{\forall x\,\neg\varphi(x)}\,\forall I}{\bot}\,\to E}{\psi}\,RAA$$

Explanation: the subderivation top left is the given one; its hypotheses are in $\Gamma \cup \{\varphi(x)\}$ (only $\varphi(x)$ is shown). Since $\varphi(x)$ (that is, all occurrences of it) is cancelled and x does not occur free in Γ or ψ, we may apply $\forall I$. From the derivation we conclude that $\Gamma, \exists x\,\varphi(x) \vdash \psi$.

We can compress the last derivation into an elimination rule for $\exists$:

$$\exists E\ \dfrac{\exists x\,\varphi(x) \qquad \begin{array}{c}\cancel{\varphi(x)}\\ \vdots\\ \psi\end{array}}{\psi}$$

with the conditions:
x not free in ψ, or in a hypothesis of the subderivation of ψ, other than $\varphi(x)$.

This is easily seen to be correct since we can always fill in the missing details, as shown in the preceding derivation.

By (*i*) we also have an introduction rule : $\exists I\ \dfrac{\varphi(t)}{\exists x\,\varphi(x)}$ for t free for x in φ.

Examples of derivations.

$$\dfrac{\dfrac{\dfrac{\overset{②}{\cancel{\exists x\,\varphi(x)}} \qquad \dfrac{\dfrac{\overset{③}{\cancel{\forall x(\varphi(x)\to\psi)}}}{\varphi(x)\to\psi}\,\forall E \qquad \overset{①}{\cancel{\varphi(x)}}}{\psi}\,\to E}{\psi}\,\exists E\ ①}{\exists x\,\varphi(x)\to\psi}\,\to I\ ②}{\forall x(\varphi(x)\to\psi)\to(\exists x\,\varphi(x)\to\psi)}\,\to I\ ③$$

$x \notin FV(\psi)$

$$\dfrac{\dfrac{\overset{③}{\cancel{\exists x(\varphi(x)\vee\psi(x))}} \qquad \dfrac{\overset{②}{\cancel{\varphi(x)\vee\psi(x)}} \qquad \dfrac{\dfrac{\overset{①}{\cancel{\varphi(x)}}}{\exists x\,\varphi(x)}}{\exists x\,\varphi(x)\vee\exists x\,\psi(x)} \qquad \dfrac{\dfrac{\overset{①}{\cancel{\psi(x)}}}{\exists x\,\psi(x)}}{\exists x\,\varphi(x)\vee\exists x\,\psi(x)}}{\exists x\,\varphi(x)\vee\exists x\,\psi(x)}\,\vee E}{\exists x\,\varphi(x)\vee\exists x\,\psi(x)}\,\exists E}{\exists x(\varphi(x)\vee\psi(x))\to\exists x\,\varphi(x)\vee\exists x\,\psi(x).}\,\to I\ ③$$

We will also sketch the alternative approach to enriching the language.

2.9.2. Theorem. Consider predicate logic with the full language and rules for all connectives, then $\vdash \exists x\, \varphi(x) \leftrightarrow \neg \forall x \neg \varphi(x)$.

Proof. Compare 1.7.3. □

It is time now to state the rules for ∀ and ∃ with more precision. We want to allow substitution of terms for some occurrences of the quantified variable in (∀E) and (∃E). The following example motivates this.

$$\cfrac{\cfrac{\forall x(x = x)}{x = x}\ \forall E}{\exists y(x = y)}\ \exists I$$

The result would not be derivable if we could only make substitutions for <u>all</u> occurrences at the same time. Yet, the result is evidently true.

The proper formulation of the rules now is

$$\forall I\ \frac{\varphi}{\forall x\, \varphi} \qquad \forall E\ \frac{\forall x\, \varphi}{\varphi[\,t/x\,]}$$

$$\exists I\ \frac{\varphi[\,t/x\,]}{\exists x\, \varphi} \qquad \exists E\ \frac{\exists x\, \varphi \quad \begin{matrix}\not{\varphi}\\ \vdots \\ \psi\end{matrix}}{\psi}$$

with the appropriate restrictions.

EXERCISES

1. Show (*i*) $\vdash \exists x(\varphi(x) \wedge \psi) \leftrightarrow \exists x\, \varphi(x) \wedge \psi$ if $x \notin FV(\psi)$
   (*ii*) $\vdash \forall x(\varphi(x) \vee \psi) \leftrightarrow \forall x\, \varphi(x) \vee \psi$ if $x \notin FV(\psi)$
   (*iii*) $\vdash \forall x\, \varphi(x) \leftrightarrow \neg \exists x \neg \varphi(x)$
   (*iv*) $\vdash \neg \forall x\, \varphi(x) \leftrightarrow \exists x \neg \varphi(x)$
   (*v*) $\vdash \neg \exists x\, \varphi(x) \leftrightarrow \forall x \neg \varphi(x)$
   (*vi*) $\vdash \exists x(\varphi(x) \to \psi) \leftrightarrow (\forall x\, \varphi(x) \to \psi)$ if $x \notin FV(\psi)$
   (*vii*) $\vdash \exists x(\varphi \to \psi(x)) \leftrightarrow (\varphi \to \exists x\, \psi(x))$ if $x \notin FV(\varphi)$
   (*viii*) $\vdash \exists x \exists y\, \varphi \leftrightarrow \exists y \exists x\, \varphi$.
   (*ix*) $\vdash \exists x\, \varphi \leftrightarrow \varphi$ if $x \notin FV(\varphi)$

2.10. NATURAL DEDUCTION AND IDENTITY

We will give rules, corresponding to the axioms $I_1 - I_4$ of section 2.6.

$$RI_1 \ \frac{}{x = x} \qquad RI_2 \ \frac{x = y}{y = x} \qquad RI_3 \ \frac{x = y \quad y = z}{y = z}$$

$$RI_4 \ \frac{x_1 = y_1, \ldots, x_n = y_n}{t(x_1, \ldots, x_n) = t(y_1, \ldots, y_n)}$$

$$\frac{x_1 = y_1, \ldots, x_n = y_n \quad \varphi(x_1, \ldots, x_n)}{\varphi(y_1, \ldots, y_n)}$$

where $y_1, \ldots, y_n$ are free for $x_1, \ldots, x_n$ in φ.

Note that we want to allow substitution of the variable y_i $(i \leqslant n)$ for *some* and not necessarily all occurrences of the variable x_i. We can express this by formulating RI_4 in the precise terms of the simultaneous substitution operator:

$$\frac{x_1 = y_1, \ldots, x_n = y_n}{t[x_1, \ldots, x_n/z_1, \ldots, z_n] = t[y_1, \ldots, y_n/z_1, \ldots, z_n]}$$

$$\frac{x_1 = y_1, \ldots, x_n = y_n \qquad \varphi[x_1, \ldots, x_n/z_1, \ldots, z_n]}{\varphi[y_1, \ldots, y_n/z_1, \ldots, z_n].}$$

Example: $\dfrac{x = y \quad x^2+y^2 > 12x}{2y^2 > 12x}$, with $\varphi = z^2+y^2 > 12x$

$\dfrac{x = y \quad x^2+y^2 > 12x}{x^2+y^2 > 12y}$, with $\varphi = x^2+y^2 > 12z$

$\dfrac{x = y \quad x^2+y^2 > 12x}{2y^2 > 12y}$, with $\varphi = z^2+y^2 > 12z$

The above are three legitimate applications of RI_4 having three different conclusions.

The rule RI_1 has no hypotheses, which may seem surprising, but which certainly is not forbidden.

The rules RI_4 have many hypotheses, as a consequence the derivation trees can look a bit more complicated. Of course one can get all the benefits from RI_4 by a restricted rule allowing only one substitution at a time.

2.10.1. Lemma. $\vdash I_i$ for $i = 1,2,3,4$.

Proof. Immediate.

We can weaken the rules RI_4 slightly by considering only the simplest terms and formulae.

2.10.2. Lemma. Let L be of type $\langle r_1,\ldots,r_n;a_1,\ldots,a_m;k\rangle$.
If the rules

$$\frac{x_1 = y_1,\ldots,x_{r_i} = y_{r_i} \quad P_i(x_1,\ldots,x_{r_i})}{P_i(y_1,\ldots,y_{r_i})}, \text{ for all } i \leqslant n,$$

and

$$\frac{x_1 = y_1,\ldots,x_{a_j} = y_{a_j}}{f_j(x_1,\ldots,x_{a_j}) = f_j(y_1,\ldots,y_{a_j})}, \text{for all } j \leqslant m,$$

are given, then the rules RI_4 are derivable.

Proof. We consider a special case. Let L have one binary predicate symbol and one unary function symbol.

(i) We show $x = y \vdash t(x) = t(y)$ by induction on t.

(a) $t(x) = f(x)$, then we are in the case of a given rule.

(b) $t(x) = f(s(x))$. Induction hypothesis : $x = y \vdash s(x) = s(y)$

$$\dfrac{\dfrac{\dfrac{\dfrac{\dfrac{x = y}{f(x) = f(y)}}{x = y \rightarrow f(x) = f(y)}}{\forall xy\,(x = y \rightarrow f(x) = f(y))}\,\forall I\ (2\times)}{s(x) = s(y) \rightarrow f(s(x)) = f(s(y))} \qquad \begin{matrix} x = y \\ \mathcal{D} \\ s(x) = s(y) \end{matrix}}{f(s(x)) = f(s(y))}$$

This shows $x = y \vdash f(s(x)) = f(s(y))$.

(ii) We show $x_1 = y_1,\ x_2 = y_2,\ \varphi(x_1,x_2) \vdash \varphi(y_1,y_2)$

(a) φ is atomic, then $\varphi = P(s(x_1,x_2),t(x_1,x_2))$.

Note that s and t can only contain one variable each.

We use the present notation just for convenience.

$$\dfrac{\begin{array}{cc} x_1=y_1 \;\; x_2=y_2 \\ D \\ s(x_1,x_2)=s(y_1,y_2) \end{array} \quad \dfrac{\dfrac{\dfrac{\dfrac{\not{x_1=y_1} \quad \not{x_2=y_2} \quad \not{P(x_1,x_2)}}{P(y_1,y_2)}}{x_1=y_1 \to (x_2=y_2 \to (P(x_1,x_2) \to P(y_1,y_2)))} \to I(3\times)}{\forall x_1x_2y_1y_2\ (x_1=y_1 \to (x_2=y_2 \to (P(x_1,x_2) \to P(y_1,y_2))))} \forall I}{s(x_1,x_2)=s(y_1,y_2) \to (t(x_1,x_2)=t(y_1,y_2) \to (P(s_x,t_x) \to P(s_y,t_y)))} \forall E}{t(x_1,x_2)=t(y_1,y_2) \to (P(s_x,t_x) \to P(s_y,t_y)) \quad (*)}$$

$$\begin{array}{c} x_1 = y_1 \quad x_2 = y_2 \\ D \\ t(x_1,x_2) = t(y_1,y_2) \quad (**) \end{array}$$

Now
$$\dfrac{(*) \qquad\qquad (**)}{P(s_x,t_x) \to P(s_y,t_y)}$$

So $x_1 = y_1,\ x_2 = y_2 \vdash P(s_x,t_x) \to P(s_y,t_y)$

where $s_x = s(x_1,x_2), \quad s_y = s(y_1,y_2)$

$t_x = t(x_1,x_2), \quad t_y = t(y_1,y_2)$.

(b) $\varphi = \sigma \to \tau$.

Induction hypothesis $x_1 = y_1,\ x_2 = y_2,\ \sigma(y_1,y_2) \vdash \sigma(x_1,x_2)$

$x_1 = y_1,\ x_2 = y_2,\ \tau(x_1,x_2) \vdash \tau(y_1,y_2)$

$$\dfrac{\begin{array}{c} \dfrac{\sigma(x_1,x_2) \to \tau(x_1,x_2) \qquad \begin{array}{c} x_1 = x_2 \quad y_1 = y_2,\ \sigma(y_1,y_2) \\ D \\ \not{\sigma(x_1,x_2)} \end{array}}{\tau(x_1,x_2)} \quad x_1 = x_2 \quad y_1 = y_2 \\ D' \\ \tau(y_1,y_2) \end{array}}{\sigma(y_1,y_2) \to \tau(y_1,y_2)}$$

So $x_1 = x_2,\ y_1 = y_2,\ \sigma(x_1,x_2) \to \tau(x_1,x_2) \vdash \sigma(y_1,y_2) \to \tau(y_1,y_2)$.

(c) $\varphi = \sigma \wedge \tau$, left to the reader.

(d) $\varphi = \forall z \psi(z,x_1,x_2)$

Induction hypothesis: $x_1 = x_2, y_1 = y_2, \psi(z,x_1,x_2) \vdash \psi(z,y_1,y_2)$

$$\dfrac{\dfrac{\forall z\ \psi(z,x_1,x_2)}{\psi(z,x_1,x_2)} \qquad x_1 = x_2 \quad y_1 = y_2}{\begin{array}{c} \mathcal{D} \\ \dfrac{\psi(z,y_1,y_2)}{\forall z\ \psi(z,y_1,y_2)} \end{array}}$$

So $x_1 = x_2, y_1 = y_2, \forall z\ \psi(z,x_1,x_2) \vdash \forall z\ \psi(z,y_1,y_2)$.

This establishes, by induction, the general rule. □

EXERCISES.

1. Show that $\forall x\ (x = x), \forall xyz\ (x = y \wedge z = y \to x = z) \vdash I_2 \wedge I_3$ (using predicate logic only).

2. Show $\vdash \exists x\ (t = x)$ for any term t.
   Explain why all functions in a structure are total (i.e. defined for all arguments), think of 0^{-1}.

3. Show $\vdash \forall z\ (z = x \leftrightarrow z = y) \to x = y$

4. Show $\vdash \forall xyz\ (x \neq y \to x \neq z \vee y \neq z)$

5. Show that in the language of identity
   $I_1, I_2, I_3 \vdash I_4$.

6. Prove the following *Duality Principle* for projective geometry (cf. section 2.7 example 4: If $\Gamma \vdash \varphi$ then also $\Gamma \vdash \varphi^d$, where Γ is the set of axioms of projective geometry and φ^d is obtained from φ by replacing each atom xIy by yIx. (Hint: check the effect of the translation d on the derivation of φ from Γ).

3. Completeness and Applications

3.1. THE COMPLETENESS THEOREM

Just as in the case of propositional logic we shall show that 'derivability' and 'semantical consequence' coincide. We will do quite a bit of work before we get to the theorem. Although the proof of the completeness theorem is not harder than, say, some proofs in analysis, we would advise the reader to read the statement of the theorem and to skip the proof at a first reading and to return to it later. It is more instructive to go to the applications and it will propably give the reader a better feeling for the subject.

The main tool in this chapter is the

3.1.1. Model Existence Lemma. If Γ is a consistent set of sentences, then Γ has a model.

A sharper version is

3.1.1a. Lemma. Let L have cardinality κ. If Γ is a consistent set of sentences, then Γ has a model of cardinality $\leqslant \kappa$.

From 3.1.1 we immediately deduce Gödel's

3.1.2. Completeness Theorem.

$$\Gamma \vdash \varphi \;\Leftrightarrow\; \Gamma \models \varphi.$$

We will now go through all the steps of the proof of the completeness theorem.

In this section we will consider sentences, unless we specifically mention non-closed formulas. Furthermore ' $\vdash$ ' will stand for 'derivability in predicate logic with identity'.

3.1.2. Definitions

(*i*) A *theory* T is a collection of sentences with the property

$T \vdash \varphi \Rightarrow \varphi \in T$ (a theory is *closed under derivability*).

(*ii*) A set Γ such that $T = \{\varphi \mid \Gamma \vdash \varphi\}$ is called an *axiom set* of the theory T. The elements of Γ are called *axioms*.

(*iii*) T is called a *Henkin theory* if for each sentence $\exists x\varphi(x)$ there is a constant c such that $\exists x\varphi(x) \to \varphi(c) \in T$ (such a c called a *witness* for x in φ).

Note that $T = \{\sigma \mid \Gamma \vdash \sigma\}$ is a theory. For, if $T \vdash \varphi$, then $\sigma_1,\ldots,\sigma_k \vdash \varphi$ for certain σ_i with $\Gamma \vdash \sigma_i$.

$$\begin{array}{ccc} D_1 & D_2 & D_k \\ \sigma_1 & \sigma_2 \ldots & \sigma_k \\ & \frac{D}{\varphi} & \end{array}$$

From the derivations $D_1,\ldots,D_k$ of $\Gamma \vdash \sigma_1,\ldots,\Gamma \vdash \sigma_k$ and D of $\sigma_1,\ldots,\sigma_k \vdash \varphi$ a derivation of $\Gamma \vdash \varphi$ is obtained, as indicated.

3.1.3. Definition. Let T and T' be theories in the languages L and L'.

(*i*) T' is an *extension* of T if $T \subseteq T'$,

(*ii*) T' is a *conservative extension* of T if $T' \cap L = T$ (i.e. all theorems of T' in the language L are already theorems of T).

Example. Consider propositional logic P in the language L with $\to,\wedge,\bot$, and propositional logic P' in the language L' with $\to,\wedge,\vee,\bot,\leftrightarrow,\neg$. Then exercise 2, section 1.7, tells us that P' is conservative over P.

Our first task is the construction of Henkin extensions of a given theory T, that is to say: extensions of T which are Henkin theories.

3.1.4. Definition. Let T be a theory with language L. We add to the language, for each sentence σ of the form $\exists x\varphi(x)$, a constant c_σ such that distinct σ's yield distinct c 's. The resulting language is L*.
T* is the theory with axiom set $T \cup \{\exists x\varphi(x) \to \varphi(c_\sigma) \mid \exists x\varphi(x)$ closed, with witness $c_\sigma\}$.

3.1.5. Lemma. T* is conservative over T.

Proof. (*a*) Let $\exists x\varphi(x) \to \varphi(c)$ be one of the new axioms.
Suppose $\Gamma, \exists x\varphi(x) \to \varphi(c) \vdash \psi$, where ψ does not contain c and where Γ is a set of sentences, none of which contains the constant c. We show $\Gamma \vdash \psi$ in a number of steps.

1. $\Gamma \vdash (\exists x\varphi(x) \to \varphi(c)) \to \psi$,

2. $\Gamma \vdash (\exists x\varphi(x) \to \varphi(y)) \to \psi$, where y is a variable that does not occur in the associated derivation. 2 follows from 1 by 2.8 exercise 4.
3. $\Gamma \vdash \forall y[(\exists x\varphi(x) \to \varphi(y)) \to \psi]$. This application of ($\forall$I) is correct, since c did not occur in Γ.
4. $\Gamma \vdash \exists y(\exists x\varphi(x) \to \varphi(y)) \to \psi$, (cf. example of 2.9).
5. $\Gamma \vdash (\exists x\varphi(x) \to \exists y\varphi(y)) \to \psi$, (2.9 exercise 1 (vii)).
6. $\vdash \exists x\varphi(x) \to \exists y\varphi(y)$.
7. $\Gamma \vdash \psi$, (from 5,6).

(b) Let $T^* \vdash \psi$ for a $\psi \in L$. By the definition of derivability $T \cup \{\sigma_1,\dots,\sigma_n\} \vdash \psi$, where the σ_i are the new axioms of the form $\exists x\varphi(x) \to \varphi(c)$.

We show $T \vdash \psi$ by induction on n. For n = 0 we are done. Let $T \cup \{\sigma_1,\dots,\sigma_{n+1}\} \vdash \psi$. Put $T' = T \cup \{\sigma_1,\dots,\sigma_n\}$, then $T', \sigma_{n+1} \vdash \psi$ and we may apply *(a)*. Hence $T \cup \{\sigma_1,\dots,\sigma_n\} \vdash \psi$.
Now by induction hypothesis $T \vdash \psi$. □

Although we have added a large number of witnesses to T, there is no evidence that T* is a Henkin theory, since by enriching the language we also add new existential statements $\exists x\tau(x)$ which may not have witnesses. In order to overcome this difficulty we iterate the above process countably many times.

3.1.6. Lemma. Define $T_0 := T$; $T_{n+1} := (T_n)^*$; then $T_\omega := \cup\{T_n \mid n \geq 0\}$ is a Henkin theory and T_ω is conservative over T.

Proof. Call the language of T_n (T_ω) L_n (L_ω).

(i) T_ω is a theory. Suppose $T_\omega \vdash \sigma$, then $\varphi_0,\dots,\varphi_n \vdash \sigma$ for certain $\varphi_0,\dots,\varphi_n \in T_\omega$.
For each $i \leq n$ $\varphi_i \in T_{m_i}$ for some m_i.
Let $m = \max\{m_i \mid i \leq n\}$. Since $T_k \subseteq T_{k+1}$ for all k, we have $T_{m_i} \subseteq T_m$ $(i \leq n)$.
Therefore $T_m \vdash \sigma$.
T_m is (by definition) a theory, so $\sigma \in T_m \subseteq T_\omega$.

(ii) T_ω is a Henkin theory. Let $\exists x\varphi(x) \in L_\omega$, then $\exists x\varphi(x) \in L_n$ for some n. By definition $\exists x\varphi(x) \to \varphi(c) \in T_{n+1}$ for a certain c. So $\exists x\varphi(x) \to \varphi(c) \in T_\omega$.

(iii) T_ω is conservative over T. Observe that $T_\omega \vdash \sigma$ if $T_n \vdash \sigma$ for some n (see (i)) and apply 3.1.5 and induction on n. □

As a corollary we get: T_ω is consistent if T is so.
For, suppose T_ω inconsistent, then $T_\omega \vdash \bot$. As T_ω is conservative over T (and

$\perp \in L$) $T \vdash \perp$. Contradiction.

Our next step is to extend T_ω as far as possible, just as we did in propositional logic (1.6.7). We state a general principle:

3.1.7. Lemma (Lindenbaum). Each consistent theory is contained in a maximally consistent theory.

Proof. We give a straightforward application of *Zorn's lemma*. Let T be consistent. Consider the set A of all consistent extensions T' of T, partially ordered by inclusion. Claim: A has a maximal element.

(1) Each chain in A has an upper bound.

Let T_i $i \in I$ be a chain. Then $T' = \cup T_i$ is a consistent extension of T containing all T_i's (exercise 2). So T' is an upper bound.

(2) Therefore A has a maximal element T_m (Zorn's lemma).

(3) T_m is a maximally consistent extension of T.

We only have to show: $T_m \subseteq T'$ and $T' \in A$, then $T_m = T'$. But this is trivial as T_m is maximal in the sense of $\subseteq$.

Conclusion: T is contained in the maximally consistent theory T_m. □

Note that in general T has many maximally consistent extensions. The above existence is far from unique (as a matter of fact the proof of its existence essentially uses the axiom of choice).

We now combine the construction of a Henkin extension with a maximally consistent extension. Fortunately the property of being a Henkin theory is preserved under taking a maximally consistent extension. For, the language remains fixed, so if for an extensional statement $\exists x\varphi(x)$ there is a witness c such that $\exists x\varphi(x) \to \varphi(c) \in T$, then, trivially, $\exists x\varphi(x) \to \varphi(c) \in T_m$.

Hence

3.1.8. Lemma. If T_m is a maximally consistent extension of T_ω, then T_m is a Henkin theory.

We now get to the proof of our main theorem

3.1.1. Model Existence Lemma. If Γ is consistent, then Γ has a model.

Proof. Let $T = \{\sigma \mid \Gamma \vdash \sigma\}$ be the theory given by Γ. Any model of T is, of course, a model of Γ.

Let T_m be a maximally consistent Henkin extension of T (which exists by the preceding lemmas), with language L_m.

We will construct a model of T_m using T_m itself. At this point the reader should realize that a language is, after all, a set, that is a set of strings of symbols. So, we will utilize this set to build the universe of a suitable model.

1. $A = \{t \in L_m \mid t \text{ is closed}\}$.
2. For each function symbol f we define a function $\hat{f}: A^n \to A$ by $\hat{f}(t_1,\dots,t_k) := f(t_1,\dots,t_k)$.
3. For each predicate symbol P we define a relation $\hat{P} \subseteq A^m$ by $\langle t_1,\dots,t_p\rangle \in \hat{P} \Rightarrow T_m \vdash P(t_1,\dots,t_p)$.
4. For each constant symbol c we define a constant $\hat{c} := c$.

Although it looks as if we have created the required model, we have to improve the result, because '=' is not interpreted as the real equality. We can only assert that

(a) the relation $t \sim s$ defined by $T_m \vdash t = s$ for $t,s \in A$ is an equivalence relation.

By lemma 2.10.1 I_1, I_2, I_3 are theorems (of T_m), so $T_m \vdash \forall x\,(x = x)$, and hence (by $\forall E$) $T_m \vdash t = t$, or $t \sim t$.

Symmetry and transitivity follow in the same way.

(b) $t_i \sim s_i \quad (i \leqslant p)$ and $\langle t_1,\dots,t_p\rangle \in \hat{P} \Rightarrow \langle s_1,\dots,s_p\rangle \in \hat{P}$.

$t_i \sim s_i \quad (i \leqslant k) \Rightarrow f(t_1,\dots,t_k) \sim f(s_1,\dots,s_k)$ for all symbols P and f.

The proof is simple: use $T_m \vdash I_4$ (lemma 2.10.1).

Once we have an equivalence relation, which, moreover, is a congruence with respect to the basic relations and functions, it is natural to introduce the quotient structure.

Denote the equivalence class of t under $\sim$ by $[t]$.

Define $\mathfrak{A} := \langle A/\!\sim, \tilde{P}_1,\dots,\tilde{P}_n, \tilde{f}_1,\dots,\tilde{f}_m, \{\tilde{c}_i \mid i \in I\}\rangle$, where

$$\tilde{P}_i := \{\langle [t_1],\dots,[t_{r_i}]\rangle \mid \langle t_1,\dots,t_{r_i}\rangle \in \hat{P}\}$$

$$\tilde{f}_j([t_1],\dots,[t_{a_j}]) = [\hat{f}_j(t_1,\dots,t_{a_j})]$$

$$\tilde{c}_i := [\hat{c}_i].$$

One has to show that the relations and functions on $A/\!\sim$ are well-defined, but that is taken care of by (b) above.

Closed terms lead a kind of double life. On the one hand they are syntactical objects, on the other hand they are the stuff that elements of the universe are made from. The two things are related by $t^{\mathfrak{A}} = [t]$. This is shown by induction on t.

(*i*) $t = c$, then $t^{\mathfrak{A}} = \tilde{c} = [\hat{c}] = [c] = [t]$,

(*ii*) $t = f(t_1,\ldots,t_k)$, then $t^{\mathfrak{A}} = \tilde{f}(t_1^{\mathfrak{A}},\ldots,t_k^{\mathfrak{A}})$ = (induction hypothesis) $= \tilde{f}([t_1],\ldots,[t_k]) = [\hat{f}(t_1,\ldots,t_k)] = [f(t_1,\ldots,t_k)]$.

Furthermore we have $\mathfrak{A} \models \varphi(t) \Leftrightarrow \mathfrak{A} \models \varphi(\overline{[t]})$, by the above and by exercise 6 section 2.4.

<u>Claim.</u> $\mathfrak{A} \models \varphi \Leftrightarrow T_m \vdash \varphi$ for all sentences in the language L_m of T_m which, by the way, is also $L(\mathfrak{A})$, since each element of $A/\sim$ has a name in L_m.
We prove the claim by induction on φ.

(*i*) φ is atomic.

$\mathfrak{A} \models P(t_1,\ldots,t_p) \Leftrightarrow \langle t_1^{\mathfrak{A}},\ldots,t_p^{\mathfrak{A}}\rangle \in \tilde{P} \Leftrightarrow \langle [t_1],\ldots,[t_p]\rangle \in \tilde{P} \Leftrightarrow$

$\Leftrightarrow \langle t_1,\ldots,t_p\rangle \in \hat{P} \Leftrightarrow T_m \vdash P(t_1,\ldots,t_p)$.

The case $\varphi = \bot$ is trivial.

(*ii*) $\varphi = \sigma \wedge \tau$. Trivial.

(*iii*) $\varphi = \sigma \rightarrow \tau$.

We recall that, by lemma 1.6.9, $T_m \vdash \sigma \rightarrow \tau \Leftrightarrow (T_m \vdash \sigma \Rightarrow T_m \vdash \tau)$.
Note that we can copy this result, since its proof only uses propositional logic, and hence remains correct in predicate logic.

$\mathfrak{A} \models \sigma \rightarrow \tau \Leftrightarrow (\mathfrak{A} \models \sigma \Rightarrow \mathfrak{A} \models \tau) \Leftrightarrow$ (induction hypothesis)
$(T_m \vdash \sigma \Rightarrow T_m \vdash \tau) \Leftrightarrow T_m \vdash \sigma \rightarrow \tau$.

(*iv*) $\varphi = \forall x\psi(x)$.

$\mathfrak{A} \models \forall x\psi(x) \Leftrightarrow \mathfrak{A} \models \neg\exists x\neg\psi(x)$, where $\exists x$ is used as an abbreviation.
$\mathfrak{A} \models \neg\exists x\neg\psi(x) \Leftrightarrow \mathfrak{A} \not\models \exists x\neg\psi(x) \Leftrightarrow \mathfrak{A} \not\models \neg\psi(\bar{a})$, for all $a \in |\mathfrak{A}| \Leftrightarrow$ for all $a \in |\mathfrak{A}|$ $\mathfrak{A} \models \psi(\bar{a})$.

Assuming $\mathfrak{A} \models \forall x\psi(x)$, we get in particular, $\mathfrak{A} \models \psi(c)$ for the witness c belonging to $\exists x\neg\psi(x)$.

Induction hypothesis: $T_m \vdash \psi(c)$.

$T_m \vdash \exists x\neg\psi(x) \rightarrow \neg\psi(c)$, so $T_m \vdash \psi(c) \rightarrow \neg\exists x\neg\psi(x)$ (contraposition), and hence $T_m \vdash \forall x\psi(x)$.

Conversely: $T_m \vdash \forall x\psi(x) \Rightarrow T_m \vdash \psi(t)$ for all closed t. By induction hypothesis $\mathfrak{A} \models \psi(t)$ for all closed t. So $\mathfrak{A} \models \psi(\overline{[t]})$ for all closed t, or $\mathfrak{A} \models \forall x\psi(x)$.

Now we see that $\mathfrak{A}$ is a model of Γ, as $\Gamma \subseteq T_m$. $\square$

In order to get an estimation of the cardinality of the model we have to compute the number of closed terms in L_m. As we did not change the language going from T_ω to T_m, we can look at the language L_ω.
We will indicate how to get the required cardinalities, given the alphabet of the original language L.
We will use the axiom of choice freely, in particular in the form of absorption laws (i.e. $\kappa+\lambda = \kappa\cdot\lambda = \max(\kappa,\lambda)$ for infinite cardinals).
Say L has type $\langle r_1,\ldots,r_n; a_1,\ldots,a_m; \kappa\rangle$.

1. Define $TERM_0 := \{c_i \mid i \in I\} \cup \{x_j \mid j \in N\}$

$$TERM_{n+1} := TERM_n \cup \{f_j(t_1,\ldots,t_{a_j}) \mid j \leqslant m,\ t_k \in TERM_n \text{ for } k \leqslant a_j\}.$$

   Then $TERM = \cup\{TERM_n \mid n \in N\}$ (exercise 5)

   $|TERM_0| = \max(\kappa,\aleph_0) = \mu$.

   Suppose $|TERM_n| = \mu$.

$$|\{f_j(t_1,\ldots,t_{a_j}) \mid t_1,\ldots,t_{a_j} \in TERM_n\}| = |TERM_n|^{a_j} = \mu^{a_j} = \mu.$$

   So $|TERM_{n+1}| = \mu + \mu + \ldots + \mu$ (m+1 times) $= \mu$.

   Finally $|TERM| = \sum_{n\in N} |TERM_n| = \aleph_0\cdot\mu = \mu$.

2. Define $FORM_0 := \{P_i(t_1,\ldots,t_{r_i}) \mid i < n,\ t_k \in TERM\} \cup \{\bot\}$

$$FORM_{n+1} := FORM_n \cup \{\varphi \square \psi \mid \square \in \{\wedge,\rightarrow\}, \varphi,\psi \in FORM_n\} \cup$$
$$\cup \{\forall x_i\varphi \mid i \in N,\ \varphi \in FORM_n\}.$$

   Then $FORM = \cup\{FORM_n \mid n \in N\}$ (exercise 5)

   As in 1, one shows $|FORM| = \mu$.

3. The set of sentences of the form $\exists x\varphi(x)$ has cardinality μ.
   It trivially is $\leqslant \mu$. Consider $A = \{\exists x_j(x_j = c_i) \mid i \in I,\ j \in N\}$.
   Clearly $|A| = \kappa\cdot\aleph_0 = \mu$. Hence the cardinality of the existential statements is μ.

4. L_1 has the constant symbols of L, plus the witnesses. By 3 the cardinality of the set of constant symbols is μ.
   Using 1 and 2 we find L_0 has μ terms and μ formulas. By induction on n each L_n has μ terms and μ formulas. Therefore L_ω has $\aleph_0\cdot\mu = \mu$ terms and formulas. L_ω is also the language of T_m.

5. L_ω has at most μ closed terms. Since L_1 has μ witnesses, L_ω has at least μ, and hence exactly μ closed terms.

6. The set of closed terms has $\leqslant \mu$ equivalence classes under $\sim$, so $||\mathfrak{A}|| \leqslant \mu$.

All this adds up to the strengthened version of the Model Existence Lemma:

Γ is consistent $\Leftrightarrow$ Γ has a model of cardinality at most the cardinality of the language.

Note the following facts:
If L has finitely many constants, then L is countable.
If L has $\kappa \geqslant \aleph_0$ constants, then $|L| = \kappa$.

The completeness theorem for predicate logic raises the same question as the completeness theorem for propositional logic: can we effectively find a derivation of φ if φ is true? The problem is that we don't have much to go on; φ is true in all structures (of the correct similarity type). Even though (in the case of a countable language) we can restrict ourselves to countable structures, the fact that φ is true in all those structures does not give the combinatorial information, necessary to construct a derivation for φ. The matter is at this stage beyond us. A treatment of the problem belongs to proof theory; Gentzen's methods or the tableau method are more suitable than ours.

In the case of predicate logic there are certain improvements on the completeness theorem. One can, for example, ask how complicated the model is that we constructed in the model existence lemma. The proper setting for those questions is found in recursion theory. We can, however, have a quick look at a simple case.

Let T be a *decidable* theory with a countable language, i.e. we have an effective method to test membership (or, what comes to the same, we can test $\Gamma \vdash \varphi$ for a set of axioms of T). Consider the Henkin theory T introduced in 3.1.6.; $\sigma \in T_\omega$ if $\sigma \in T_n$ for a certain n. This number n can be read off from σ by inspection of the witnesses occurring in σ.

From the witnesses we can also determine which axioms of the form $\exists x\varphi(x) \rightarrow \varphi(c)$ are involved. Let $\{\tau_1,\ldots,\tau_n\}$ be the set of axioms required for the derivation of σ, then $T \cup \{\tau_1,\ldots,\tau_n\} \vdash \sigma$. By the rules of logic this reduces to $T \vdash \tau_1 \wedge \ldots \wedge \tau_n \rightarrow \sigma$. Since the constants c_i are new with respect to T, this is equivalent to $T \vdash \forall z_1,\ldots,z_k(\tau'_1 \wedge \ldots \wedge \tau'_n \rightarrow \sigma')$ for suitable variables $z_1,\ldots,z_k$, where $\tau'_1,\ldots,\tau'_n,\sigma'$ are obtained by substitution. Thus we see that $\sigma \in T_\omega$ is decidable. The next step is the formation of a maximal extension T_m.

Let $\varphi_0, \varphi_1, \varphi_2, \ldots$ be an enumeration of all sentences of T_ω. We add sentences to T_ω in steps.

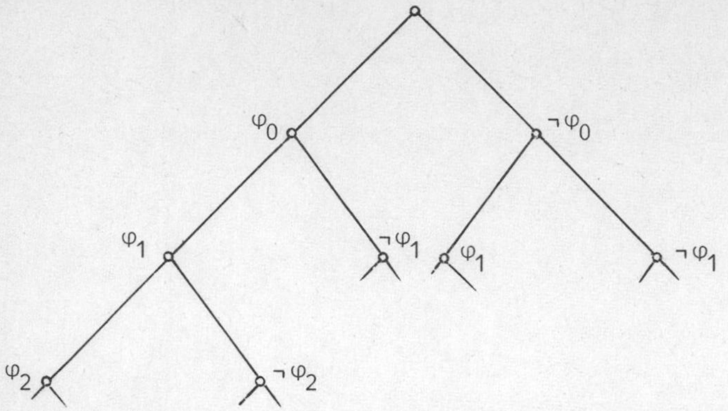

$$\text{step } 0\text{: } T_0 = \begin{cases} T_\omega \cup \{\varphi_0\} & \text{if } T \cup \{\varphi_0\} \text{ is consistent,} \\ T_\omega \cup \{\neg\, \varphi_0\} & \text{else,} \end{cases}$$

$$\text{step } n+1\text{: } T_{n+1} = \begin{cases} T_n \cup \{\varphi_{n+1}\} & \text{if } T_n \cup \{\varphi_{n+1}\} \text{ is consistent,} \\ T_n \cup \{\neg\, \varphi_{n+1}\} & \text{else,} \end{cases}$$

$T^0 = \bigcup_{n \geqslant 0} T_n$ (T^0 is given by a suitable infinite path in the tree).

It is easily seen that T^0 is maximally consistent. Moreover, T^0 is decidable. To test $\varphi_n \in T^0$ we have to test $\varphi_n \in T_n$, or $T_{n-1} \cup \{\varphi_n\}$ is consistent, i.e. $T_{n-1} \cup \{\varphi_n\} \vdash \bot$.

Given the decidability of T_ω, we conclude that $T_{n-1} \cup \{\varphi_n\} \vdash \bot$ is decidable. So T^0 is decidable.

The model $\mathfrak{A}$ constructed in 3.1.1 is therefore also decidable in the following sense: the operations and relations of $\mathfrak{A}$ are decidable, which means that $\langle [t_1], \ldots, [t_p] \rangle \in \tilde{P}$ and $\tilde{f}([t_1], \ldots, [t_k]) = [t]$ are decidable.

Summing up we say that a decidable consistent theory has a decidable model (this can be made more precise by replacing 'decidable' by 'recursive').

EXERCISES

1. Consider the language of groups. $T = \{\sigma \mid \mathfrak{A} \models \sigma\}$, where $\mathfrak{A}$ is a fixed non-

trivial group. Show that T is not a Henkin theory.

2. Let $\{T_i \mid i \in I\}$ be a set of theories, linearly ordered by inclusion. Show that $T = \bigcup\{T_i \mid i \in I\}$ is a theory which extends each T_i.
If each T_i is consistent, then T is consistent.

3. Show that

$$\lambda_n \vdash \sigma \Leftrightarrow \sigma \text{ holds in all models with at least n elements,}$$
$$\mu_n \vdash \sigma \Leftrightarrow \sigma \text{ holds in all models with at most n elements,}$$
$$\lambda_n \wedge \mu_n \vdash \sigma \Leftrightarrow \sigma \text{ holds in all models with exactly n elements,}$$
$$\{\lambda_n | n \in N\} \vdash \sigma \Leftrightarrow \sigma \text{ holds in all infinite models,}$$

(for a definition of λ_n, μ_n cf. section 2.7).

4. Show that $T = \{\sigma \mid \lambda_2 \vdash \sigma\} \cup \{c_1 \neq c_2\}$ in a language with = and two constant symbols c_1, c_2, is a Henkin theory.

5. Show $TERM = \bigcup\{TERM_n \mid n \in N\}$,
$FORM = \bigcup\{FORM_n \mid n \in N\}$ (cf. 1.1.5).

3.2. COMPACTNESS AND SKOLEM-LÖWENHEIM

Unless specified otherwise, we consider sentences in this section. From the Model Existence Lemma we get the following

3.2.1. Compactness theorem.

Γ has a model $\Leftrightarrow$ each finite subset Δ of Γ has a model.

An equivalent formulation is

Γ has no model $\Leftrightarrow$ some finite $\Delta \subseteq \Gamma$ has no model.

Proof. We consider the second version.
$\Leftarrow$ Trivial.
$\Rightarrow$ Suppose Γ has no model, then by the model existence lemma Γ is inconsistent, i.e. $\Gamma \vdash \bot$. Therefore there are $\sigma_1,\ldots,\sigma_n \in \Gamma$ such that $\sigma_1,\ldots,\sigma_n \vdash \bot$. This shows that $\Delta = \{\sigma_1,\ldots,\sigma_n\}$ has no model. □

Let us introduce a bit of notation: $Mod(\Gamma) = \{\mathfrak{A} \mid \mathfrak{A} \models \sigma \text{ for all } \sigma \in \Gamma\}$. For convenience we will often write $\mathfrak{A} \models \Gamma$ for $\mathfrak{A} \in Mod(\Gamma)$.

In general Mod(Γ) is not a set (in the technical sense of set theory: Mod(Γ) is, in general, a proper class). We will not worry about that since the notation is only used as an abbreviation.

Conversely, let K be a class of structures (we have fixed the similarity type), then $Th(K) = \{\sigma \mid \mathfrak{A} \models \sigma \text{ for all } \mathfrak{A} \in K\}$. We call Th(K) the *theory of* K.

We adopt the convention (already used in section 2.7) not to include the identity axioms in a set Γ; these will always be satisfied.
We write $Mod(\varphi_1,\ldots,\varphi_2)$ instead of $Mod(\{\varphi_1,\ldots,\varphi_n\})$.

Examples.

1. $Mod(\forall xy(x \leq y \wedge y \leq x \leftrightarrow x = y), \forall xyz(x \leq y \wedge y \leq z \rightarrow x \leq z))$ is the class of posets.

2. Let G be the class of all groups.
   Th(G) is the theory of groups.

We can consider the set of integers with the usual additive group structure, but also with the ring structure, so there are two structures $\mathfrak{A}$ and $\mathfrak{B}$, of which the first one is in a sense a part of the second (category theory uses a forgetful functor to express this). We say that $\mathfrak{A}$ is a *reduct* of $\mathfrak{B}$, or $\mathfrak{B}$ is an *expansion* of $\mathfrak{A}$.

In general

3.2.2. Definition. $\mathfrak{A}$ is a *reduct* of $\mathfrak{B}$ ($\mathfrak{B}$ an *expansion* of $\mathfrak{A}$) if $|\mathfrak{A}| = |\mathfrak{B}|$ and moreover all relations, functions and constants of $\mathfrak{A}$ occur also as relations, functions and constants of $\mathfrak{B}$.

Notation: $(\mathfrak{A}, S_1,\ldots,S_n, g_1,\ldots,g_m, \{a_j \mid j \in J\})$ is the expansion of $\mathfrak{A}$ with the indicated extras.

In the early days of logic (before "model theory" was introduced) Skolem (1920) and Löwenheim (1915) studied the possible cardinalities of models of consistent theories. The following generalization follows immediately from the preceding results.

3.2.3. Downward Skolem-Löwenheim theorem.
Let Γ be a set of sentences in a language of cardinality κ, and let $\kappa < \lambda$.

If Γ has a model of cardinality λ, then Γ has a model of cardinality κ.

Proof. Add to the language L of Γ a set of fresh constants (not occurring in the alphabet of L) $\{c_i \mid i \in I\}$ of cardinality κ, and consider $\Gamma' = \Gamma \cup \{c_i \neq c_j \mid i,j \in I,\ i \neq j\}$. Claim: $\mathrm{Mod}(\Gamma') \neq \emptyset$.

Consider a model $\mathfrak{A}$ of Γ of cardinality λ. We expand $\mathfrak{A}$ to $\mathfrak{A}'$ by adding κ distinct constants (this is possible: $|\mathfrak{A}|$ contains a subset of cardinality κ). $\mathfrak{A}' \in \mathrm{Mod}(\Gamma)$ (cf. exercise 2) and $\mathfrak{A}' \models c_i \neq c_j (i \neq j)$.
Consequently $\mathrm{Mod}(\Gamma') \neq \emptyset$.
The cardinality of the language of Γ' is κ.
By the model existence lemma Γ' has a model $\mathcal{B}'$ of cardinality $\leqslant \kappa$, but, by the axioms $c_i \neq c_j$, the cardinality is also $\geqslant \kappa$. Hence $\mathcal{B}'$ has cardinality κ. Now take the reduct $\mathcal{B}$ of $\mathcal{B}'$ in the language of Γ, then $\mathcal{B} \in \mathrm{Mod}(\Gamma)$ (exercise 2). □

Examples.

1. The theory of real numbers, $\mathrm{Th}(\mathbb{R})$, in the language of fields, has a countable model.

2. Consider Zermelo-Fraenkel's set theory ZF. If $\mathrm{Mod}(ZF) \neq \emptyset$, then ZF has a countable model. This fact was discovered by Skolem. Because of its baffling nature, it was called Skolem's paradox. One can prove in ZF the existence of uncountable sets (e.g. the continuum), how can ZF then have a countable model? The answer is simple: countability as seen from outside and from inside the model is not the same. To establish countability one needs a bijection to the natural numbers. Apparently a model can be so poor that it misses some bijections which do exist outside the model.

3.2.4. Upward Skolem-Löwenheim theorem.
Let Γ have a language L of cardinality κ, and $\mathfrak{A} \in \mathrm{Mod}(\Gamma)$ with cardinality $\lambda \geqslant \kappa$.
For each $\mu > \lambda$ Γ has a model of cardinality μ.

Proof. Add to L μ fresh constants c_i, $i \in I$ and consider $\Gamma' = \Gamma \cup \{c_i \neq c_j \mid i \neq j,\ i,j \in I\}$. Claim: $\mathrm{Mod}(\Gamma') \neq \emptyset$. We apply the compactness theorem.
Let $\Delta \subseteq \Gamma'$ be finite. Say Δ contains new axioms with constants $c_{i_0}, \ldots, c_{i_k}$, then $\Delta \subseteq \Gamma \cup \{c_{i_p} \neq c_{i_q} \mid p,q \leqslant k\} = \Gamma_0$. Clearly each model of Γ_0 is a model of Δ (exercise 1(i)).
Now take $\mathfrak{A}$ and expand it to $\mathfrak{A}' = (\mathfrak{A}, a_1, \ldots, a_k)$, where the a_i are distinct.

Then obviously $\mathfrak{A}' \in Mod(\Gamma_0)$, so $\mathfrak{A}' \in Mod(\Delta)$. By the compactness theorem there is a $\mathfrak{B}' \in Mod(\Gamma')$. The reduct $\mathfrak{B}$ of $\mathfrak{B}'$ to the (type of) language L is a model of Γ. From the extra axioms in Γ' it follows that $\mathfrak{B}'$, and hence $\mathfrak{B}$, has cardinality $\geq \mu$.
We now apply the downward Skolem-Löwenheim theorem and obtain the existence of a model of Γ of cardinality μ. □

We now list a number of applications.

3.2.5. Peano's arithmetic has non-standard models.

Let $\mathcal{P}$ be the class of all Peano structures. Put $PA = Th(\mathcal{P})$. By the completeness theorem $PA = \{\sigma \mid \Sigma \vdash \sigma\}$ where Σ is the set of axioms listed in section 2.7, example 6. PA has a model of cardinality $\aleph_0$ (the standard model $\mathfrak{N}$), so by the upward Skolem-Löwenheim theorem it has models of every $\kappa > \aleph_0$. These models are clearly not isomorphic to $\mathfrak{N}$.
For more see 3.3.10.

3.2.6. Finite and infinite models.

Lemma. If Γ has arbitrarily large finite models, then Γ has an infinite model.

Proof. Put $\Gamma' = \Gamma \cup \{\lambda_n \mid n > 1\}$, where λ_n expresses the sentence "there are at least n distinct elements", cf. section 2.7, example 1.
Apply the compactness theorem. Let $\Delta \subseteq \Gamma'$ be finite, and let λ_m be the sentence λ_n in Δ with the largest index n. Verify that $Mod(\Delta) \supset Mod(\Gamma \cup \{\lambda_m\})$. Now Γ has arbitrarily large finite models, so Γ has a model $\mathfrak{A}$ with at least m elements, i.e. $\mathfrak{A} \in Mod(\Gamma \cup \{\lambda_m\})$. So $Mod(\Delta) \neq \emptyset$.
By compactness $Mod(\Gamma') \neq \emptyset$, but in virtue of the axioms λ_n, a model of Γ is infinite. Hence Γ', and therefore Γ, has an infinite model. □

We get the following simple

Corollary. Consider a class K of structures which has arbitrarily large finite models (and hence also infinite models). Then, in the language of the class, there is no set Σ of sentences, such that
$\mathfrak{A} \in Mod(\Sigma) \Leftrightarrow \mathfrak{A}$ is finite. □

Proof. Immediate.

We can paraphrase the result as follows: the class of finite structures in such a class K is not axiomatizable in first order logic.

We all know that finiteness can be expressed in a language that contains variables for sets or functions (e.g. Dedekind's definition), so the inability to characterize the notion of finite is a specific defect of first-order logic. We say that *finiteness is not a first-order property*.

The corollary applies to numerous classes, e.g. groups, rings, fields, posets, sets (identity structures).

3.2.7. Axiomatizability and finite axiomatizability.

Definition. A class K of structures is (finitely) *axiomatizable* if there is a (finite) set Γ such that $K = \mathrm{Mod}(\Gamma)$.

We say that Γ *axiomatizes* K; the sentences of Γ are called *axioms* (cf. 3.1.2).

Examples. For the classes of posets, ordered sets, groups. rings, Peano-structures the axiom sets Γ are listed in section 2.7.

The following fact is very useful:

Lemma *(a)* If $K = \mathrm{Mod}(\Gamma)$ and K is finitely axiomatizable, then K is axiomatizable by a finite subset of Γ.

Proof. Let $K = \mathrm{Mod}(\Delta)$ for a finite Δ, then $K = \mathrm{Mod}(\sigma)$, where σ is the conjunction of all sentences of Δ (exercise 3). Then $\sigma \models \psi$ for all $\psi \in \Gamma$ and $\Gamma \models \sigma$, hence also $\Gamma \vdash \sigma$. Thus there are finitely many $\psi_1,\ldots,\psi_k \in \Gamma$ such that $\psi_1,\ldots,\psi_k \vdash \sigma$.

Claim $K = \mathrm{Mod}(\psi_1,\ldots,\psi_k)$.

(i) $\{\psi_1,\ldots,\psi_k\} \subseteq \Gamma$ so $\mathrm{Mod}(\Gamma) \subseteq \mathrm{Mod}(\psi_1,\ldots,\psi_k)$.

(ii) From $\psi_1,\ldots,\psi_k \vdash \sigma$ it follows that $\mathrm{Mod}(\psi_1,\ldots,\psi_k) \subseteq \mathrm{Mod}(\sigma)$.

Using (i) and (ii) we conclude $\mathrm{Mod}(\psi_1,\ldots,\psi_k) = K$. □

This lemma is instrumental in proving non-finite-axiomatizability results. We need one more fact.

Lemma *(b)* K is finitely axiomatizable $\Leftrightarrow$ K and its complement K^c are both axiomatizable.

Proof. $\Rightarrow$. Let $K = \mathrm{Mod}(\varphi_1,\ldots,\varphi_n)$, then $K = \mathrm{Mod}(\varphi_1 \wedge \ldots \wedge \varphi_k)$.
$\mathfrak{A} \in K^c$ (complement of K) $\Leftrightarrow$ $\mathfrak{A} \not\models \varphi_1 \wedge \ldots \wedge \varphi_n$ $\Leftrightarrow$ $\mathfrak{A} \models \neg(\varphi_1 \wedge \ldots \wedge \varphi_n)$. So

$K^c = \mathrm{Mod}(\neg(\varphi_1 \wedge \ldots \wedge \varphi_n))$.

$\Leftarrow$. Let $K = \mathrm{Mod}(\Gamma)$, $K^c = \mathrm{Mod}(\Delta)$.

$K \cap K^c = \mathrm{Mod}(\Gamma \cup \Delta) = \emptyset$ (exercise 1).

By compactness, there are $\varphi_1,\ldots,\varphi_n \in \Gamma$ and $\psi_1,\ldots,\psi_m \in \Delta$ such that

$\mathrm{Mod}(\varphi_1,\ldots,\varphi_n,\psi_1,\ldots,\psi_m) = \emptyset$,

or $\quad \mathrm{Mod}(\varphi_1,\ldots,\varphi_n) \cap \mathrm{Mod}(\psi_1,\ldots,\psi_m) = \emptyset, \quad (1)$

$K = \mathrm{Mod}(\Gamma) \subseteq \mathrm{Mod}(\varphi_1,\ldots,\varphi_n) \quad (2)$

$K^c = \mathrm{Mod}(\Delta) \subseteq \mathrm{Mod}(\psi_1,\ldots,\psi_m) \quad (3)$

(1), (2), (3) $\Rightarrow K = \mathrm{Mod}(\varphi_1,\ldots,\varphi_n)$. $\square$

We now get a number of corollaries.

Corollary 1. The class of all infinite sets (identity structures) is axiomatizable, but not finitely axiomatizable.

Proof. $\mathfrak{A}$ is infinite $\Leftrightarrow$ $\mathfrak{A} \in \mathrm{Mod}(\{\lambda_n \mid n \in N\})$.

So the axiom set is $\{\lambda_n \mid n \in N\}$.

On the other hand the class of finite sets is not axiomatizable, so, by lemma (b), the class of infinite sets is not finitely axiomatizable.

Corollary 2.

(*i*) The class of field of characteristic p (>0) is finitely axiomatizable.

(*ii*) The class of fields of characteristic 0 is axiomatizable but not finitely axiomatizable.

(*iii*) The class of fields of positive characteristic is not axiomatizable.

Proof.

(*i*) The theory of fields has a finite set Δ of axioms. $\Delta \cup \{\bar{p} = 0\}$ axiomatizes the class F_p of fields of characteristic p (where $\bar{p}$ stands for $1 + 1 + \ldots + 1, (p\times)$).

(*ii*) $\Delta \cup \{\bar{2} \neq 0, \bar{3} \neq 0, \ldots, \bar{p} \neq 0, \ldots\}$ axiomatizes the class F_0 of characteristic 0. Suppose F_0 was finitely axiomatizable, then by lemma (a) F_0 was axiomatizable by $\Gamma = \Delta \cup \{\bar{p}_1 \neq 0, \ldots, \bar{p}_k \neq 0\}$, where $p_1,\ldots,p_k$ are primes (not necessarily the first k one). Let q be a prime greater than all p_i (Euclid). Then $Z/(q)$ (the integers modulo q) is a model of Γ, but $Z/(q)$ is not a field of characteristic 0. Contradiction.

(*iii*) follows immediately from (ii) and lemma (b).

Corollary 3. The class A_c of all algebraically closed fields is axiomatizable, but not finitely axiomatizable.

Proof. Let $\sigma_n = \forall y_1 \ldots y_n \exists x(x^n + y_1 x^{n-1} + \ldots + y_{n-1}x + y_n = 0)$.
Then $\Gamma = \Delta \cup \{\sigma_n \mid n \geq 1\}$ (Δ as in corollary 2) axiomatizes A_c.

To show non-finite axiomatizability, apply the compactness theorem to Γ and find a field in which a certain polynomial does not factorize. □

Corollary 4. The class of all torsion-free abelian groups is axiomatizable, but not finitely axiomatizable.

Proof. Exercise 15.

Remark: In lemma (a) we used the completeness theorem and in lemma (b) the compactness theorem. The advantage of using only the compactness theorem is that one avoids the notion of provability altogether. The reader might object that this advantage is rather artifical since the compactness theorem is a corollary to the completeness theorem. This is true in our presentation; one can, however, derive the compactness theorem by purely model theoretic means (using ultraproducts, cf. Chang-Keisler, 4.1.11), so there are situations where one has to use the compactness theorem. For the moment the choice between using the completeness theorem or the compactness theorem is largely a matter of taste or convenience.

By way of illustration we will give an alternative proof of lemma (a) using the compactness theorem.

Proof. Again we have $Mod(\Gamma) = Mod(\sigma)$ (*).
Consider $\Gamma' = \Gamma \cup \{\neg\sigma\}$.

$$\begin{aligned} \mathfrak{A} \in Mod(\Gamma') &\Leftrightarrow \mathfrak{A} \in Mod(\Gamma) \text{ and } \mathfrak{A} \models \neg\sigma, \\ &\Leftrightarrow \mathfrak{A} \in Mod\,\Gamma \text{ and } \mathfrak{A} \notin Mod(\sigma). \end{aligned}$$

In view of (*) we have $Mod(\Gamma') = \emptyset$.

By the compactness theorem there is a finite subset Δ of Γ' with $Mod(\Delta) = \emptyset$. It is no restriction to suppose that $\neg\sigma \in \Delta$, hence $Mod(\psi_1,\ldots,\psi_k,\neg\sigma) = \emptyset$. It now easily follows that $Mod(\psi_1,\ldots,\psi_k) = Mod(\sigma) = Mod(\Gamma)$.

3.2.8. Ordering sets.

One easily shows that each finite set can be ordered, for infinite sets this is harder. A simple trick is presented below.

Theorem. Each infinite set can be ordered.

Proof. Let $|X| = \kappa \geq \aleph_0$. Consider Γ, the set of axioms for linear order (section 2.7 no 2). Γ has a countable model, e.g. $\mathbb{N}$. By the upward Skolem-Löwenheim theorem Γ has a model $\mathfrak{A} = \langle A,<\rangle$ of cardinality κ. Since X and A have the same cardinality there is a bijection $f: X \to A$. Define $x < x' := f(x) < f(x')$. Evidently, $<$ is a linear order. □

In the same way one gets:
Each infinite set can be densely ordered.
The same trick works for axiomatizable classes in general.

EXERCISES.

1. Show (*i*) $\Gamma \subseteq \Delta \Rightarrow \mathrm{Mod}(\Delta) \subseteq \mathrm{Mod}(\Gamma)$,
   (*ii*) $K_1 \subseteq K_2 \Rightarrow \mathrm{Th}(K_2) \subseteq \mathrm{Th}(K_1)$,
   (*iii*) $\mathrm{Mod}(\Gamma \cup \Delta) = \mathrm{Mod}(\Gamma) \cap \mathrm{Mod}(\Delta)$,
   (*iv*) $\mathrm{Th}(K_1 \cup K_2) = \mathrm{Th}(K_1) \cap \mathrm{Th}(K_2)$,
   (*v*) $K \subseteq \mathrm{Mod}(\Gamma) \Leftrightarrow \Gamma \subseteq \mathrm{Th}(K)$,
   (*vi*) $\mathrm{Mod}(\Gamma \cap \Delta) \supseteq \mathrm{Mod}(\Gamma) \cup \mathrm{Mod}(\Delta)$,
   (*vii*) $\mathrm{Th}(K_1 \cap K_2) \supseteq \mathrm{Th}(K_1) \cup \mathrm{Th}(K_2)$.

   Show that in (vi) and (vii) $\supseteq$ cannot be replaced by $=$.

2. Show (*i*) $\Gamma \subseteq \mathrm{Th}(\mathrm{Mod}(\Gamma))$,
   (*ii*) $K \subseteq \mathrm{Mod}(\mathrm{Th}(K))$,
   (*iii*) $\mathrm{Th}(\mathrm{Mod}(\Gamma))$ is a theory with axiom set Γ.

3. If $\mathfrak{A}$ with language L is a reduct of $\mathfrak{B}$, then $\mathfrak{A} \models \sigma \Leftrightarrow \mathfrak{B} \models \sigma$ for $\sigma \in L$.

4. $\mathrm{Mod}(\varphi_1,\ldots,\varphi_n) = \mathrm{Mod}(\varphi_1 \wedge \ldots \wedge \varphi_n)$.

5. $\Gamma \models \varphi \Rightarrow \Delta \models \varphi$ for a finite subset $\Delta \subseteq \Gamma$.
   (Give one proof using completeness, another proof using compactness on $\Gamma \cup \{\neg\sigma\}$).

6. Show that *well-ordering* is not a first-order notion.
   Suppose that Γ axiomatizes the class of well-orderings.
   Add countably many constants c_i and show that $\Gamma \cup \{c_{i+1} < c_i \mid i \in \mathbb{N}\}$ has a model.

7. If Γ has only finite models, then there is an n such that each model has at most n elements.

8. Let L have the binary predicate symbol P.
$\sigma := \forall x\, \neg P(x,x) \wedge \forall xyz(P(x,y) \wedge P(y,z) \rightarrow P(x,z)) \wedge \forall x \exists y P(x,y)$.
Show that Mod(σ) contains only infinite models.

9. Show that $\sigma \vee \forall xy(x = y)$ has infinite models and a finite model, but no arbitrarily large finite models (σ as in 8).

10. Let L have one unary function symbol.
    (*i*) Write down a sentence φ such that $\mathfrak{A} \models \varphi \Leftrightarrow f^{\mathfrak{A}}$ is a surjection.
    (*ii*) Idem for an injection.
    (*iii*) Idem for a bijection (permutation).
    (*iv*) Use (ii) to formulate a sentence σ such that $\mathfrak{A} \models \sigma \Rightarrow$ is infinite (Dedekind).
    (*v*) Show that each infinite set carries a permutation without fixed points (cf. the proof of 3.2.8).

11. Show: σ holds for fields of characteristic zero,
$\Rightarrow \sigma$ holds for all fields of characteristic $q > p$ for a certain p.

12. Consider a sequence of theories T_i such that $T_i \neq T_{i+1}$ and $T_i \subseteq T_{i+1}$. Show that $\bigcup \{T_i \mid i \in N\}$ is not finitely axiomatizable.

13. If T_1 and T_2 are theories such that Mod$(T_1 \cup T_2) = \emptyset$, then there is a σ such that $T_1 \models \sigma$ and $T_2 \models \neg\sigma$.

14. (*i*) A group can be ordered $\Leftrightarrow$ each finitely generated subgroup can be ordered.
    (*ii*) An abelian group $\mathfrak{A}$ can be ordered $\Leftrightarrow$ $\mathfrak{A}$ is torsion free.
    (Hint: look at all closed atoms of L($\mathfrak{A}$) true in $\mathfrak{A}$.)

15. Prove Corollary 4.

16. Show that each countable, ordered set can be embedded in the rationals.

17. Show that the class of trees cannot be axiomatized. Here we define a tree as a structure $\langle T, \leqslant, t \rangle$, where $\leqslant$ is a partial order, such that for each a the predecessors form a finite chain $a = a_n < a_{n-1} < \ldots < a_1 < a_0 = t$.
t is called the top.

18. A graph (with symmetric and irreflexive R) is called k-colourable if we can

paint the vertices with k-different colours such that adjacent vertices have distinct colours. We formulate this by adding k unary predicates $C_1,\dots,C_k$, plus the following axioms

$$\forall x \bigvee_i C_i(x), \quad \bigwedge_{i\neq j} \neg(C_i(x) \wedge C_j(x)),$$
$$\bigwedge_i \forall xy(C_i(x) \wedge C_i(y) \rightarrow \neg R(x,y)).$$

Show that a graph is k-colourable if each finite subgraph is k-colourable (de Bruyn-Erdös).

3.3. SOME MODEL THEORY

In model theory one investigates the various properties of models (structures), in particular in connection with the features of their language. One could say that algebra is a part of model theory. Some parts of algebra indeed belong to model theory, other parts only in the sense of the limiting case in which the role of language is negligible. It is the interplay between language and models that makes model theory fascinating.
Here, however, we will only discuss the very beginnings of the topic.

In algebra one does not distinguish structures which are isomorphic; the nature of the objects is purely accidental. In logic we have another criterion: we distinguish between two structures by exhibiting a sentence which holds in one but not in the other. So, if $\mathfrak{A} \models \sigma \Leftrightarrow \mathfrak{B} \models \sigma$ for all σ, then we cannot (logically) distinguish $\mathfrak{A}$ and $\mathfrak{B}$.

3.3.1. Definition.

(*i*) f: $|\mathfrak{A}| \rightarrow |\mathfrak{B}|$ is a *homomorphism* if for all P_i $\langle a_1,\dots,a_k\rangle \in P_i^{\mathfrak{A}} \Rightarrow \langle f(a_1),\dots,f(a_k)\rangle \in P_i^{\mathfrak{B}}$, for all F_j, $f(F_j^{\mathfrak{A}}(a_1,\dots,a_p)) = F_j^{\mathfrak{B}}(f(a_1),\dots,f(a_p))$ and $f(c_i^{\mathfrak{A}}) = c_i^{\mathfrak{B}}$, for all c_i.

(*ii*) f is an *isomorphism* if it is a homomorphism which is bijective and satisfies $\langle a_1,\dots,a_n\rangle \in P_i^{\mathfrak{A}} \Leftrightarrow \langle f(a_1),\dots,f(a_n)\rangle \in P_i^{\mathfrak{B}}$, for all P_i.

We write $f: \mathfrak{A} \rightarrow \mathfrak{B}$ if f is a homomorphism from $\mathfrak{A}$ to $\mathfrak{B}$. $\mathfrak{A} \cong \mathfrak{B}$ stands for "$\mathfrak{A}$ is isomorphic to $\mathfrak{B}$", i.e. there is an isomorphism $f: \mathfrak{A} \rightarrow \mathfrak{B}$.

3.3.2. Definition. $\mathfrak{A}$ and $\mathfrak{B}$ are *elementarily equivalent* if for all sentences σ, $\mathfrak{A} \models \sigma \Leftrightarrow \mathfrak{B} \models \sigma$.

Notation: $\mathfrak{A} \equiv \mathfrak{B}$. Note that $\mathfrak{A} \equiv \mathfrak{B} \Leftrightarrow Th(\mathfrak{A}) = Th(\mathfrak{B})$.

3.3.3. Lemma. $\mathfrak{A} \cong \mathfrak{B} \rightarrow \mathfrak{A} \equiv \mathfrak{B}$.

Proof. exercise 2. □

3.3.4. Definition. $\mathfrak{A}$ is a *substructure* (submodel) of $\mathfrak{B}$ (of the same type) if

$|\mathfrak{A}| \subseteq |\mathfrak{B}|$; $P_i^{\mathfrak{B}} \cap |\mathfrak{A}|^n = P_i^{\mathfrak{A}}$;

$F_j^{\mathfrak{B}} \upharpoonright |\mathfrak{A}|^n = F_j^{\mathfrak{A}}$ and $c_i^{\mathfrak{A}} = c_i^{\mathfrak{B}}$ (n is the number of arguments).

Notation: $\mathfrak{A} \subseteq \mathfrak{B}$.

Note that it is not sufficient for $\mathfrak{A}$ to be contained in $\mathfrak{B}$ "as a set"; the relations and functions of $\mathfrak{B}$ have to be extensions of the corresponding ones on $\mathfrak{A}$.

Examples. The field of rationals is a substructure of the field of reals, but not of the ordered field of reals.
Let $\mathfrak{A}$ be the additive group of rationals, $\mathfrak{B}$ the multiplicative group of non-zero rationals. Although $|\mathfrak{B}| \subseteq |\mathfrak{A}|$. $\mathfrak{B}$ is not a substructure of $\mathfrak{A}$.

The well-known notions of subgroups, subrings, subspaces, all satisfy the above definition.

The notion of elementary equivalence only requires that sentences (which do not refer to specific elements, except for constants) are simultaneously true in two structures. We can sharpen the notion, by considering $\mathfrak{A} \subseteq \mathfrak{B}$ and by allowing reference to elements of $|\mathfrak{A}|$.

3.3.5. Definition. $\mathfrak{A}$ is an *elementary substructure* of $\mathfrak{B}$ (or $\mathfrak{B}$ is an *elementary extension* of $\mathfrak{A}$) if $\mathfrak{A} \subseteq \mathfrak{B}$ and for all $\varphi(x_1,\dots,x_n)$ in L and $a_1,\dots,a_n \in |\mathfrak{A}|$, $\mathfrak{A} \models \varphi(\overline{a}_1,\dots,\overline{a}_n) \Leftrightarrow \mathfrak{B} \models \varphi(\overline{a}_1,\dots,\overline{a}_n)$.

Notation: $\mathfrak{A} \prec \mathfrak{B}$.

We say that $\mathfrak{A}$ and $\mathfrak{B}$ have the same true sentences *with parameters in* $\mathfrak{A}$.

3.3.6. Fact. $\mathfrak{A} \prec \mathfrak{B} \Rightarrow \mathfrak{A} \equiv \mathfrak{B}$.

The converse does not hold (cf. exercise 4).

Since we will often join all elements of $|\mathfrak{A}|$ to $\mathfrak{A}$ as constants, it is convenient to have a special notation for the enriched structure: $\hat{\mathfrak{A}} = (\mathfrak{A}, \{\bar{a} \mid a \in |\mathfrak{A}|\})$.

If one wants to describe a certain structure $\mathfrak{A}$, one has to specify all the basic relationships and functional relations. This can be done in the language $L(\mathfrak{A})$ belonging to $\mathfrak{A}$ (which, incidentally, *is* the language of the type of $\hat{\mathfrak{A}}$).

3.3.7. Definition. *The diagram*, $\mathrm{Diag}(\mathfrak{A})$, is the set of closed atoms and negations of closed atoms of $L(\mathfrak{A})$ which are true in $\mathfrak{A}$.

Example.

1. $\mathfrak{A} = \langle N \rangle$. $\mathrm{Diag}(\mathfrak{A}) = \{\bar{n} = \bar{n} \mid n \in N\} \cup \{\bar{n} \neq \bar{m} \mid n \neq m;\ n,m \in N\}$.

2. $\mathfrak{B} = \langle \{1,2,3\}, < \rangle$. (natural order).
$\mathrm{Diag}(\mathfrak{B}) = \{\bar{1} = \bar{1},\ \bar{2} = \bar{2},\ \bar{3} = \bar{3}.\ \bar{1} \neq \bar{2},\ \bar{1} \neq \bar{3},\ \bar{2} \neq \bar{3},\ \bar{2} \neq \bar{1},\ \bar{3} \neq \bar{1},\ \bar{3} \neq \bar{2},$
$\bar{1} < \bar{2},\ \bar{1} < \bar{3},\ \bar{2} < \bar{3},\ \neg\bar{2} < \bar{1},\ \neg\bar{3} < \bar{1},\ \neg\bar{3} < \bar{2},\ \neg\bar{1} < \bar{1},\ \neg\bar{2} < \bar{2},\ \neg\bar{3} < \bar{3}\}$.

Diagrams are useful for lots of purposes. We demonstrate one here.

We say that $\mathfrak{A}$ is *isomorphically embedded* in $\mathfrak{B}$ if there is an isomorphism f from $\mathfrak{A}$ onto a substructure of $\mathfrak{B}$.

3.3.8. Lemma. $\mathfrak{A}$ is isomorphically embedded in $\mathfrak{B} \Leftrightarrow \hat{\mathfrak{B}}$ is a model of $\mathrm{Diag}(\mathfrak{A})$.

Proof. $\Rightarrow$: Let f be an isomorphic embedding of $\mathfrak{A}$ in $\mathfrak{B}$, then
$\mathfrak{A} \models P_i(\bar{a}_1,\dots,\bar{a}_n) \Leftrightarrow \mathfrak{B} \models P_i(\overline{f(a_1)},\dots,\overline{f(a_n)})$ and
$\mathfrak{A} \models t(\bar{a}_1,\dots,\bar{a}_n) = s(\bar{a}_1,\dots,\bar{a}_n) \Leftrightarrow \mathfrak{B} \models t(\overline{f(a_1)},\dots) = s(\overline{f(a_1)},\dots)$ (cf. exercise 2.). By interpreting $\bar{a}$ as $f(a)$ in $\hat{\mathfrak{B}}$ (i.e. $\bar{a}^{\mathfrak{B}} = f(a)$), we immediately see $\hat{\mathfrak{B}} \models \mathrm{Diag}(\mathfrak{A})$.

$\Leftarrow$: Let $\hat{\mathfrak{B}} \models \mathrm{Diag}(\mathfrak{A})$. Define a mapping $f\colon |\mathfrak{A}| \to |\mathfrak{B}|$ by $f(a) = \bar{a}^{\mathfrak{B}}$.
Then, clearly, f satisfies the conditions of definition 3.3.1 on relations and functions (since they are given by atoms and negations of atoms). Moreover if $a_1 \neq a_2$ then $\mathfrak{A} \models \neg\bar{a}_1 = \bar{a}_2$, so $\hat{\mathfrak{B}} \models \neg\bar{a}_1 = \bar{a}_2$.
Hence $\bar{a}_1^{\mathfrak{B}} \neq \bar{a}_2^{\mathfrak{B}}$, and thus $f(a_1) \neq f(a_2)$.

This shows that f is an isomorphism. $\square$

We will often identify $\mathfrak{A}$ with its image under an isomorphic embedding into

$\mathcal{B}$, so that we may consider $\mathfrak{A}$ as a substructure of $\mathcal{B}$.

We have a similar criterion for elementary extension. We say that $\mathfrak{A}$ is *elementarily embeddable* in $\mathcal{B}$ if $\mathfrak{A} \cong \mathfrak{A}'$ and $\mathfrak{A}' \prec \mathcal{B}$ for some $\mathfrak{A}'$. Again, we often simplify matters by just writing $\mathfrak{A} \prec \mathcal{B}$, when we mean "elementarily embeddable".

3.3.9. Lemma. $\mathfrak{A} \prec \mathcal{B} \Leftrightarrow \hat{\mathcal{B}} \models Th(\hat{\mathfrak{A}})$.

N.B. $\mathfrak{A} \prec \mathcal{B}$ holds "up to isomorphism". $\hat{\mathcal{B}}$ is supposed to be of a similarity type which admits at least constants for all constant symbols of $L(\mathfrak{A})$.

Proof. $\Rightarrow$. Let $\varphi(\bar{a}_1,\dots,\bar{a}_n) \in Th(\hat{\mathfrak{A}})$, then $\hat{\mathfrak{A}} \models \varphi(\bar{a}_1,\dots,\bar{a}_n)$, and hence $\hat{\mathcal{B}} \models \varphi(\bar{a}_1,\dots,\bar{a}_n)$. So $\hat{\mathcal{B}} \models Th(\hat{\mathfrak{A}})$.
$\Leftarrow$. By 3.3.8 $\mathfrak{A} \subseteq \mathcal{B}$ (up to isomorphism).
The reader can easily finish the proof now. □

We now give some applications.

3.3.10. *Non-standard models of arithmetic.*

Recall that $\mathfrak{N} = \langle N,+,\cdot,S,0\rangle$ is the *standard model* of arithmetic. We know that it satisfies Peano's axioms (cf. example 6, section 2.7). We use the abbreviations introduced in section 2.7.

Let us now construct a non-standard model.
Consider $T = Th(\mathfrak{N})$. By the Skolem-Löwenheim theorem T has an uncountable model $\mathfrak{M}$. Since $\mathfrak{M} \models Th(\hat{\mathfrak{N}})$, we have, by 3.3.9, $\mathfrak{N} \prec \mathfrak{M}$.
Note that $\mathfrak{N} \not\cong \mathfrak{M}$ (why ?). We will have a closer look at the way in which $\mathfrak{N}$ is embedded in $\mathfrak{M}$.

We note that
$$\mathfrak{N} \models \forall xyz(x < y \wedge y < z \rightarrow x < z) \qquad (1)$$
$$\mathfrak{N} \models \forall xy(x < y \vee x = y \vee y < x) \qquad (2)$$
$$\mathfrak{N} \models \forall x(\bar{0} \leqslant x) \qquad (3)$$
$$\mathfrak{N} \models \neg\exists x(\bar{n} < x \wedge x < \overline{n+1}) \qquad (4)$$

Hence, $\mathfrak{N}$ being an elementary substructure of $\mathfrak{M}$, we have (1) and (2) for $\mathfrak{M}$, i.e. $\mathfrak{M}$ is linearly ordered. From $\mathfrak{N} \prec \mathfrak{M}$ and (3) we conclude that $\bar{0}$ is the first element of $\mathfrak{M}$. Furthermore, (4) with $\mathfrak{N} \prec \mathfrak{M}$ tells us that there are no elements of $\mathfrak{M}$ between the "standard natural numbers".

As a result we see that $\mathfrak{N}$ is an initial segment of $\mathfrak{M}$:

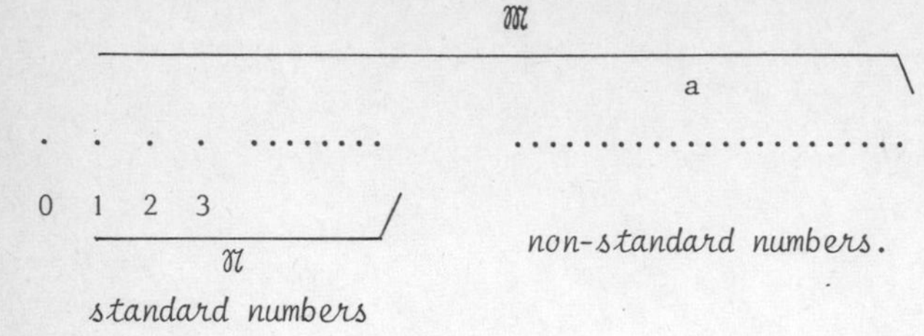

Remark: it is important to realize that (1) - (4) are not only *true in the standard model*, but even provable in *PA*. This implies that they hold not only in elementary extensions of $\mathfrak{N}$, but in *all* Peano structures. The price one has to pay is the actual proving of (1) - (4) in *PA*, which is more cumbersome than the mere establishing their validity in $\mathfrak{N}$. However, anyone who can give an informal proof of these simple properties will find out that it is just one more (tedious, but not difficult) step to formalize the proof in our natural deduction system. Step-by-step proofs are outlined in the exercises 27, 28.

So all elements of $|\mathfrak{M}| - |\mathfrak{N}|$, the *non-standard numbers*, come after the standard ones.

Since $\mathfrak{N}$ is uncountable, there is at least one non-standard number a. Note that for all n $n < a$, so $\mathfrak{M}$ has a *non-archimedean order* (recall that $n = 1 + 1 + \ldots \ldots + 1$ (n×)).

We see that the successor S(n) (= n+1) of a standard number is standard. Furthermore $\mathfrak{N} \models \forall x(x \neq \overline{0} \rightarrow \exists y(y+\overline{1} = x))$, so, since $\mathfrak{N} \prec \mathfrak{M}$, also $\mathfrak{M} \models \forall x(x \neq \overline{0} \rightarrow \exists y(y+\overline{1} = x))$, i.e. in $\mathfrak{M}$ each number, distinct from zero, has a (unique) predecessor. Since a is non-standard it is distinct from zero, hence it has a predecessor, say a_1. Since successors of standard numbers are standard, a_1 is non-standard. We can repeat this procedure indefinitely and obtain an infinite descending sequence $a > a_1 > a_2 > a_3 > \ldots$ of non-standard numbers.

Conclusion: $\mathfrak{M}$ is not well-ordered.

However, non-empty *definable* subsets of $\mathfrak{M}$ *do* possess a least element. For, such a set is of the form $\{b \mid \mathfrak{M} \models \varphi(\overline{b})\}$ where $\varphi \in L(\mathfrak{N})$, and we know $\mathfrak{N} \models \exists x\varphi(x) \rightarrow \exists x(\varphi(x) \wedge \forall y(\varphi(y) \rightarrow x \leq y))$.
This sentence also holds in $\mathfrak{M}$ and it tells us that $\{b \mid \mathfrak{M} \models \varphi(\overline{b})\}$ has a least element if it is not empty.

The above construction not merely gave a non-standard Peano structure (cf. 3.2.5), but also a non-standard model of *true arithmetic*, i.e. it is a model of all sentences true in the standard model. Moreover, it is an elementary extension.

The non-standard models of *PA* that are elementary extensions of $\mathfrak{N}$ are the ones that can be handled most easily, since the facts from the standard model carry over. There are also quite a number of properties that have been established for non-standard models in general.
We treat two of them here:

Theorem. *The set of standard numbers in a non-standard model is not definable.*

Suppose there is a $\varphi(x)$ in the language of *PA*, such that: $\mathfrak{M} \models \varphi(\overline{a}) \Leftrightarrow$ a is a standard natural number, then $\neg\varphi(x)$ defines the non-standard numbers. Since *PA* proves the *least number principle*, we have $\mathfrak{M} \models \exists x(\neg\varphi(x) \wedge \forall y < x(\varphi(y)))$, or there is a least non-standard number. However, as we have seen above, this is not the case. So there is no such definition.

A simple consequence is the

Overspill Lemma: If $\varphi(\overline{n})$ holds in a non-standard model for infinitely many finite numbers n, then $\varphi(a)$ holds for at least one infinite number a.

Suppose that $\varphi(\overline{a})$ holds for no infinite a, then $\exists y(x < y \wedge \varphi(y))$ defines the set of standard natural numbers in the model.
This contradicts the preceding result.

Our technique of constructing models yields various non-standard models of Peano's arithmetic. We have at this stage no means to decide if all models of *PA* are elementarily equivalent or not. The answer to this question is provided by Gödel's incompleteness theorem, which states that there is a sentence γ such that $PA \nvdash \gamma$ and $PA \nvdash \neg\gamma$. Quite recently the incompleteness of *PA* has been re-established by quite different means by Paris-Kirby-Harrington, Kripke, and others. As a result we have now examples for γ, which belong to 'normal mathematics', whereas Gödel's γ, although purely arithmetical, can be considered as slightly artificial, cf. *Barwise*, Handbook of Mathematical Logic, D8.
PA has a decidable (recursive) model, namely the standard model. That, however, is the only one. By a theorem of Tennenbaum all non-standard models of *PA* are undecidable (not recursive).

3.3.11. *Non-standard real numbers.*

Similarly to the previous subsection, we can introduce non-standard models

for the real number system.
We use the language of the ordered field R of real numbers, and for convenience we use the function symbol, $|\ \ |$, for the absolute value function.

By the Skolem-Löwenheim theorem there is a model $*\mathcal{R}$ of $Th(\hat{\mathcal{R}})$ such that $*\mathcal{R}$ has greater cardinality than $\mathcal{R}$. Applying 3.3.9, we see that $\mathcal{R} \prec *\mathcal{R}$, so $*\mathcal{R}$ is an ordered field, containing the standard real numbers. For cardinality reasons there is an element $a \in |*\mathcal{R}| - |\mathcal{R}|$. For the element a there are two possibilities:

(i) $|a| > |r|$ for all $r \in |\mathcal{R}|$,

(ii) there is an $r \in |\mathcal{R}|$ such that $|a| < r$.

In the second case $\{u \in |\mathcal{R}| \mid u < |a|\}$ is a bounded, non-empty set, which therefore has a supremum s (in $\mathcal{R}$).
Since $|a|$ is non-standard number, there is no standard number between s and $|a|$. By ordinary algebra, there is no standard number between 0 and $||a| - s|$. Hence $||a| - s|^{-1}$ is larger than all standard numbers. So in case (ii) there is also a non-standard number greater than all standard numbers.

Elements satisfying the condition (i) above, are called *infinite* and elements satisfying (ii) are called *finite* (note that the standard numbers are finite).

We now list a number of facts, leaving the (fairly simple) proofs to the reader.

1. $*\mathcal{R}$ has a non-archimedean order.
2. There are numbers a such that for all positive standard r, $0 < |a| < r$. We call such numbers *infinitesimals*.
3. a is infinitesimal $\Leftrightarrow$ a^{-1} is infinite.
4. For each non-standard finite number a there is a unique standard number st(a) such that a-st(a) is infinitesimal.

Infinitesimals can be used for elementary calculus in the Leibnizian way. We will give a few examples.
Consider an expansion $\mathcal{R}'$ of R with a predicate for $\mathcal{N}$ and a function v. Let $*\mathcal{R}'$ be the corresponding non-standard model such that $\mathcal{R}' \prec *\mathcal{R}'$. We are actually considering two extensions at the same time. $\mathcal{N}$ is contained in $\mathcal{R}'$, i.e. singled out by a special predicate N. Hence $\mathcal{N}$ is extended, along with $\mathcal{R}'$ to $*\mathcal{N}$. As is to be expected $*\mathcal{N}$ is an elementary extension of N (cf. exercise 14). Therefore we may safely operate in the traditional manner with real numbers and natural numbers. In particular we have in $*\mathcal{R}'$ also infinite natural numbers available.

We want v to be a sequence, i.e. we are only interested in the values of v for natural number arguments. The concepts of convergence, limit, etc. can be taken from analysis.

We will use the notation of the calculus. The reader should try to give a correct notation.

Here is one example: $\exists m \forall n > m(|v_n - v_m| < \varepsilon)$ stands for $\exists x(N(x) \wedge \forall y(N(y) \wedge y > x \rightarrow |v(y) - v(x)| < \varepsilon)$.
Properly speaking we should relativize quantifiers over natural numbers (cf. 2.5.9), but it is more convenient to use variables of several sorts.

5. The sequence v (or (v_n)) converges in $\mathcal{R}'$ iff for all infinite natural numbers n,m $|v_n - v_m|$ is infinitesimal.

Proof. (v_n) converges in $\mathcal{R}'$ if $\mathcal{R}' \models \forall \varepsilon > 0\ \exists n \forall m > n(|v_n - v_m| < \varepsilon)$. Assume that (v_n) converges. Choose for $\varepsilon > 0$ an $n(\varepsilon) \in |\mathcal{R}'|$ such that

$$\mathcal{R}' \models \forall m > n(|v_n - v_m| < \varepsilon).$$

Then also $^*\mathcal{R}' \models \forall m > n(|v_n - v_m| < \varepsilon)$.
In particular, if m,m' are infinite, then $m,m' > n(\varepsilon)$ for all ε, so $|v_m - v_{n(\varepsilon)}| < \varepsilon$ and $|v_{m'} - v_{n(\varepsilon)}| < \varepsilon$ for all ε.
Hence $|v_m - v_{m'}| < 2\varepsilon$ for all ε. This means that $|v_m - v_{m'}|$ is infinitesimal.

Conversely, if $|v_n - v_m|$ is infinitesimal for all infinite n,m, then $^*\mathcal{R}' \models \forall m > n(|v_n - v_m| < \varepsilon)$ where n is infinite and ε standard, positive.
So $^*\mathcal{R}' \models \exists n \forall m > n(|v_n - v_m| < \varepsilon)$, for each standard $\varepsilon > 0$.
Now, since $\mathcal{R}' \prec {}^*\mathcal{R}'$, $\mathcal{R}' \models \exists n \forall m > n(|v_n - v_m| < \varepsilon)$ for $\varepsilon > 0$, so

$$\mathcal{R}' \models \forall \varepsilon > 0\ \exists n \forall m > n(|v_n - v_m| < \varepsilon).$$

Hence (v_n) converges. □

6. $\lim_{n \to \infty} v_n = a \Leftrightarrow |a - v_n|$ is infinitesimal for infinite n.

Proof. Similar to 5. □

We have only been able to touch on "non-standard analysis". For an extensive treatment, see *Robinson*, *Stroyan-Luxemburg*.

We can now strengthen the Skolem-Löwenheim theorems.

3.3.12. Downward Skolem-Löwenheim theorem.

Let the language L of $\mathfrak{A}$ have cardinality κ, and suppose $\mathfrak{A}$ has cardinality $\lambda \geq \kappa$. Then there is a structure $\mathcal{B}$ of cardinality κ such that $\mathcal{B} \prec \mathfrak{A}$.

Proof. See corollary 3.4.11.

3.3.13. Upward Skolem-Löwenheim theorem.

Let the language L of $\mathfrak{A}$ have cardinality κ and suppose $\mathfrak{A}$ has cardinality $\lambda \geqslant \kappa$. Then for each $\mu > \lambda$ there is a structure $\mathfrak{B}$ of cardinality μ, such that $\mathfrak{A} \prec \mathfrak{B}$.

Proof. Apply the old upward Skolem-Löwenheim theorem to $\mathrm{Th}(\hat{\mathfrak{A}})$. □

In the completeness proof we used maximally consistent theories. In model theory these are called complete theories. As a rule the notion is defined with respect to axiom sets.

3.3.14. Definition. The theory with axioms Γ is called *complete* if for each sentence σ in the language of Γ, $\Gamma \vdash \sigma$ or $\Gamma \vdash \neg\sigma$.

A complete theory leaves, so to speak, no questions open, but it does not prima facie restrict the class of models. In the old days mathematicians would try to characterize some model up to isomorphism, i.e. to give a set of axioms such that $\mathfrak{A}, \mathfrak{B} \in \mathrm{Mod}(\Gamma) \Rightarrow \mathfrak{A} \cong \mathfrak{B}$. The Skolem-Löwenheim theorems have taught us that this is (barring the finite case) unattainable. There is, however, a significant notion:

3.3.15. Definition. Let κ be a cardinal. A theory is κ-categorical if any two of its models of cardinality κ are isomorphic, and if it has at least one model of cardinality κ.

Categoricity in some cardinality is not as unusual as one might think. We list some examples.

1. The theory of infinite sets (identity structures) is κ-categorical for all infinite κ.

Proof. Trivial, because 'isomorphic' here means "of the same cardinality".

2. The theory of densely ordered sets without end-points is $\aleph_0$-categorical.

Proof. See any textbook on set-theory. Cantor proved it by the back-and-forth method. □

3. The theory of divisible torsion-free abelian groups is κ-categorical for $\kappa > \aleph_0$.

Proof. Check that a divisible torsion-free abelian groups is a vector space over the rationals. Use the fact that vector spaces of the same dimension (over the same field) are isomorphic. □

4. The theory of algebraically closed fields (of a fixed characteristic) is κ-categorical for $\kappa > \aleph_0$.

Proof. Use Steinitz' theorem: two algebraically closed fields of the same characteristic and the same uncountable transcendence degree are isomorphic. □

The connection between categoricity and completeness, for countable languages, is given by

3.3.16. Vaught's theorem.

If T has no finite models and is κ-categorical for some κ, then T is complete.

Proof. Suppose T is not complete. Then there is a σ such that $T \nvdash \sigma$ and $T \nvdash \neg\sigma$. By the model existence lemma, there are $\mathfrak{A}$ and $\mathfrak{B}$ in Mod(T) such that $\mathfrak{A} \models \sigma$ and $\mathfrak{B} \models \neg\sigma$. Since $\mathfrak{A}$ and $\mathfrak{B}$ are infinite we can apply the Skolem-Löwenheim theorem (upwards or downwards), so as to obtain $\mathfrak{A}'$ and $\mathfrak{B}'$, or cardinality κ, such that $\mathfrak{A} \equiv \mathfrak{A}'$ and $\mathfrak{B} \equiv \mathfrak{B}'$. But then $\mathfrak{A}' \cong \mathfrak{B}'$ and hence $\mathfrak{A}' \equiv \mathfrak{B}$, so $\mathfrak{A} \equiv \mathfrak{B}$. This contradicts $\mathfrak{A} \models \sigma$ and $\mathfrak{B} \models \neg\sigma$. □

As a consequence we see that the following theories are complete:

1. the theory of infinite sets;
2. the theory of densely ordered sets without end-points;
3. the theory of divisible torsion-free abelian groups;
4. the theory of algebraically closed fields of fixed characteristic.

A corollary of the last fact was known as *Lefschetz' principle*: if a sentence σ, in the first-order language of fields, holds for the complex numbers, it holds for all algebraically closed fields of characteristic zero.
As a matter of fact, σ can be proved by any means available, not necessarily algebraic.

3.3.17. Decidability.

We have seen in chapter I that there is an effective method to test whether a proposition is provable - by means of the truth table technique, since "truth = provability".

It would be wonderful to have such a method for predicate logic. Church has shown that there is no such method (if we identify "effective" with "recursive") for general predicate logic. But there might be special theories which are decidable. A technical study of decidability belongs to recursion theory. Here we will sketch a few informal considerations.

If T has a decidable set of axioms Γ, then there is an effective method for listing all theorems of T.

One can obtain such a listing as follows:

(a) Make an effective list $\sigma_1, \sigma_2, \sigma_3, \ldots$ of all axioms of T (this is possible because Γ is decidable).

1. write down all derivations of size 1, using σ_1,
2. write down all derivations of size 2, using σ_1, σ_2,

⋮

n. write down all derivations of size n, using $\sigma_1, \ldots, \sigma_n$

⋮

Each time we get only finitely many theorems and each theorem is eventually derived. The process is clearly effective (although not efficient).

We now observe

3.3.18. Lemma. If Γ and Γ^c (complement of Γ) are effectively listable, then Γ is decidable.

Proof. Generate the lists of Γ and Γ^c simultaneously. In finitely many steps we will either find σ in the list for Γ or in the list for Γ^c. So for each σ we can decide in finitely many steps whether $\sigma \in \Gamma$ or not. □

As a corollary we get the

3.3.19. Theorem. If T is effectively axiomatizable and complete, then T is decidable.

Proof. Since T is complete, we have $\Gamma \vdash \sigma$ or $\Gamma \vdash \neg\sigma$ for each σ (where Γ axiomatizes T).

So $\sigma \in T^c \Leftrightarrow \Gamma \nvdash \sigma \Leftrightarrow \Gamma \vdash \neg\sigma$.

From the above sketch it follows that T and T^c are effectively listable. By the lemma T is decidable.

Application. The following theories are decidable:

(1) the theory of infinite sets;

(2) the theory of densely ordered sets without end-points;

(3) the theory of divisible, torsion free abelian groups;

(4) the theory of algebraically closed fields of fixed characteristic.

Proof. See the consequences of Vaught's theorem (3.3.16),
The effective listings are left to the reader (the simplest case is, of course, that of a finitely axiomatizable theory, e.g. (1), (2)). □

We will finally present one more application of the non-standard approach, by giving a non-standard proof of

3.3.20. König's Lemma. A denumerable, finitary tree has an infinite path.

A finitary tree, or *fan*, has the property that each node has only finitely many immediate successors ('zero successors' is included).
By contraposition one obtains from König's lemma the so-called *fan theorem* (which was discovered first):

If in a fan all paths are finite then the length of the paths is bounded.

If one considers the tree as a topological space, with its canonical topology (basic open set "are" nodes), then König's lemma is the Bolzano-Weierstrasz theorem and the fan-theorem states the compactness.

We will now proceed to a non-standard proof of König's lemma.

Let T be a fan, and let T* be a proper elementary extension (use 3.3.13).

(1) the relation "... is an immediate successor of ..." can be expressed in the language of partial order:
$x <_i y := x < y \wedge \forall z(x \leqslant z \leqslant y \rightarrow x = z \vee y = z)$ where, as usual, $x < y$ stands for $x \leqslant y \wedge x \neq y$.

(2) If a is standard, then its immediate successors in T* are also standard.

Since T is finitary, we can indicate $a_1, \ldots, a_n$ such that
$T \models \forall x(x <_i \bar{a} \leftrightarrow \bigvee_{1\leqslant k\leqslant n} \bar{a}_k = x)$.

By $T \prec T^*$, we also have $T^* \models \forall x(x <_i \bar{a} \leftrightarrow \bigvee_{1\leqslant k\leqslant n} \bar{a}_k = x)$, so if b is an immediate successor of a in T*, then $b = a_k$ for some $k \leq n$, i.e. b is standard.

Note that a node without successors in T has no successors in T* either, for $T \models \forall x(x \leq \overline{a} \rightarrow x = \overline{a}) \Leftrightarrow T^* \models \forall x(x \leq \overline{a} \leftrightarrow x = \overline{a})$.

(3) In T we have that a successor of a node is an immediate successor of that node or a successor of an immediate successor, i.e.

$$T \models \forall xy(x < y \rightarrow \exists z(x \leq z \underset{i}{<} y)). \qquad (*)$$

This is the case since for nodes a and b with $a < b$, b must occur in the finite chain of all predecessors of a. So let $a = a_n < a_{n-1} < \ldots < a_i = b < a_{i-1} < \ldots$, then $a \leq a_{i+1} \underset{i}{<} b$.

Since the desired property is expressed by a first-order sentence (*), (3) also holds for T*.

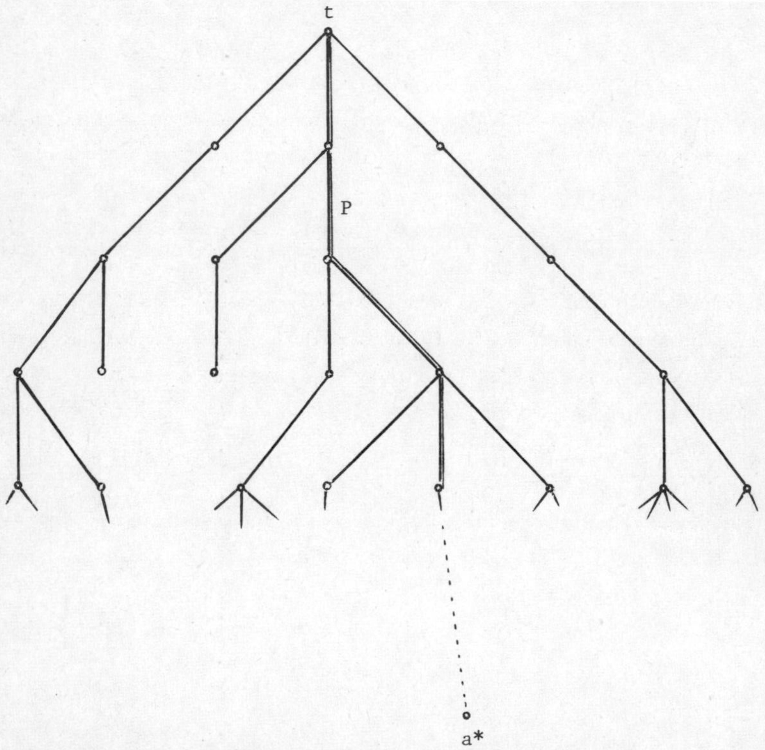

(4) Let a* be a non-standard element of T*. We claim that $P = \{a \in |T| \mid a^* < a\}$ is an infinite path (i.e. a chain).

(*i*) P is linearly ordered since $T \models \forall xyz(x \leq y \wedge x \leq z \rightarrow y \leq z \vee z \leq y)$ and hence for any $p, q \in P \subseteq |T^*|$ we have $p \leq q$ or $q \leq p$.

(*ii*) Suppose P is finite with last element b, then b has a successor and hence an immediate successor in T* which is a predecessor of a*.

By (2) this immediate successor belongs to P. Contradiction. Hence P is infinite.

This establishes that T has an infinite path. □

3.3.21. Quantifier Elimination.

Some theories have the pleasant property that they allow the reduction of formulas to a particularly simple form: one in which no quantifiers occur. Without going into a general theory of quantifier elimination, we will demonstrate the procedure in a simple case: *the theory* $\mathcal{DO}$ *of dense order without end points*.

Let $FV(\varphi) = \{y_1,\ldots,y_n\}$, where all variables actually occur in φ. By standard methods we obtain a prenex normal form φ' of φ, such that $\varphi' := Q_1x\, Q_2x \ldots Q_mx_m\psi(x_1,\ldots,x_m,y_1,\ldots,y_n)$, where each Q_i is one of the quantifiers $\forall,\exists$. We will eliminate the quantifiers starting with the innermost one.

Consider the case $Qm = \exists$. We bring ψ into disjunctive normal form $\bigvee\psi_j$, where each ψ_j is a conjunction of atoms and negations of atoms.
First we observe that the negations of atoms can be eliminated in favor of atoms, since $\mathcal{DO} \vdash \neg z = z' \leftrightarrow (z < z' \vee z' < z)$ and $\mathcal{DO} \vdash \neg z < z' \leftrightarrow (z = z' \vee z' < z)$.
So we may assume that the ψ_j's contain only atoms.
By plain predicate logic we can replace $\exists x_m \bigvee\psi_j$ by the equivalent formula $\bigvee\exists x_m\psi_j$.

Notation: for the rest of this example we will use $\sigma \overset{*}{\leftrightarrow} \tau$ as an abbreviation for $\mathcal{DO} \vdash \sigma \leftrightarrow \tau$.

We have just seen that it suffices to consider only formulas of the form $\exists x_m \bigwedge\sigma_p$, where each σ_p is atomic. A systematic look at the conjuncts will show us what to do.

(1) If x_m does not occur in $\bigwedge\sigma_p$, we can delete the quantifier (cf. 2.5.2).

(2) Otherwise, collect all atoms containing x_m and regroup the atoms, such that we get $\bigwedge\sigma_p \overset{*}{\leftrightarrow} \bigwedge_i x_m < u_i \wedge \bigwedge_j v_j < x_m \wedge \bigwedge_k w_k = x_m \wedge \chi$, where χ does not contain x_m. Abbreviate this formula as $\tau \wedge \chi$.
By predicate logic we have $\exists x_m(\tau \wedge \chi) \overset{*}{\leftrightarrow} \exists x_m\tau \wedge \chi$ (cf. 2.5.3). Since we

want to eliminate $\exists x_m$, it suffices to consider $\exists x_m \tau$ only.

Now the matter has been reduced to bookkeeping. Bearing in mind that we are dealing with a linear order, we will exploit the information given by τ concerning the relative position of the u_i, v_j, w_k's with respect to x_m.

(2a) $\tau := \bigwedge x_m < u_i \wedge \bigwedge v_j < x_m \wedge \bigwedge w_k = x_m$.

Then $\exists x_m \tau \overset{*}{\leftrightarrow} \tau'$, with $\tau' := \bigwedge w_0 < u_i \wedge \bigwedge v_j < w_0 \wedge \bigwedge w_0 = w_k$

(where w_0 is the first variable among the w_k's).

The equivalence follows immediately by a model theoretic argument (i.e. $\mathcal{DO} \models \exists x_m \tau \leftrightarrow \tau'$).

(2b) $\tau := \bigwedge x_m < u_i \wedge \bigwedge v_j < x_m$.

Now the properties of $\mathcal{DO}$ are essential. Observe that $\exists x_m (\bigwedge x_m < \bar{a}_i \wedge \bigwedge \bar{b}_j < x_m)$ holds in a *densely ordered* set if and only if all the a_i's lie to the right of the b_j's. So we get (by completeness) $\exists x_m \tau \overset{*}{\leftrightarrow} \bigwedge_{i,j} v_j < u_i$.

(2c) $\tau := \bigwedge x_m < u_i \wedge \bigwedge w_k = x_m$.

Then $\exists x_m \tau \overset{*}{\leftrightarrow} \bigwedge x_m < u_i \wedge \bigwedge w_k = w_0$.

(2d) $\tau := \bigwedge v_j < x_m \wedge \bigwedge w_k = x_m$.

Cf. (2c).

(2e) $\tau := \bigwedge x_m < u_i$.

Observe that $\exists x_m \tau$ holds in all ordered sets without a left endpoint. So we have $\exists x_m \tau \overset{*}{\leftrightarrow} \top$, since we work in $\mathcal{DO}$.

(2f) $\tau := \bigwedge v_j < x_m$.

Cf. (2e).

(2g) $\tau := \bigwedge w_k = x_m$.

Then $\exists x_m \tau \overset{*}{\leftrightarrow} \bigwedge w_0 = w_k$.

Remarks. *(i)* The cases (2b), (2e) and (2f) make essential use of $\mathcal{DO}$.

(ii) It is often possible to introduce shortcuts, e.g. when a variable (other than x_m) occurs in two of the big conjuncts we have

$\exists x_m \tau \overset{*}{\leftrightarrow} \bot$.

If the innermost quantifier is universal, we reduce it to an existential one by $\forall x_m \varphi \leftrightarrow \neg \exists x_m \neg \varphi$.
Now it is clear how to eliminate the quantifiers one by one.

Example.

$$\exists xy(x < y \wedge \exists z(x < z \wedge z < y \wedge \forall u(u \neq z \rightarrow u < y \vee u = x))).$$

$$\overset{*}{\leftrightarrow} \exists xyz\forall u[x < y \wedge x < z \wedge z < y \wedge (u = z \vee u < y \vee u = x)].$$

$$\overset{*}{\leftrightarrow} \exists xyz \neg \exists u[\neg x < y \vee \neg x < z \vee x < z \vee \neg z \vee y \vee (\neg u = z \wedge \neg u < y \wedge \neg u = x)].$$

$$\overset{*}{\leftrightarrow} \exists xyz \neg \exists u[x = y \vee y < x \vee x = z \vee z < x \vee z = y \vee y < z \vee$$
$$\vee ((u < z \vee z < u) \wedge (u = y \vee y < u) \wedge (u < x \vee x < u))].$$

$$\overset{*}{\leftrightarrow} \exists xyz \neg \exists u[x = y \vee y < x \vee x = z \vee z < x \vee z = y \vee y < z \vee$$
$$(u < z \wedge u = y \wedge u < x) \vee (u < z \wedge u = y \wedge x < u) \vee (u < z \wedge y < u \wedge u < x) \vee$$
$$\vee (u < z \wedge y < u \wedge x < u) \vee (z < u \wedge u = y \wedge u < x) \vee (z < u \wedge u = y \wedge x < u) \vee$$
$$\vee (z < u \wedge y < u \wedge u < x) \vee (z < u \wedge y < u \wedge x < u)].$$

$$\overset{*}{\leftrightarrow} \exists xyz \neg[x = y \vee y < x \vee x = z \vee z < x \vee z = y \vee y < z \vee$$
$$\vee \exists u(u < z \wedge u = y \wedge u < x) \vee \exists u(u < z \wedge u = y \wedge x < u) \vee$$
$$\ldots\ldots\ldots\ldots\ldots\ldots \vee \exists u(z < u \wedge y < u \wedge x < u)].$$

$$\overset{*}{\leftrightarrow} \exists xyz \neg[x = y \vee \ldots \vee y < z \vee (y < z \wedge y < x) \vee (y < z \wedge x < y) \vee$$
$$\vee (y < z \wedge y < x) \vee (y < z \wedge x < z) \vee (z < y \wedge y < x) \vee$$
$$\vee (z < y \wedge x < y) \vee (z < x \wedge y < x) \vee \top].$$

$$\overset{*}{\leftrightarrow} \exists xyz(\neg \top).$$

$$\overset{*}{\leftrightarrow} \bot.$$

Evidently the above quantifier elimination for the theory of dense order without endpoints provides an alternative proof of its decidability. For, if φ is a sentence, then φ is equivalent to an open sentence φ'. Given the language of $\mathcal{DO}$ it is obvious that φ' is equivalent to either $\top$ or $\bot$. Hence, we have an algorithm for deciding $\mathcal{DO} \vdash \varphi$. Note that we have an obtained more:

$\mathcal{DO}$ is complete, since $\mathcal{DO} \vdash \varphi \leftrightarrow \bot$ or $\mathcal{DO} \vdash \varphi \leftrightarrow \top$, so $\mathcal{DO} \vdash \neg\varphi$ or $\mathcal{DO} \vdash \varphi$.

In general we cannot expect that much from quantifier elimination; e.g. the theory of algebraically closed fields admits quantifier elimination, but it is not complete (because the characteristic has not been fixed in advance); the open sentences may contain unprovable and unrefutable atoms such as $7 = 12$, $23 = 0$.

We may conclude from the existence of a quantifier elimination a certain model theoretic property, introduced by Abraham Robinson, which has turned out to be important for applications in algebra (cf. the Handbook of Mathematical Logic, A_4).

3.3.22. Definition. A theory T is *model complete* if for $\mathfrak{A}, \mathfrak{B} \in Mod(T)$.
$\mathfrak{A} \subseteq \mathfrak{B} \Rightarrow \mathfrak{A} \prec \mathfrak{B}$.

We can now immediately obtain the following

3.3.23. Theorem. If T admits quantifier elimination, then T is model complete.

Proof. Let $\mathfrak{A}$ and $\mathfrak{B}$ be models of T, such that $\mathfrak{A} \subseteq \mathfrak{B}$. We must show that $\mathfrak{A} \models \varphi(\bar{a}_1,\ldots,\bar{a}_n) \Leftrightarrow \mathfrak{B} \models \varphi(\bar{a}_1,\ldots,\bar{a}_n)$ for all $a_1,\ldots,a_n \in |\mathfrak{A}|$, where $FV(\varphi) = \{x_1,\ldots,x_n\}$.
Since T admits quantifier elimination, there is a quantifier free $\psi(x_1,\ldots,x_n)$ such that $T \vdash \varphi \leftrightarrow \psi$.
Hence it suffices to show $\mathfrak{A} \models \psi(\bar{a}_1,\ldots,\bar{a}_n) \Leftrightarrow \mathfrak{B} \models \psi(\bar{a}_1,\ldots,\bar{a}_n)$ for a quantifier free ψ. A simple induction ψ establishes this equivalence. □

Some theories T have a particular model that is, up to isomorphism, contained in every model of T. We call such a model a *prime model* of T.

Examples.
(*i*) The rationals form a prime model for the theory of dense ordering without endpoints;
(*ii*) The field of the rationals is the prime model of the theory of fields of characteristic zero;
(*iii*) The standard model is the prime model of Peano's arithmetic.

3.3.24. Theorem. A model complete theory with a prime model is complete.

Proof. Left to the reader. □

EXERCISES.

1. Let $\mathfrak{A} = \langle A,\leqslant\rangle$ be a poset. Show that $Diag(\mathfrak{A}) \cup \{\forall xy(x \leqslant y \vee y \leqslant x\}$ has a model. (Hint: use compactness).
Conclude that every poset can be linearly ordered by an extension of its ordering.

2. If $f: \mathfrak{A} \cong \mathfrak{B}$ and $FV(\varphi) = \{x_1,\ldots,x_n\}$, show

$\mathfrak{A} \models \varphi[\bar{a}_1,\ldots,\bar{a}_n/x_1,\ldots,x_n] \;\Leftrightarrow\; \mathfrak{B} \models \varphi[\overline{f(a_1)},\ldots,\overline{f(a_n)}/x_1,\ldots,x_n]$.

In particular, $\mathfrak{A} \equiv \mathfrak{B}$.

3. Let $\mathfrak{A} \subseteq \mathfrak{B}$. φ is called *universal* (*existential*) if φ is prenex with only universal (existential) quantifiers
   (*i*) Show that for universal sentences φ $\mathfrak{B} \models \varphi \Rightarrow \mathfrak{A} \models \varphi$.
   (*ii*) Show that for existential sentences φ $\mathfrak{A} \models \varphi \Rightarrow \mathfrak{B} \models \varphi$.

   (Application: a substructure of a group is a group. This is one reason to use the similarity type $\langle -;2,1;1\rangle$ for groups, instead of $\langle -;2;0\rangle$, or $\langle -;2;1\rangle$, as some authors do).

4. Let $\mathfrak{A} = \langle N,<\rangle$, $\mathfrak{B} = \langle N - \{0\},<\rangle$.
   Show (*i*) $\mathfrak{A} \cong \mathfrak{B}$;
   (*ii*) $\mathfrak{A} \equiv \mathfrak{B}$;
   (*iii*) $\mathfrak{B} \subseteq \mathfrak{A}$;
   (*iv*) not $\mathfrak{B} \prec \mathfrak{A}$.

5. (Tarski). Let $\mathfrak{A} \subseteq \mathfrak{B}$. Show $\mathfrak{A} \prec \mathfrak{B} \;\Leftrightarrow$ for all $\varphi \in L$ and $a_1,\ldots,a_n \in |\mathfrak{A}|$, $\mathfrak{B} \models \exists y\varphi(y,\bar{a}_1,\ldots,\bar{a}_n) \;\Rightarrow$ there is an element $b \in |\mathfrak{A}|$ such that $\mathfrak{B} \models \varphi(\bar{b},\bar{a}_1,\ldots,\bar{a}_n)$, where $FV(\varphi(y,\bar{a}_1,\ldots,\bar{a}_n)) = \{y\}$.

   Hint: for $\Leftarrow$ show
   (*i*) $t^{\mathfrak{A}}(\bar{a}_1,\ldots,\bar{a}_n) = t^{\mathfrak{B}}(\bar{a}_1,\ldots,\bar{a}_n)$ for $t \in L$,
   (*ii*) $\mathfrak{A} \models \varphi(\bar{a}_1,\ldots,\bar{a}_n) \;\Leftrightarrow\; \mathfrak{B} \models \varphi(\bar{a}_1,\ldots,\bar{a}_n)$ for $\varphi \in L$ by induction on φ (use only $\vee, \neg, \exists$).

6. Another construction of a non-standard model of arithmetic: Add to the language L of arithmetic a new constant c. Show $\Gamma = Th(\hat{\mathfrak{N}}) \cup \{c > \bar{n} \mid n \in |\mathfrak{N}|\}$ has a model $\mathfrak{M}$. Show that $\mathfrak{M} \not\cong \mathfrak{N}$. Can $\mathfrak{M}$ be countable?

7. Consider the ring $\mathbb{Z}$ of integers. Show that there is an $\mathfrak{A}$ such that $\mathbb{Z} \prec \mathfrak{A}$ and $\mathbb{Z} \not\cong \mathfrak{A}$ (a non-standard model of the integers).
   Show that $\mathfrak{A}$ has an "infinite prime number", p_∞.
   Let (p_∞) be the principal ideal in $\mathfrak{A}$ generated by p_∞. Show that $\mathfrak{A}/(p_\infty)$ is a field F. (Hint: look at $\forall x$ ("x not in (p_∞)" $\rightarrow \exists yz(xy = 1 + zp_\infty)$), give a proper formulation and use elementary equivalence). What is the characteristic of F? (This yields a non-standard construction of the rationals from the integers: consider the prime field).

8. Deduce from the non-standard model of arithmetic that "well-ordering" is not

a first-order concept.

9. Deduce from the non-standard model of the reals that "archimedean ordered field" is not a first-order concept.

10. Consider the language of identity with constants $c_i\ (i \in N)$
$\Gamma = \{I_1, I_2, I_3\} \cup \{c_i \neq c_j \mid i,j \in N,\ i \neq j\}$. Show that the theory of Γ is κ-categorical for $\kappa > \aleph_0$, but not $\aleph_0$-categorical.

11. Show that the condition "no finite models" in Vaughts's theorem is necessary (look at the theory of identity).

12. Let $X \subseteq |\mathfrak{A}|$. Define $X_0 = X \cup C$ where C is the set of constants of $\mathfrak{A}$,
$X_{n+1} = X_n \cup \{f(a_1,\ldots,a_m) \mid f \text{ in } \mathfrak{A},\ a_1,\ldots,a_m \in X_n\}$,
$X_\omega = \cup\{X_n \mid n \in N\}$.
Show that $\mathfrak{B} = \langle X_\omega, R_1 \cap X_\omega^{r_1},\ldots,R_n \cap X_\omega^{r_n},\ f_1 \upharpoonright X_\omega^{a_1},\ldots,f_m \upharpoonright X_\omega^{a_m}, \{c_i \mid i \in I\}\rangle$ is a substructure of $\mathfrak{A}$. We say that $\mathfrak{B}$ is the substructure generated by X. Show that $\mathfrak{B}$ is the smallest substructure of $\mathfrak{A}$ containing X; $\mathfrak{B}$ can also be characterized as the intersection of all substructures containing X.

13. Let $^*\mathcal{R}$ be a non-standard model of $\mathrm{Th}(\mathcal{R})$. Show that st(cf. 3.3.10) is a homomorphism from the ring of finite numbers onto $\mathcal{R}$. What is the kernel?

14. Consider $\mathcal{R}' = \langle \mathcal{R}, N, \ ,+,\cdot,-,^{-1},0,1\rangle$, where N is the set of natural numbers. $L(\mathcal{R}')$ has a predicate symbol N and, we can, restricting ourselves to + and $\cdot$, recover arithmetic by relativizing our formulas to N (cf. 2.5.9).
Let $\mathcal{R}' \prec {}^*\mathcal{R}' = \langle {}^*\mathcal{R}, {}^*N, \ldots\rangle$. Show that $\mathfrak{N} = \langle N, <, +, \cdot, 0, 1\rangle \prec \langle {}^*N, <, +, \cdot, 0, 1\rangle = {}^*\mathfrak{N}$.
(Hint: consider for each $\varphi \in L(\mathfrak{N})$ the relativized $\varphi^N \in L(\mathcal{R}')$).

15. Show that any Peano-structure contains $\mathfrak{N}$ as a substructure.

16. Let L have at least one constant. Let $\sigma = \exists x_1 \ldots x_n \varphi(x_1,\ldots,x_n)$ and
$\Sigma_\sigma = \{\varphi(t_1,\ldots,t_n) \mid t_i \text{ closed in } L\}$, where φ is open.
   (i) $\models \sigma \Leftrightarrow$ Each $\mathfrak{A}$ is a model of at least one sentence in Σ_σ.
   (hint: for each $\mathfrak{A}$, look at the substructure generated by $\emptyset$).
   (ii) Consider Σ_σ as a set of propositions. Show that for each valuation v (in the sense of propositional logic) there is a model $\mathfrak{A}$ such that $v(\varphi(t_1,\ldots,t_n)) = v^{\mathfrak{A}}(\varphi(t_1,\ldots,t_n))$ for all $\varphi(t_1,\ldots,t_n) \in \Sigma_\sigma$.
   (iii) Show that $\vdash \sigma \Leftrightarrow\ \vdash \bigvee_{i=1}^{m} \varphi(t_1^i,\ldots,t_n^i)$ for a certain m (hint: use exercise

9, section 1.6).

17. Let $\mathfrak{A}$, $\mathfrak{B} \in \mathrm{Mod}(T)$ and $\mathfrak{A} \equiv \mathfrak{B}$.
Show that $\mathrm{Diag}(\mathfrak{A}) \cup \mathrm{Diag}(\mathfrak{B}) \cup T$ is consistent (use the compactness theorem).
Conclude that there is a model of T in which both $\mathfrak{A}$ and $\mathfrak{B}$ can be isomorphically embedded.

18. Consider the class K of all structures of type $\langle 1;-;0\rangle$ with a denumerable unary relation. Show that $T = \mathrm{Th}(K)$ is κ-categorical for $\kappa > \aleph_0$, and not $\aleph_0$-categorical.

19. Consider a theory T of identity with axioms λ_n for all $n \in N$. In which cardinalities is T categorical? Show that T is complete and decidable. Compare the result with exercise 10.

20. Show that the theory of dense order without end-points is not categorical in the cardinality of the continuum.

21. Consider the structure $\mathfrak{A} = \langle R, <, f\rangle$, where $<$ is the natural order, and where f is a unary function. Let L be the corresponding language. Show that there is no sentence σ in L such that $\mathfrak{A} \models \sigma \Leftrightarrow f(r) > 0$ for all $r \in R$.
(hint: consider isomorphisms $x \mapsto x+k$).

22. Let $\mathfrak{A} = \langle A, \sim\rangle$, where $\sim$ is an equivalence relation with denumerably many equivalence classes, all of which are infinite. Show that $\mathrm{Th}(\mathfrak{A})$ is $\aleph_0$-categorical. Axiomatize $\mathrm{Th}(\mathfrak{A})$. Is there a finite axiomatization? Is $\mathrm{Th}(\mathfrak{A})$ κ-categorical for $\kappa > \aleph_0$?

23. Let L be a language with one unary function symbol f. Find a sentence τ_n, which says that "f has a loop of length n", i.e. $\mathfrak{A} \models \tau_n \Leftrightarrow$ there are $a_1,\ldots,a_n \in |\mathfrak{A}|$ such that $f^{\mathfrak{A}}(a_i) = a_{i+1}$ $(i < n)$ and $f^{\mathfrak{A}}(a_n) = a_1$. Consider a theory T with axiom set $\{\beta, \neg\tau_1, \neg\tau_2, \neg\tau_3, \ldots, \neg\tau_n, \ldots\}$ $(n \in \omega)$, where β expresses "f is bijective".
Show that T is κ-categorical for $\kappa > \aleph_0$. (hint: consider the partition $\{(f^{\mathfrak{A}})^i(a) \mid i \in \omega\}$ in a model $\mathfrak{A}$). Is T $\aleph_0$-categorical?
Show that T is complete and decidable. Is T finitely axiomatizable?

24. Put $T_\forall = \{\sigma \mid T \vdash \sigma$ and σ is universal$\}$.
Show that $T_\forall$ axiomatizes the theory of all substructures of models of T. Note

that one part follows from exercise 3. For the converse: let $\mathfrak{A}$ be a model of $T_\forall$ and consider Diag($\mathfrak{A}$) $\cup$ T. Use compactness.

25. We say that a theory is *preserved under substructures* if $\mathfrak{A} \subseteq \mathfrak{B}$ and $\mathfrak{B} \in$ Mod(T) implies $\mathfrak{A} \in$ Mod(T).
(Łos-Tarski). Show that T is preserved under substructures iff T can be axiomatized by universal sentences (use exercise 24).

26. Let $\mathfrak{A} \equiv \mathfrak{B}$, show that there exists a $\mathfrak{C}$ such that $\mathfrak{A} \prec \mathfrak{C}$, $\mathfrak{B} \prec \mathfrak{C}$ (up to isomorphism). Hint: assume that the set of new constants of $\hat{\mathfrak{A}}$ is disjoint with the set of new constants of $\hat{\mathfrak{B}}$.
Show that Th($\hat{\mathfrak{A}}$) $\cup$ Th($\hat{\mathfrak{B}}$) has a model.

27. Show that the ordening $<$, defined by $x < y := \exists u(y = x+Su)$ is provably transitive in Peano's Arithmetic, i.e. $PA \vdash \forall xyz(x < y \wedge y < z \rightarrow x < z)$.

28. Show (*i*) $PA \vdash \forall x(0 \leqslant x)$
(use induction on x),
(*ii*) $PA \vdash \forall x(x = 0 \vee \exists y(x = Sy))$
(use induction on x),
(*iii*) $PA \vdash \forall xy(x+y = y+x)$,
(*iv*) $PA \vdash \forall y(x < y \rightarrow Sx \leqslant y)$
(use induction on y),
(*v*) $PA \vdash \forall xy(x < y \vee x = y \vee y < x)$
(use induction x, the case of x = 0 is simple, for the step from x to Sx use (iv)),
(*vi*) $PA \vdash \forall y \neg \exists x(y < x \wedge x < Sy)$
(compare with (iv)).

29. (*i*) Show that the theory I_∞ of identity with "infinite universe" (cf. section 3.1, exercise 3 or exercise 19 above) admits quantifier elimination.
(*ii*) Show that I_∞ has a prime model.

3.4. SKOLEM FUNCTIONS, OR HOW TO ENRICH YOUR LANGUAGE

In mathematical arguments one often finds passages such as "... there is an x such that $\varphi(x)$ holds. Let a be such an element, then we see that ...".

In terms of our logic, this amounts to the introduction of a constant whenever the existence of some element satisfying a certain condition has been established. The problem is: does one thus strengthen the theory in an essential way? In a precise formulation: suppose $T \vdash \exists x\varphi(x)$. Introduce a (new) constant a and replace T by $T' = T \cup \{\varphi(a)\}$. Question: is T' conservative over T, i.e. does $T' \vdash \psi \Rightarrow T \vdash \psi$ hold, for ψ not containing a?
We have dealt with a comparable problem in the context of Henkin models, (section 3.1), so we can use the experience obtained there.

3.4.1. Theorem. Let T be a theory with language L, such that $T \vdash \exists x\varphi(x)$ ($FV(\varphi) = \{x\}$), and let c be a constant not occurring in L. Then $T \cup \{\varphi(c)\}$ is conservative over T.

Proof. By lemma 3.1.5, $T' = T \cup \{\exists x\varphi(x) \rightarrow \varphi(c)\}$ is conservative over T. If $\psi \in L$ and $T \cup \{\varphi(c)\} \vdash \psi$, then $T' \cup \{\exists x\varphi(x)\} \vdash \psi$, or $T' \vdash \exists x\varphi(x) \rightarrow \psi$. Since T' is conservative over T we have $T \vdash \exists x\varphi(x) \rightarrow \psi$. Using $T \vdash \exists x\varphi(x)$, we get $T \vdash \psi$. For an alternative proof see exercise 6. □

The above is but a special case of a very common piece of practice; if one, in the process of proving a theorem establishes that "for each x there is a y such that $\varphi(x,y)$", then it is very convenient to introduce a function f that picks a y for each x, such that $\varphi(x,f(x))$ holds for each x. This technique usually invokes the axiom of choice. We can put the same question in this case: If $T \vdash \forall x\exists y\varphi(x,y)$ introduce a function symbol f and replace T by $T' = T \cup \forall x\varphi(x,f(x))$. Question: Is T' conservative over T?

The idea of enriching the language, as indicated above, goes back to Skolem.

3.4.2. Definition. Let φ be a formula of the language L with $FV(\varphi) = \{x_1,\dots,x_n,y\}$. Associate with φ an n-ary function symbol f_φ, called the *Skolem function* (symbol) of φ. The sentence $\forall x_1 \dots x_n(\exists y\varphi(x_1,\dots,x_n,y) \rightarrow \varphi(x_1,\dots,x_n,f_\varphi(x_1,\dots,x_n)))$ is called the *Skolem axiom* for φ.

Note that the witness of section 3.1 is a special case of a Skolem function (take n = 0): f_φ is a constant.

3.4.3. Definition. If T is a theory with language L, then $T^* = T \cup \{\sigma \mid \sigma$ is a Skolem axiom for some formula of L$\}$ is the Skolem extension of T and its language L* extends L by including all Skolem functions for L. If $\mathfrak{A}$ is of the type of L and $\mathfrak{A}^*$ and expansion of $\mathfrak{A}$ of the type of L*, such that $\mathfrak{A}^* \models \sigma$ for all Skolem axioms σ of L and $|\mathfrak{A}| = |\mathfrak{A}^*|$, then $\mathfrak{A}^*$ is called a *Skolem expansion* of $\mathfrak{A}$.

The interpretation in $\mathfrak{A}^*$ of a Skolem function symbol is called a Skolem function.

Note that a Skolem expansion contains infinitely many functions, so it is a mild extension of our notion of structure.
The analogue of 3.1.5 is

3.4.4. Theorem. *(i)* T^* is conservative over T,
(ii) each $\mathfrak{A} \in Mod(T)$ has a Skolem expansion $\mathfrak{A}^* \in Mod(T^*)$.

Proof. We first show (ii). We only consider the case of formulas with $FV(\varphi) = \{x_1,\ldots,x_n,y\}$ for $n \geqslant 1$. The case $n = 0$ is similar, but simpler. It requires the introduction of new constants in $\mathfrak{A}$ (cf. exercise 6).

Let $\mathfrak{A} \in Mod(T)$ and $\varphi \in L$ with $FV(\varphi) = \{x_1,\ldots,x_n,y\}$. We want to find a Skolem function for φ in $\mathfrak{A}$.
Define $V_{a_1,\ldots,a_n} = \{b \in |\mathfrak{A}| \mid \mathfrak{A} \models \varphi(\bar{a}_1,\ldots,\bar{a}_n,\bar{b})\}$.
Apply AC to the set $\{V_{a_1,\ldots,a_n} \mid V_{a_1,\ldots,a_n} \neq \emptyset\}$: there is a choice function F such that $F(V_{a_1,\ldots,a_n}) \in V_{a_1,\ldots,a_n} \neq \emptyset$.
Define a Skolem function by

$$F_\varphi(a_1,\ldots,a_n) = \begin{cases} F(V_{a_1,\ldots,a_n}) & \text{if } V_{a_1,\ldots,a_n} \neq \emptyset, \\ e & \text{else} \end{cases}$$

where $e \in |\mathfrak{A}|$.

Now it is a routine matter to check that indeed
$\mathfrak{A}^* \models \forall x_1 \ldots x_n(\exists y\varphi(x_1,\ldots,x_n,y) \rightarrow \varphi(x_1,\ldots,x_n,f_\varphi(x_1,\ldots,x_n)))$, where $F_\varphi = f_\varphi^{\mathfrak{A}^*}$, and where $\mathfrak{A}^*$ is the expansion of $\mathfrak{A}$ with all Skolem functions F_φ (including the "Skolem constants", i.e. witnesses).
(i) follows immediately from (ii): Let $T \nvdash \psi$ (with $\psi \in L$), then there is an $\mathfrak{A}$ such that $\mathfrak{A} \not\models \psi$. Since $\psi \in L$, we also have $\mathfrak{A}^* \not\models \psi$ (cf. section 3.2, exercise 3), hence $T^* \nvdash \psi$. □

Remark: It is not necessary (for 3.4.4) to extend L with *all* Skolem function symbols. We may just add Skolem function symbols for some given set S of formulas of L. We then speak of the Skolem extension of T with respect to S (or with respect to φ if $S = \{\varphi\}$).

The following corollary confirms that we can introduce Skolem functions in the course of a mathematical argument, without essentially strengthening the theory.

3.4.5. Corollary. If $T \vdash \forall x_1 \dots x_n \exists y \varphi(x_1,\dots,x_n,y)$, where $FV(\varphi) = \{x_1,\dots,x_n,y\}$, then $T' = T \cup \{\forall x_1 \dots x_n \varphi(x_1,\dots,x_n,f_\varphi(x_1,\dots,x_n))\}$ is conservative over T.

Proof. Observe that

$$T'' = T \cup \{\forall x_1 \dots x_n (\exists y \varphi(x_1,\dots,x_n,y) \rightarrow \varphi(x_1,\dots,x_n),f_\varphi(x_1,\dots,x_n))\} \vdash$$
$$\forall x_1 \dots x_n \varphi(x_1,\dots,x_n,f_\varphi(x_1,\dots,x_n)).$$

So $T' \vdash \psi \Rightarrow T'' \vdash \psi$. Now apply 3.4.4. □

The introduction of a Skolem extension of a theory T results in the "elimination" of the existential quantifier in prefixes of the form $\forall x,\dots,x_n \exists y$. The iteration of this process on prenex normal forms eventually results in the elimination of all existential quantifiers.

The Skolem functions in an expanded model are by no means unique. If, however, $\mathfrak{A} \models \forall x_1 \dots x_n \exists ! y \varphi(x_1,\dots,x_n,y)$, then the Skolem function for φ is uniquely determined; we even have $\mathfrak{A}^* \models \forall x_1 \dots x_n,y(\varphi(x_1,\dots,x_n,y) \leftrightarrow y = f_\varphi(x_1,\dots,x_n))$.

We say that φ *defines* the function F_φ in $\mathfrak{A}^*$, and $\forall x_1 \dots x_n(\varphi(x_1,\dots,x_n,y) \leftrightarrow y = f_\varphi(x_1,\dots,x_n))$ is called the *definition* of F_φ in $\mathfrak{A}^*$.

We may reasonably expect that with respect to Skolem functions the $\forall\exists!$ - combination yields better results than the $\forall\exists$-combination. The following theorem tells us that we get substantially more than just a conservative extension result.

3.4.6. Theorem. Let $T \vdash \forall x_1 \dots x_n \exists ! y \varphi(x_1,\dots,x_n,y)$, where $FV(\varphi) = \{x_1,\dots,x_n,y\}$, and let f be an n-ary symbol not occurring in T or φ. Then $T^+ = T \cup \{\forall x_1 \dots x_n y(\varphi(x_1,\dots,x_n,y) \leftrightarrow y = f(x_1,\dots,x_n))\}$ is conservative over T.

There is a translation $\tau \rightarrow \tau^0$ from $L^* = (L \cup \{f\})$ into L, such that

(1) $T^+ \vdash \tau \leftrightarrow \tau^0$,

(2) $T^+ \vdash \tau \Leftrightarrow T \vdash \tau^0$,

(3) $\tau = \tau^0$ for $\tau \in L$.

Proof. *(i)* We will show that f acts just like a Skolem function, in fact T^+ is equivalent to the theory T' of Corollary 3.4.5 (taking f for f_φ).

(a) $T^+ \vdash \forall x_1 \dots x_n \varphi(x_1,\dots,x_n,f(x_1,\dots,x_n))$.

For, $T^+ \vdash \forall x_1 \ldots x_n \exists y \varphi(x_1,\ldots,x_n,y)$ and

$$T^+ \vdash \forall x_1 \ldots x_n \exists y \varphi(x_1,\ldots,x_n,y) \leftrightarrow y = f(x_1,\ldots,x_n) .$$

Now a simple exercise in natural deduction, involving RI_4, yields (a). Therefore $T' \subseteq T^+$.

(*b*) $y = f(x_1,\ldots,x_n), \forall x_1 \ldots x_n \varphi(x_1,\ldots,x_n,f(x_1,\ldots,x_n)) \vdash \varphi(x_1,\ldots,x_n,y)$

so $T' \vdash y = f(x_1,\ldots,x_n) \rightarrow \varphi(x_1,\ldots,x_n,y)$ and

$\varphi(x_1,\ldots,x_n,y), \forall x_1 \ldots x_n \varphi(x_1,\ldots,x_n,f(x_1,\ldots,x_n))$,
$\forall x_1 \ldots x_n \exists ! y \varphi(x_1,\ldots,x_n,y) \vdash y = f(x_1,\ldots,x_n)$,

so $T' \vdash \varphi(x_1,\ldots,x_n,y) \rightarrow y = f(x_1,\ldots,x_n)$.

Hence $T' \vdash \forall x_1 \ldots x_n (\varphi(x_1,\ldots,x_n,y) \leftrightarrow y = f(x_1,\ldots,x_n))$.

So $T^+ \subseteq T'$, and hence $T' = T^+$.

Now, by 3.4.5, T^+ is conservative over T.

(*ii*) The idea, underlying the translation, is to replace occurrences of f(—) by a new variable and to eliminate f. Let $\tau \in L^*$ and let f(—) be a term in not containing f in any of its subterms.
Then $\vdash \tau(\ldots,f(—),\ldots) \leftrightarrow \exists y(y = f(—) \wedge \tau(\ldots,y,\ldots))$, where y does not occur in τ, and $T^* \vdash \tau(\ldots,f(—),\ldots) \wedge \exists y(\varphi(—,y) \wedge \tau(\ldots,y,\ldots))$.
The right-hand side contains one occurrence of f less than τ. Iteration of the procedure leads to the required f-free formula τ^0. The reader can provide the details of a precise inductive definition of τ^0; note that one need only consider atomic τ (the translation extends trivially to all formulas). Hint: define something like "f-depth" of terms and atoms.
From the above description of τ^0 it immediately follows that $T' \vdash \tau \leftrightarrow \tau^0$. Now (2) follows from (i) and (1). Finally (3) is evident. □

As a special case we get the *explicit definition* of a function.

3.4.7. Corollary. Let $FV(t) = \{x_1,\ldots,x_n\}$ and $f \notin L$. Then
$T^+ = T \cup \{\forall x_1 \ldots x_n (t = f(x_1,\ldots,x_n))\}$ is conservative over T.

Proof. We have $\forall x_1 \ldots x_n \exists ! y(y = t)$, so the definition of f, as in 3.4.6, becomes $\forall x_1 \ldots x_n y(y = t \leftrightarrow y = f(x_1,\ldots,x_n))$, which, by the predicate and identity rules, is equivalent to $\forall x_1 \ldots x_n (t = f(x_1,\ldots,x_n))$. □

We call $f(x_1,\ldots,x_n) = t$ the *explicit definition* of f.

One can also add new predicate symbols to a language in order to replace formulas by atoms.

3.4.8. Theorem. Let $FV(\varphi) = \{x_1,\dots,x_n\}$ and let Q be a predicate symbol not in L. Then

(i) $T^+ = T \cup \{\forall x_1 \dots x_n(\varphi \leftrightarrow Q(x_1,\dots,x_n))\}$ is conservative over T.

(ii) there is a translation $\tau \to \tau^0$ from $L \cup \{Q\}$ into L such that

(1) $T^+ \vdash \tau \leftrightarrow \tau^0$,

(2) $T^+ \vdash \tau \Leftrightarrow T \vdash \tau^0$,

(3) $\tau = \tau^0$ for $\tau \in L$.

Proof. Similar to, but simpler than, the above.
We indicate the steps; the details are left to the reader.

(a) Let $\mathfrak{A}$ have the type of L. Expand $\mathfrak{A}$ to $\mathfrak{A}^+$ by adding a relation $Q^+ = \{\langle a_1,\dots,a_n\rangle \mid \mathfrak{A} \models \varphi(\overline{a}_1,\dots,\overline{a}_n)\}$.

(b) Show $\mathfrak{A} \models T \Leftrightarrow \mathfrak{A}^+ \models T^+$ and conclude (i).

(c) Imitate the translation of 3.4.6. □

We call the extensions shown in 3.4.6, 3.4.7 and 3.4.8, *extensions by definition*. The sentences

$$\forall x_1 \dots x_n y(\varphi \leftrightarrow y = f(x_1,\dots,x_n)),$$

$$\forall x_1 \dots x_n(f(x_1,\dots,x_n) = t),$$

$$\forall x_1 \dots x_n(\varphi \leftrightarrow Q(x_1,\dots,x_n)).$$

are called the *defining axioms* for f and Q respectively.

Extension by definition belongs to the daily practice of mathematics (and science in general). If a certain notion, definable in a given language, plays an important role in our considerations, then it is convenient to have a short, handy notation for it.
Think of "x is a prime number", "x is equal to y or less than y", "z is the maximum of x and y", etc.

Examples. *1. Characteristic functions*

Consider a theory T with (at least) two constants c_0, c_1, such that $T \vdash c_0 \neq c_1$. Let $FV(\varphi) = \{x_1,\dots,x_n\}$, then $T \vdash \forall x_1 \dots x_n \exists ! y((\varphi \wedge y = c_1) \vee (\neg\varphi \wedge y = c_0))$. (Show this directly or use the completeness theorem).

The defining axiom for the characteristic function, K_φ, is $\forall x_1 \dots x_n y[((\varphi \wedge y = c_1) \vee (\neg\varphi \wedge y = c_0)) \leftrightarrow y = K_\varphi(x_1,\dots,x_n))$.

2. *Definition by (primitive) recursion*

In arithmetic one often introduces functions by recursion, e.g. $x!, x^y$. The study of these and similar functions belongs to recursion theory; here we only note that we can conservatively add symbols and axioms for them. *Fact* (Gödel, Davis, Matijasevich): each recursive function is definable in *PA*, in the sense that there is a formula φ of *PA* such that

(*i*) $PA \vdash \forall x_1 \dots x_n \exists ! y\varphi(x_1,\dots,x_n,y)$ and

(*ii*) for $k_1,\dots,k_n,m \in N$ $f(k_1,\dots,k_n) = m \Rightarrow PA \vdash \varphi(\bar{k}_1,\dots,\bar{k}_n,\bar{m})$.

For details see *Davis*, 1958; *Manin*, 1977.

Before ending this chapter, let us briefly return to the topic of Skolem functions and Skolem expansions. As we remarked before, the introduction of Skolem functions allows us to dispense with certain existential quantifiers in formulas. We will exploit this idea to rewrite formulas as universal formulas (in an extended language!).

First we transform the formula φ into prenex normal form φ'. Let us suppose that $\varphi' = \forall x_1 \dots x_n \exists y \psi(x_1,\dots,x_n,y,x_1,\dots,z_k)$, where $z_1,\dots,z_k$ are all the free variables in φ. Now consider

$$T^* = T \cup \{\forall x_1 \dots x_n z_1 \dots z_k (\exists y \psi(x_1,\dots,x_n,y,z_1,\dots,z_k) \to \psi(x_1,\dots,x_n,f(x_1,\dots,x_n,z_1,\dots,z_k),z_1,\dots,z_k))\}.$$

By theorem 3.4.4 T^* is conservative over T, and it is a simple exercise in logic to show that $T^* \vdash \forall x_1 \dots x_n \exists y \psi(\text{—},y,\text{—}) \leftrightarrow \forall x_1 \dots x_n \psi(\text{—},f(\dots),\text{—})$.

We now repeat the process and eliminate the next extential quantifier in the prefix of ψ. In finitely many steps we obtain a formula φ^s in prenex normal form without existential quantifiers, which, in a suitable conservative extention of T obtained by a series of Skolem expansions, is equivalent to φ.

Warning: the *Skolem form* φ^s differs in kind from other normal forms, in the sense that it is not *logically equivalent* to φ.

Theorem 3.4.4 shows that the adding of Skolem Axioms to a theory is conservative, so we can safely operate with Skolem forms. The Skolem φ^s has the property that is satisfiable if and only if φ is so. (cf. exercise 4). Therefore it is sometimes called the Skolem form for satisfiability. There is a dual Skolem form φ_s (cf. exercise 5), which is valid if and only if φ is so. φ_s is called the Skolem form for validity.

Example. $\forall x_1 \exists y_1 \exists y_2 \forall x_2 \exists y_3 \forall x_3 \forall x_4 \exists y_4 \ \varphi\ (x_1,x_2,x_3,x_4,y_1,y_2,y_3,y_4,z_1,z_2)$.

step 1. Eliminate y_1:

$\forall x_1 \exists y_2 \forall x_2 \exists y_3 \forall x_3 \forall x_4 \exists y_4\ \varphi(x_1,x_2,x_3,x_4,f(x_1,z_1,z_2),y_2,y_3,y_4,z_1,z_2)$

step 2. Eliminate y_2:

$\forall x_1 x_2 \exists y_3 \forall x_3 x_4 \exists y_4\ \varphi(\ldots,f(x_1,z_1,z_2),g(x_1,z_1,z_2),y_3,y_4,z_1,z_2)$

step 3. Eliminate y_3:

$\forall x_1 x_2 x_3 x_4 \exists y_4\ \varphi(\ldots,f(x_1,z_1,z_2),g(x_1,z_1,z_2),h(x_1,z_2,z_1,z_2),y_4,z_1,z_2)$

step 4. Eliminate y_4:

$\forall x_1 x_2 x_3 x_4\ \varphi(\ldots,f(x_1,z_1,z_2),g(x_1,z_1,z_2),h(x_1,x_2,z_1,z_2),k(x_1,x_2,x_3,x_4,z_1,z_2),z_1,z_2)$.

In Skolem expansions we have functions available which pick elements for us. We can exploit this to obtain elementary extensions.

3.4.9. Theorem. Consider $\mathfrak{A}$ and $\mathfrak{B}$ of the same type.
If $\mathfrak{B}^*$ is a Skolem expansion of $\mathfrak{B}$ and $\mathfrak{A}^* \subseteq \mathfrak{B}^*$, where $\mathfrak{A}^*$ is some expansion of $\mathfrak{A}$, then $\mathfrak{A} \prec \mathfrak{B}$.

Proof. We use exercise 5 of section 3.3. Let $a_1,\ldots,a_n \in |\mathfrak{A}|$
$\mathfrak{B} \models \exists y\varphi(y,\bar{a}_1,\ldots,\bar{a}_n) \Leftrightarrow \mathfrak{B}^* \models \varphi(f_\varphi(\bar{a}_1,\ldots,\bar{a}_n),\bar{a}_1,\ldots,\bar{a}_n)$, where f_φ is the Skolem function for φ.
Since $\mathfrak{A}^* \subseteq \mathfrak{B}^*$, $f_\varphi^{\mathfrak{A}^*}(a_1,\ldots,a_n) = f_\varphi^{\mathfrak{B}^*}(a_1,\ldots,a_n)$ and so
$b = (f_\varphi(\bar{a}_1,\ldots,\bar{a}_n))^{\mathfrak{B}^*} = (f_\varphi(\bar{a}_1,\ldots,\bar{a}_n))^{\mathfrak{A}^*} \in |\mathfrak{A}|$.
Hence $\mathfrak{B}^* \models \varphi(\bar{b},\bar{a}_1,\ldots,\bar{a}_n)$. This shows $\mathfrak{A} \prec \mathfrak{B}$. □

3.4.10. Definition. Let $X \subseteq |\mathfrak{A}|$. The *Skolem Hull* $\mathfrak{S}_X$ of X is the substructure of $\mathfrak{A}$ which is the reduct of the structure generated by X in the Skolem expansion $\mathfrak{A}^*$ of $\mathfrak{A}$ (cf. exercise 12, section 3.3).

In other words $\mathfrak{S}_X$ is the smallest substructure of $\mathfrak{A}$, containing X, which is closed under all Skolem functions (including the constants).

3.4.11. Corollary. For all $X \subseteq |\mathfrak{A}|$ $\mathfrak{S}_X \prec \mathfrak{A}$.

We now immediately get the strengthening of the downward Skolem-Löwenheim theorem formulated in theorem 3.3.12, by observing that the cardinality of a substructure generated by X is the maximum of the cardinalities of X and of the language. (This holds too in the present case, where infinitely many Skolem functions are added to the language.)

EXERCISES.

1. Consider again the example concerning the characteristic function.
   (*i*) Show $T^+ \vdash \forall x_1 \ldots x_n(\varphi \leftrightarrow K_\varphi(x_1,\ldots,x_n) = c_1)$.
   (*ii*) Translate $K_\varphi(x_1,\ldots,x_n) = K_\varphi(y_1,\ldots,y_n)$.
   (*iii*) Show $T^+ \vdash \forall x_1 \ldots x_n y_1,\ldots,y_n(K_\varphi(x_1,\ldots,x_n) = K_\varphi(y_1,\ldots,y_n))$
   $\leftrightarrow \forall x_1 \ldots x_n \varphi(x_1,\ldots,x_n) \vee \forall x_1 \ldots x_n \neg\varphi(x_1,\ldots,x_n)$.

2. Determine the Skolem forms of
   (*a*) $\forall y \exists x(2x^2 + yx - 1 = 0)$,
   (*b*) $\forall \varepsilon \exists \delta(\varepsilon > 0 \rightarrow (\delta > 0 \wedge \forall x(|x - \overline{a}| < \delta \rightarrow |f(x) - f(\overline{a})| < \varepsilon)$,
   (*c*) $\forall x \exists y(x = f(y))$,
   (*d*) $\forall xy(x < y \rightarrow \exists u(u < x) \wedge \exists v(y < v) \wedge \exists w(x < w \wedge w < y))$,
   (*e*) $\forall x \exists y(x = y^2 \vee x = -y^2)$.

3. Let σ^s be the Skolem form of σ. Consider only sentences.
   (*i*) Show that $\Gamma \cup \{\sigma^s\}$ is conservative over $\Gamma \cup \{\sigma\}$.
   (*ii*) Put $\Gamma^s = \{\sigma^s \mid \sigma \in \Gamma\}$. Show that for finite Γ, Γ^s is conservative over Γ.
   (*iii*) Show that Γ^s is conservative over Γ for arbitrary Γ.

4. φ with $FV(\varphi) = \{x_1,\ldots,x_n\}$ is called *satisfiable* if there is an $\mathfrak{A}$ and $a_1,\ldots,a_n \in |\mathfrak{A}|$ such that $\mathfrak{A} \models \varphi(\overline{a}_1,\ldots,\overline{a}_n)$. Show that φ is satisfiable iff φ^s is satisfiable.

5. Let σ be a sentence in prenex normal form. We define the *dual Skolem form* σ_s of σ as follows: let $\sigma = (Q_1x_1)\ldots(Q_nx_n)\tau$, where τ is open and Q_i are quantifiers. Consider $\sigma' = (\overline{Q}_1x_1)\ldots(\overline{Q}x_n)\neg\tau$ where $\overline{Q}_i = \forall,\exists$ iff $Q_i = \exists,\forall$. Suppose $(\sigma')^s = (\overline{Q_{i_1}x_{i_1}})\ldots(\overline{Q}_{i_k}x_{i_k})\neg\tau'$; then $\sigma_s = (Q_{i_1}x_{i_1})\ldots(Q_{i_k}x_{i_k})\,\tau'$.

   In words: eliminate from σ the universal quantifiers and their variables just as the existential ones in the case of the Skolem form.
We end up with an existential sentence.
Example: $(\forall x \exists y \forall z \varphi(xyx))_s = \exists y \varphi(c,y,f(y))$.

We suppose that L has at least one constant symbol.
(*a*) Show that for all (prenex) sentences σ,
   $\models \sigma$ iff $\models \sigma_s$.

   (Hint: look at exercise 4). Hence the name: "Skolem form for *validity*".

(*b*) Prove *Herbrand's theorem*: $\vdash \sigma \Leftrightarrow \vdash \bigvee_{i=1}^{m} \sigma'_s(t_1^i,\ldots,t_n^i)$, for some m where σ'_s

is obtained from σ_s by deleting the quantifiers. The t_j^i ($i \leq m$, $j \leq n$) are certain closed terms in the dual Skolem expansion of L.
Hint: look at $\neg(\neg\sigma)^s$. Use exercise 16, section 3.3.

6. Let $T \vdash \exists x\varphi(x)$, with $FV(\varphi) = \{x\}$. Show that any model $\mathfrak{A}$ of T can be expanded to a model $\mathfrak{A}^*$ of T with an extra constant c that that $\mathfrak{A}^* \models \varphi(c)$.
Use this for an alternative proof of 3.4.1.

7. Consider I_∞, the theory of identity "with infinite universe with axioms $\lambda_n (n \in N)$ and I'_∞ with extra constants $c_i (i \in N)$ and axioms $c_i \neq c_j$ for $i \neq j$, $i,j \in N$. Show that I'_∞ is conservative over I_∞.

4. Second-Order Logic

In first-order predicate logic the variables range over *elements* of a structure, in particular the quantifiers are interpreted in the familiar way as "for all elements a of $|\mathfrak{A}|$ ..." and "there exists an element a of $|\mathfrak{A}|$ ...". We will now allow a second kind of variable ranging over subsets of the universe and its cartesian products, i.e. relations over the universe.

The introduction of these second-order variables is not the result of an unbridled pursuit of generality; one is often forced to take all subsets of a structure into consideration. Examples are "each bounded non-empty set of reals has a supremum", "each non-empty set of natural numbers has a smallest element", "each ideal is contained in a maximal ideal". Already the introduction of the reals on the basis of the rationals requires quantification over sets of rationals, as becomes clear from the theory of Dedekind cuts.

Instead of allowing variables for (and quantification over) sets, one can also allow variables for functions. However, since we can reduce functions to sets (or relations), we will restrict ourselves here to second-order logic with set variables.

When dealing with second-order arithmetic we can restrict our attention to variables ranging over subsets $\mathbb{N}$, since there is a coding of finite sequences of numbers to numbers, e.g. via Gödels β-function, or via exponents. In general we will,however, allow for variables for relations.

The introduction of the syntax of second-order logic is so similar to that of first-order logic that we will leave most of the details to the reader.

The *alphabet* consists of symbols for

(*i*) individual variables — $x_0, x_1, x_2, \ldots$,

(*ii*) individual constants — $c_0, c_1, c_2, \ldots$, and for each $n \geq 0$

and for each $n \geq 0$

(*iii*) n-ary set (predicate) variables — $X^n_0, X^n_1, X^n_2, \ldots$,

(*iv*) n-ary set (predicate) constants — $\bot, P^n_0, P^n_1, P^n_2, \ldots$,

(*v*) connectives — $\wedge, \rightarrow, \vee, \neg, \leftrightarrow, \exists, \forall$,

Finally we have the usual auxiliary symbols: (,), ’ .

Remark: There are denumerably many variables of each kind. The number of constants may be arbitrarily large.

Formulas are inductively defined by:

(i) $X_i^0, P_i^0, \bot \in$ FORM,

(ii) for $n > 0$ $X^n(t_1,\ldots,t_n) \in$ FORM,
$P^n(t_1,\ldots,t_n) \in$ FORM,
where t_i is an individual variable or constant,

(iii) FORM is closed under the propositional connectives,

(iv) FORM is closed under first- and second-order quantification.

Notation: we will in the case of set variables X^1 also write $x \in X^1$ instead of $X^1(x)$, and we will often omit the superscript.

The semantics of second-order logic is defined in the same manner as in the case of first-order logic.

4.1. Definition. A *second-order structure* is a sequence

$\mathfrak{A} = \langle A, A^*, c^*, R^* \rangle$, where

$A^* = \langle A_n \mid n \in N \rangle$, $c^* = \{c_i \mid i \in N\} \subseteq A$

$R^* = \langle R_i^n \mid i,n \in N \rangle$,

such that $A_n \subseteq P(A^n)$, $R_i^n \in A_n$.

In words: a second-order structure consists of a universe A of individuals and second-order universes of n-ary relations ($n \geqslant 0$), individual constants and set (relation) constants, belonging to the various universes.

In case each A_n contains *all* n-ary relations (i.e. $A_n = P(A^n)$), we call *full*.

Since we have listed $\bot$ as a 0-ary predicate constant, we must accomodate it in the structure $\mathfrak{A}$.

In accordance with the customary definitions of set theory, we write $0 = \emptyset$, $1 = \{0\}$ and $2 = \{0,1\}$. Also we take $A^0 = 1$, and hence $A_0 \subseteq P(A^0) = P(1) = 2$. By convention we assign 0 to $\bot$. Since we also want a distinct 0-ary predicate (proposition) $\top := \neg \bot$, we put $1 \in A_0$. So, in fact, $A_0 = P(A^0) = 2$.

Now, in order to define *validity in* $\mathfrak{A}$, we mimic the procedure of first-order logic. Given a structure $\mathfrak{A}$, we introduce an extended language $L(\mathfrak{A})$ with names $\overline{S}$ for all elements S of A and A_n ($n \in N$). The constants R_i^n are interpretations of the corresponding constant symbols P_i^n.

We define $\mathfrak{A} \models \varphi$ for closed φ.

4.2. Definition. (*i*) $\mathfrak{A} \models \overline{S}$ if $S = 1$,

(*ii*) $\mathfrak{A} \models \overline{S}^n(\overline{s}_1,\ldots,\overline{s}_n)$ if $\langle s_1,\ldots,s_n \rangle \in S^n$,

(*iii*) the propositional connectives are interpreted as usual (cf. 1.2.1, 2.4.5),

(*iv*) $\mathfrak{A} \models \forall x\varphi(x)$ if $\mathfrak{A} \models \varphi(\overline{s})$ for all $s \in A$,

$\mathfrak{A} \models \exists x\varphi(x)$ if $\mathfrak{A} \models \varphi(\overline{s})$ for some $s \in A$,

(*v*) $\mathfrak{A} \models \forall X^n\varphi(X^n)$ if $\mathfrak{A} \models \varphi(\overline{S}^n)$ for all $S^n \in A_n$,

$\mathfrak{A} \models \exists X^n\varphi(X^n)$ if $\mathfrak{A} \models \varphi(\overline{S}^n)$ for some $S^n \in A_n$.

If $\mathfrak{A} \models \varphi$, we say that φ is *true*, or valid, in $\mathfrak{A}$.

As in first-order logic we have a natural deduction system, which consists of the usual rules for first-order logic, plus extra rules for second-order quantifiers.

$$\forall^2 I \ \frac{\varphi}{\forall X^n\varphi} \qquad\qquad \forall^2 E \ \frac{\forall X^n\varphi}{\varphi^*}$$

$$\exists^2 I \ \frac{\varphi^*}{\exists X^n\varphi} \qquad\qquad \exists^2 E \ \frac{\exists X^n\varphi \quad \begin{matrix}[\varphi]\\ \vdots \\ \psi\end{matrix}}{\psi}$$

where the conditions on $\forall^2 I$ and $\exists^2 E$ are the usual ones, and φ^* is obtained from φ by replacing each occurrence of $X^n(t_1,\ldots,t_n)$ by $\sigma(t_1,\ldots,t_n)$ for a certain formula σ, such that no free variables among the t_i become bound after the substitution.

Note that $\exists^2 I$ gives us the traditional

Comprehension Schema:

$$\exists X^n \forall x_1 \ldots x_n[\varphi(x_1,\ldots,x_n) \leftrightarrow X^n(x_1,\ldots,x_n)],$$

where X^n may not occur free in φ.

Proof. $$\frac{\forall x_1\ldots x_n[\varphi(x_1,\ldots,x_n) \leftrightarrow \varphi(x_1,\ldots,x_n)]}{\exists X^n\forall_1\ldots x_n[\varphi(x_1,\ldots,x_n) \leftrightarrow X^n(x_1,\ldots,x_n)]}\ \exists^2 I$$

Since the topline is derivable, we have a proof of the desired principle.

Conversely, $\exists^2 I$ follows from the comprehension principle, given the ordinary rules of logic. The proof is sketched here ($\vec{x}$ and $\vec{t}$ stand for sequences of variables or terms).

$$\dfrac{\exists X^n \forall\vec{x}[\sigma(\vec{x}) \leftrightarrow X^n(\vec{x})] \qquad \dfrac{\dfrac{\dfrac{\forall\vec{x}[\sigma(\vec{x}) \leftrightarrow X^n(\vec{x})]}{\sigma(\vec{t}) \leftrightarrow X^n(\vec{t})} \quad \cancel{\varphi(\ldots,\sigma(\vec{t}),\ldots)}}{\varphi(\ldots,X^n(\vec{t}),\ldots)}\,\dagger}{\exists X^n\ \varphi(\ldots,X^n(\vec{t}),\ldots)}\,*}{\exists X^n\ \varphi(\ldots,X^n(\vec{t}),\ldots)}$$

In † a number of steps are involved, i.e. those necessary for the Substitution Theorem. In * we have applied a harmless ∃-introduction, in the sense that we went from a instance involving a variable to an existence statement, exactly as in first-order logic. This seems to beg the question, as we want to justify $\exists^2$-introduction. However, on the basis of the ordinary quantifier rules we have justified something much stronger than * on the assumption of the Comprehension Schema, namely the introduction of the existential quantifier, given a *formula* σ and not merely a variable or a constant.

Since we can define $\forall^2$ from $\exists^2$ a similar argument works for $\forall^2 E$.

The extra strength of the second-order quantifier rules lies in $\forall^2 I$ and $\exists^2 E$. We can make this precise by considering second-order logic as a special kind of first-order logic (i.e. "flattening" 2nd-order logic). The basic idea is to introduce special predicates to express the relation between a predicate and its arguments.

So let us consider a first-order logic with a sequence of predicates $Ap_0, Ap_1, Ap_2, Ap_3, \ldots$, such that each Ap_n is (n+1)-ary. We think of $Ap_n(x,y_1,\ldots,y_n)$ as $x^n(y_1,\ldots,y_n)$.

For n = 0 we get $Ap_0(x)$ as a first-order version of X^0, but that is in accordance with our intentions. X^0 is a proposition (i.e. something that can be assigned a truth value), and so is $Ap_0(x)$. We now have a logic in which all variables are first-order, so we can apply all the results from the preceding chapters.

For the sake of a natural simulation of second-order logic we add unary predicates $V, U_0, U_1, U_2, \ldots$, to be thought of as "is an element", "is a o-ary predicate (i.e. proposition)" "is a 1-ary predicate", etc.

We now have to indicate a list of axioms of our first-order system that embody the characteristic properties of second-order logic.

(*i*) $\forall xyz(U_i(x) \wedge U_j(y) \wedge V(z) \rightarrow x \neq y \wedge y \neq z \wedge z \neq x)$ for all $i \neq j$.
(i.e. the U_i's are pairwise disjoint, and disjoint from V).

(*ii*) $\forall xy_1 \ldots y_n(Ap_n(x,y_1,\ldots,y_n) \rightarrow U_n(x) \wedge \bigwedge_i V(y_i))$, for $n \geqslant 1$.
(i.e. if $x,y_1,\ldots,y_n$ are in the relation Ap_n, then think of x as a predicate, and the y_i's as elements).

(*iii*) $V(C_0)$, $V(C_2 i+1)$, for $i \geqslant 0$, and $U_n(C_{3^i \cdot 5^n})$, for $i, n \geqslant 0$.
(i.e. certain constants are designated as "elements" and "predicates").

(*iv*) $\forall z_1 \ldots z_m \exists x \forall y_1 \ldots y_n\ (\varphi \leftrightarrow Ap_n(x,y_1,\ldots,y_n))$, where $x \neq FV(\varphi)$.
(the first-order version of the comprehension schema. We assume that $FV(\varphi) \subseteq \{z_1,\ldots,z_m,y_1,\ldots,y_n\}$

(*v*) $\neg\, Ap_0(C_0)$.
(so there is a 0-ary predicate for 'falsity').

We claim that the first-order theory given by the above axioms represents second-order logic in the following precise way: we can translate second-order logic in the language of the above theory such that derivability is faithfully preserved.

The translation is obtained by assigning suitable symbols to the various symbols of the alphabet of second-order logic and defining an inductive procedure for converting composite strings of symbols.

We put $(x_i)^* := x_2 i+1$,

$(c_i)^* := c_2 i+1$, for $i \geqslant 0$

$(X_i^n)^* := x_{3^i \cdot 5^n}$,

$(P_i^n)^* := c_{3^i \cdot 5^n}$, for $i \geqslant 0$, $n > 0$

$(X_i^0)^* := Ap_0(x_{3^i})$, for $i \geqslant 0$

$(P_i^0)^* := Ap_0(c_{3^i})$, for $i \geqslant 0$

$(\bot)^* := Ap_0(c_0)$

Furthermore $(\varphi \,\square\, \psi) := \varphi^* \,\square\, \psi^*$ for binary connections $\square$

$(\neg\,\varphi)^* := \neg\,\varphi^*$

and $(\forall x_i\ \varphi(x_i))^* := \forall x_i^*(V(x_i^*) \to \varphi^*(x_i^*))$

$(\exists x_i\ \varphi(x_i))^* := \exists x_i^*(V(x_i^*) \wedge \varphi^*(x_i^*))$

$(\forall X_i^n\ \varphi(X_i^n))^* := \forall (X_i^n)^*(U_n((X_i^n)^*) \to \varphi^*((X_i^n)^*))$

$(\exists X_i^n\ \varphi(X_i^n))^* := \exists (X_i^n)^*(U_n((X_i^n)^*) \wedge \varphi^*((x_i^n)^*))$.

It is a tedious but routine job to show that $\vdash_2 \varphi \Leftrightarrow \vdash_1 \varphi^*$, where 2 and 1 refer to derivability in the respective second-order and first-order systems.

Note that the above translation could be used as an excuse for not doing second-order logic at all, were it not for the fact that first-order version is not nearly so natural as the second-order one. Moreover, it obscures a number of interesting and fundamental features, e.g. validity in all principal models, see below, makes sense for the second-order version, whereas it is rather an extraneous matter with the first-order version.

4.3. Definition. A second-order structure $\mathfrak{A}$ is called a *model* of second-order logic if the comprehension schema is valid in $\mathfrak{A}$.
If $\mathfrak{A}$ is full (i.e. $A_n = P(A^n)$ for all n), then we call $\mathfrak{A}$ a *principal* (or *standard*) model.

From the notion of model we get two distinct notions of "second-order validity": *(i)* true in all models, *(ii)* true in all principal models.

Recall that $\mathfrak{A} \models \varphi$ was defined for arbitrary second-order structures; we will use $\models \varphi$ for "true in all models".

By the standard induction on derivations we get

$\vdash_2 \varphi \Rightarrow \models \varphi$

Using the above translation into first-order logic we also get $\models \varphi \Rightarrow \vdash_2 \varphi$.

Combining these results we get

4.4. The completeness theorem $\vdash_2 \varphi \Leftrightarrow \models \varphi$

Obviously, we also have $\models \varphi \Rightarrow \varphi$ is true in all principal models. The converse, however, is not the case. We can make this plausible by the following argument:

(i) We can define the notion of a unary function in second-order logic, and hence the notions 'bijective' and 'surjective'. Using these notions we can formulate a sentence σ, which states "the universe (of individuals) is

finite" (any injection of the universe into itself is a surjection).

(*ii*) Consider $\Gamma = \{\sigma\} \cup \{\lambda_n \mid n \in N\}$. Γ is consistent, because each finite subset $\{\sigma, \lambda_{n_1}, \ldots, \lambda_{n_k}\}$ is consistent, since it has a second-order model, namely the principal model over a universe with n elements, where $n = \max\{n_1, \ldots, n_k\}$.

So, by the completeness theorem above Γ has a second-order model.

Suppose now that Γ has a principal model $\mathfrak{A}$. Then $\mathfrak{A} \models \sigma$ means that $|\mathfrak{A}|$ is actually Dedekind finite, and (assuming the axiom of choice) *finite*. Say $\mathfrak{A}$ has n_0 elements, then $\mathfrak{A} \not\models \lambda_{n_0+1}$. Contradiction.
So Γ has no principal model. Hence the completeness theorem fails for validity w.r.t. principal models (and likewise compactness).

To find a sentence that holds in all principal models, but fails in some model a more refined argument is required.

A peculiar feature of second-order logic is the definability of all the usual connectives in terms of $\forall$ and $\to$.

4.5. Theorem. (a) $\vdash_2 \bot \leftrightarrow \forall X^0 . X^0$,

(b) $\vdash_2 \varphi \wedge \psi \leftrightarrow \forall X^0((\varphi \to (\psi \to X^0)) \to X^0)$,

(c) $\vdash_2 \varphi \vee \psi \leftrightarrow \forall X^0((\varphi \to X^0) \wedge (\psi \to X^0) \to X^0)$,

(d) $\vdash_2 \exists x\varphi \leftrightarrow \forall X^0(\forall x(\varphi \to X^0) \to X^0)$,

(e) $\vdash_2 \exists X^n\varphi \leftrightarrow \forall X^0(\forall X^n(\varphi \to X^0) \to X^0)$.

Proof. (a) is obvious.

(b)

$$\dfrac{\dfrac{\dfrac{\dfrac{\dfrac{\dfrac{[\varphi \wedge \psi]}{\varphi} \quad [\varphi \to (\psi \to X^0)]}{\psi \to X^0} \quad \dfrac{[\varphi \wedge \psi]}{\psi}}{X^0}}{(\varphi \to (\psi \to X^0)) \to X^0}}{\forall X^0[(\varphi \to (\psi \to X^0)) \to X^0]}}{\varphi \wedge \psi \to \forall X^0[(\varphi \to (\psi \to X^0)) \to X^0]}$$

Conversely,

$$\dfrac{\dfrac{\dfrac{\dfrac{\cancel{\varphi}\quad\cancel{\psi}}{\varphi\wedge\psi}}{\psi\to(\varphi\wedge\psi)}}{\varphi\to(\psi\to(\varphi\wedge\psi))}\qquad\dfrac{\forall X^0((\varphi\to(\psi\to X^0))\to X^0)}{\varphi\to(\psi\to(\varphi\wedge\psi))\to\varphi\wedge\psi}\ \forall^2 E}{\varphi\wedge\psi}$$

(d)

$$\dfrac{\dfrac{\exists x\varphi(x)\qquad\dfrac{\dfrac{\cancel{\varphi(x)}\qquad\dfrac{\cancel{\forall x(\varphi(x)\to X)}}{\varphi(x)\to X}}{X}}{\forall x(\varphi(x)\to X)\to X}}{\forall x(\varphi(x)\to X)\to X}}{\forall X[\forall x(\varphi(x)\to X)\to X]}$$

Conversely,

$$\dfrac{\dfrac{\dfrac{\dfrac{\cancel{\varphi(x)}}{\exists x\varphi(x)}}{\varphi(x)\to\exists x\varphi(x)}}{\forall x(\varphi(x)\to\exists x\varphi(x))}\qquad\dfrac{\forall X[\forall x(\varphi(x)\to X)\to X]}{\forall x(\varphi(x)\to\exists x\varphi(x))\to\exists x\varphi(x)}}{\exists x\varphi(x)}$$

(c) and (e) are left to the reader. □

In second-order logic we also have natural means to define identity for individuals. The underlying idea, going back to Leibniz, is that equals have exactly the same properties.

4.6. <u>Definition</u>. $x = y := \forall X(X(x) \leftrightarrow X(y))$

This defined identity has the desired properties, i.e. it satisfies $I_1, -, I_4$.

4.7. <u>Theorem</u>. (*i*) $\vdash_2 x = x$

(*ii*) $\vdash_2 x = y \to y = x$

(*iii*) $\vdash_2 x = y \wedge y = z \to x = z$

(*iv*) $\vdash x = y \to \varphi(x) \to \varphi(y)$

Proof. Obvious. □

In case the logic already has an identity relation for individuals, say $\doteq$, we can show

4.8. Theorem $\vdash_2 x \doteq y \leftrightarrow x = y$.

Proof. $\rightarrow$ is obvious, by I_4.
$\leftarrow$ is obtained as follows:

$$\dfrac{x \doteq x \qquad \dfrac{\forall X(X(x) \leftrightarrow X(y))}{x \doteq x \leftrightarrow x \doteq y}}{x \doteq y}$$

In $\forall^2$E we have substituted $z = x$ for $X(z)$. □

We can also use second-order logic to extend Peano's Arithmetic to second-order arithmetic.

We consider a second-order logic with (first-order) identity and one binary predicate constant S, which represents, intuitively, the successor relation.
The following special axioms are added:

(1) $\exists! x \forall y \neg S(y,x)$

(2) $\forall x \exists! y S(x,y)$

(3) $\forall xyz(S(x,z) \wedge S(y,z) \rightarrow x = y)$

For convenience we extend the language with numerals and the successor function. This extension is conservative anyway, under the following axioms:

(*i*) $\forall y \neg S(y,\bar{0})$

(*ii*) $S(\bar{n},\overline{n+1})$

(*iii*) $y = x^+ \leftrightarrow S(x,y)$

We now write down the *induction axiom* (N.B., not a schema, as in first-order arithmetic, but a proper axiom!).

(4) $\forall X(X(0) \wedge \forall x(X(x) \rightarrow X(x^+)) \rightarrow \forall x X(x))$

The extension from first-order to second-order arithmetic is *not* conservative. It is, however, beyond our modest means to prove this fact.

One can also use the idea behind the induction axiom to give an (inductive) definition of the class of natural numbers in a second-order logic with axioms (1), (2), (3): N is the smallest class containing 0 and closed under the successor operation.

Let $\nu(x) := \forall X[(X(0) \wedge \forall y(X(y) \to X(y^+)) \to \forall y X(y)) \to X(x)]$

Then, by the comprehension axiom

$$\exists Y \forall x(\nu(x) \leftrightarrow Y(x))$$

As yet we cannot assert the existence of a unique Y satisfying $\forall x(\nu(x) \leftrightarrow Y(x))$, since we have not yet introduced identity for second-order terms.

Therefore, let us add identity relations for the various second-order terms, plus their obvious axioms.

Now we can formulate the

Axioms of Extensionality

$$\forall \vec{x}(X^n(\vec{x}) \leftrightarrow Y^n(\vec{x})) \leftrightarrow X^n = Y^n$$

So, finally, with the help of the axiom of extensionality, we can assert $\exists! Y \forall x(\nu(x) \leftrightarrow Y(x))$. Thus we can conservatively add a unary predicate constant N with axiom $\forall x(\nu(x) \leftrightarrow N(x))$.

The axiom of extensionality is on the one hand rather basic — it allows definition by abstraction ("the set of all x, such that ..."), on the other hand rather harmless — we can always turn a second-order model without extensionality into one with extensionality by taking a quotient with respect to the equivalence relation induced by = .

For more information second-order logic and models the reader is referred to *Church*, *Robbin* and *Kreisel-Krivine*.

EXERCISES

1. Show that the restriction on X^n in the comprehension schema cannot be dropped (consider $\neg X(x)$).

2. Show $\Gamma \vdash_2 \varphi \Leftrightarrow \Gamma^* \vdash_1 \varphi^*$ (where $\Gamma^* = \{\psi^* | \psi \in \Gamma\}$)
   Hint: use induction on the derivation, with the comprehension schema and simplified $\forall$, $\exists$-rules. For the quantifier rules it is convenient to consider

an intermediate step consisting of a replacement of the free variable by a fresh constant of the proper kind.

3. Prove (c) and (e) of theorem 4.5.

4. Prove theorem 4.7.

5. Give a formula $\varphi(X^2)$ which states that X^2 is a function.

6. Give a formula $\varphi(X^2)$ which states that X^2 is a linear order.

7. Give a sentence σ which states that the individuals can be linearly ordered without having a last element (σ can serve as an infinity axiom).

8. Given second-order arithmetic with the successor function, give axioms for addition as a ternary relation.

9. Let a second-order logic with a binary predicate constant $<$ be given, with extra axioms that make $<$ a dense linear ordering without end points. We write $x < y$ for $<(x,y)$.
   X is a *Dedekind Cut* if $\exists x X(x) \wedge \exists x \neg X(x) \wedge \forall x(X(x) \wedge y < x \rightarrow X(y))$.
   Define a partial ordering on the Dedekind cuts by putting $X \leqslant X' :=$ $\forall x(X(x) \rightarrow X'(x))$. Show that this partial order is total.

10. Consider the first-order version of second-order logic (involving the predicates Ap_n, U_n, V) with the axiom n of extensionality. Any model $\mathfrak{A}$ of this first-order theory can be "embedded" in the principal second-order model over $I_{\mathfrak{A}} = \{a \in |\mathfrak{A}| \mid \mathfrak{A} \models V(\bar{a})\}$, as follows.
    Define for any $r \in U_n$

    $$f(r) = \{\langle a_1, \ldots a_n \rangle \mid \mathfrak{A} \models Ap_n(\bar{r}, \bar{a}_1, \ldots, \bar{a}_n)\}$$

    Show that f establishes an "isomorphix" embedding of $\mathfrak{A}$ into the corresponding principal model.

    Hence principals models can be viewed as unique maximal models of second-order logic.

11. Formulate the axiom of choice — for each number x there is a set X ... — in second-order arithmetic.

5. Intuitionistic Logic

5.1. CONSTRUCTIVE REASONING

In the preceding chapters, we have been guided by the following, seemingly harmless extrapolation from our experience with finite sets: infinite universes can be surveyed in their totality. In particular can we in a global manner determine if $\mathfrak{A} \models \exists x\varphi(x)$ holds, or not. To adapt Hermann Weyl's phrasing: we are used to think of infinite sets not merely as defined by a property, but as a set whose elements are so to speak spread out in front of us so that we can run through them just as an officer in the police office goes through his file. This view of the mathematical universe is an attractive but rather unrealistic idealization. If one takes our limitations in the face of infinite totalities serious, then one has to read a statement like "there is a prime number greater than $10^{10^{10}}$" in a stricter way than "it is impossible that the set of primes is exhausted before $10^{10^{10}}$". For, we cannot inspect the set of natural numbers in a glance and detect a prime. We have to exhibit a prime p greater than $10^{10^{10}}$.

Similarly, one might be convinced that a certain problem (e.g. the determination of the saddle point of a zero-sum game has a solution on the basis of an abstract theorem (such as Brouwer's fixed point theorem). Nonetheless one cannot *exhibit* a solution. What one needs is a *constructive* method (proof) that determines the solution.

One more example to illustrate the restrictions of abstract methods. Consider the problem "Are there two irrational numbers a and b such that a^b is rational ?" We apply the following smart reasoning: suppose $\sqrt{2}^{\sqrt{2}}$ is rational, then we have solved the problem. Should $\sqrt{2}^{\sqrt{2}}$ be irrational then $(\sqrt{2}^{\sqrt{2}})^{\sqrt{2}}$ is rational. In both cases there is a solution, so the answer to the problem is: Yes. However, should somebody ask us to provide such a pair a,b, then we have to engage in some serious number theory in order to come up with the right choice between the numbers mentioned above.

Evidently statements can be read in an inconstructive way, as we did in the preceding chapters, and in a constructive way. We will in the present chapter briefly sketch the logic one uses in constructive reasoning. In mathematics the practice of constructive procedures and reasoning has been advocated by a number of people, but the founding fathers of constructive mathematics clearly are

L. Kronecker and L.E.J. Brouwer. The latter presented a complete program for the rebuilding of mathematics on a constructive basis. Brouwer's mathematics (and the accompanying logic) is called *intuitionistic*, and in this context the traditional inconstructive mathematics (and logic) is called *classical*.

There are a number of philosophical issues connected with intuitionism, for which we refer the reader to the literature, of *Dummett*, *Heyting*, *Troelstra- van Dalen*.

Since we can no longer base our interpretations of logic on the fiction that the mathematical universe is a predetermined totality which can be surveyed as a whole, we have to provide a heuristic interpretation of the logical connectives in intuitionistic logic. We will base our heuristics on the interpretation put forward by A. Heyting.

The point of departure is that a statement φ is considered to be true (or to hold) if we have a proof for it. By a proof we mean a mathematical construction that establishes φ, not a deduction in some formal system. For example, a proof of '$2+3=5$' consists of the successive constructions of 2,3 and 5, followed by a construction that adds 2 and 3, followed by a construction that compares the outcome of this addition and 5.

The primitive notion is here "a proves φ", where we understand by a proof a (for our purpose unspecified) construction. We will now indicate how proofs of composite statements depend on proofs of their parts.

a proves $\varphi\wedge\psi$:= a is a pair $\langle b,c\rangle$ such that b proves φ and c proves ψ.

a proves $\varphi\vee\psi$:= a is a pair $\langle b,c\rangle$ such that b is a natural number and if $b=0$ then c proves φ, if $b\neq 0$ then c proves ψ.

a proves $\varphi\rightarrow\psi$:= a is a construction that converts any proof p of φ into a proof a(p) of ψ.

no a proves $\perp$.

In order to deal with the quantifiers we assume that some domain D of objects is given.

a proves $\forall x\varphi(x)$:= a is a construction such that for each $d\in D$ a(d) proves $\varphi(\bar{d})$.

a proves $\exists x\varphi(x)$:= a is a pair $\langle b,c\rangle$ such that $b\in D$ and c proves $\varphi(\bar{b})$.

The above explanation of the connectives serves as a means of giving the reader a feeling for what is and what is not correct in intuitionistic logic.

Examples: 1. $\varphi\wedge\psi\rightarrow\varphi$ is true, for let $\langle a,b\rangle$ be a proof of $\varphi\wedge\psi$, then the construction c with $c(a,b)=a$ converts a proof of $\varphi\wedge\psi$ into a proof of φ. So c proves $(\varphi\wedge\psi\rightarrow\varphi)$.

2. $(\varphi \wedge \psi \to \sigma) \to (\varphi \to (\varphi \to \sigma))$. Let a prove $\varphi \wedge \psi \to \sigma$, i.e. a converts each proof $\langle b,c \rangle$ of $\varphi \wedge \psi$ into a proof a(b,c) of σ. Now the required proof p of $\varphi \to (\psi \to \sigma)$ is a construction that converts each proof b of φ into a proof p(b) of $\psi \to \sigma$. So p(b) is a construction that converts a proof c of ψ into a proof (p(b))(c) of σ. Recall that we had a proof a(b,c) of σ, so put (p(b))(c) = a(b,c), let q be given by q(c) = a(b,c). Then p is defined by p(b) = q(c). Clearly, the above contains the description of a construction that converts a into a proof p of $\varphi \to (\psi \to \sigma)$. (For those who know λ-conversion: $p = \lambda b.\lambda c.a(b,c)$, so $\lambda a.\lambda b.\lambda c.a(b,c)$ is the proof we are looking for).

3. $\neg\exists x\varphi(x) \to \forall x\neg\varphi(x)$.

We will now argue a bit more informal. Suppose we have a construction a that reduces a proof of $\exists x\varphi(x)$ to a proof of $\bot$. We want a construction p that produces for each $d \in D$ a proof of $\varphi(\bar{d}) \to \bot$, i.e. a construction that converts a proof of $\varphi(\bar{d})$ into a proof of $\bot$. So let b be a proof of $\varphi(\bar{d})$, then $\langle d,b \rangle$ is a proof of $\exists x\varphi(x)$, and a(d,b) is a proof of $\bot$. Hence p with (p(d))(b) = a(d,b) is a proof of $\forall x\neg\varphi(x)$. This provides us with a construction that converts a into p.

The reader may try to justify some statements for himself, but he should not worry if the details turn out to be too complicated. A convenient handling of these problems requires a bit more machinery than we have at hand (e.g. λ-notation). Note, by the way, that the whole procedure is not unproblematic since we assume a number of closure properties of the class of constructions.

Now that we have given a rough heuristics of the meaning of the logical connectives in intuitionistic logic, let us move on to a formalization. As it happens, the systems of natural deduction is almost right. The only rule that lacks constructive content is that of Reduction and Absurdum. As we have seen (p. 40), an application of RAA yields $\vdash \neg\neg\varphi \to \varphi$, but for $\neg\neg\varphi \to \varphi$ to hold informally we need a construction that transforms a proof of $\neg\neg\varphi$ into a proof of φ. Now a proves $\neg\neg\varphi$ if a transforms each proof b of $\neg\varphi$ into a proof of $\bot$, i.e. there cannot be a proof b of $\neg\varphi$. b itself should be a construction that transforms each proof c of φ into a proof of $\bot$. So we know that there cannot be a construction that turns a proof of φ into a proof of $\bot$, but that is a long way from the required proof! (cf. ex. 1)

5.2. INTUITIONISTIC PROPOSITIONAL AND PREDICATE LOGIC

We adopt all the rules of natural deduction for the connectives $\vee, \wedge, \to, \bot, \exists, \forall$, with the exception of the rule RAA. In order to cover both propositional and predicate logic in one sweep we allow in the alphabet (cf. 2.3, p. 61.) 0-ary predicate symbols, usually called proposition symbols.

Strictly speaking we deal with a derivability notion different from the one introduced earlier (cf. p. 38), since RAA is dropped, therefore we should use a distinct notation, e.g. $\vdash_i$. However, we will continue to use $\vdash$ when no confusion arises.

We can now adopt all results of the preceding parts that did not make use of RAA.

The following list may be helpful:

5.2.1. Lemma.

(1) $\vdash \varphi \wedge \psi \leftrightarrow \psi \wedge \varphi$ (p. 34)

(2) $\vdash \varphi \vee \psi \leftrightarrow \psi \vee \varphi$

(3) $\vdash (\varphi \wedge \psi) \wedge \sigma \leftrightarrow \varphi \wedge (\psi \wedge \sigma)$

(4) $\vdash (\varphi \vee \psi) \vee \sigma \leftrightarrow \varphi \vee (\psi \vee \sigma)$

(5) $\vdash \varphi \vee (\psi \wedge \sigma) \leftrightarrow (\varphi \vee \psi) \wedge (\varphi \vee \sigma)$

(6) $\vdash \varphi \wedge (\psi \vee \sigma) \leftrightarrow (\varphi \wedge \psi) \vee (\varphi \wedge \sigma)$ (p. 54)

(7) $\vdash \varphi \rightarrow \neg\neg\varphi$ (p. 34)

(8) $\vdash (\varphi \rightarrow (\psi \rightarrow \sigma)) \leftrightarrow (\varphi \wedge \psi \rightarrow \sigma)$ (p. 34)

(9) $\vdash \varphi \rightarrow (\psi \rightarrow \varphi)$ (p. 39)

(10) $\vdash \varphi \rightarrow (\neg\varphi \rightarrow \psi)$ (p. 39)

(11) $\vdash \neg(\varphi \vee \psi) \leftrightarrow \neg\varphi \wedge \neg\psi$

(12) $\vdash \neg\varphi \vee \neg\psi \rightarrow \neg(\varphi \wedge \psi)$

(13) $\vdash (\neg\varphi \vee \psi) \rightarrow (\varphi \rightarrow \psi)$

(14) $\vdash (\varphi \rightarrow \psi) \rightarrow (\neg\psi \rightarrow \neg\varphi)$ (p. 39)

(15) $\vdash (\varphi \rightarrow \psi) \rightarrow ((\psi \rightarrow \sigma) \rightarrow (\varphi \rightarrow \sigma))$ (p. 39)

(16) $\vdash \bot \leftrightarrow (\varphi \wedge \neg\varphi)$ (p. 39)

(17) $\vdash \exists x(\varphi(x) \vee \psi(x)) \leftrightarrow \exists x\varphi(x) \vee \exists x\psi(x)$

(18) $\vdash \forall x(\varphi(x) \wedge \psi(x)) \leftrightarrow \forall x\varphi(x) \wedge \forall x\psi(x)$

(19) $\vdash \neg\exists x\varphi(x) \leftrightarrow \forall x\neg\varphi(x)$

(20) $\vdash \exists x\neg\varphi(x) \rightarrow \neg\forall x\varphi(x)$

(21) $\vdash \forall x(\varphi \rightarrow \psi(x)) \leftrightarrow (\varphi \rightarrow \forall x\psi(x))$

(22) $\vdash \exists x(\varphi \rightarrow \psi(x)) \rightarrow (\varphi \rightarrow \exists x\psi(x))$

(23) $\vdash (\varphi \vee \forall x\psi(x)) \rightarrow \forall x(\varphi \vee \psi(x))$

(24) $\vdash (\varphi \wedge \exists x\psi(x)) \leftrightarrow \exists x(\varphi \wedge \psi(x))$

(25) $\vdash \exists x(\varphi(x) \rightarrow \psi) \rightarrow (\forall x\varphi(x) \rightarrow \psi)$

(26) $\vdash \forall x(\varphi(x) \rightarrow \psi) \leftrightarrow (\exists x\varphi(x) \rightarrow \psi)$

(Observe that (19) and (20) are special cases of (26) and (25)).

All of those theorems can be proved by means of straight forward application of the rules. Some well-known theorems are conspicuously absent, and in some cases there is only an implication one way; we will show later that the implication cannot, in general, be reversed.

From a constructive point of view RAA is used to derive strong conclusions from weak premises. E.g. in $\neg(\varphi \wedge \psi) \vdash \neg\varphi \vee \neg\varphi$ the premise is weak (something has no proof) and the conclusion is strong, it asks for an effective decision. One cannot expect to get such results in intuitionistic logic. Instead there is a collection of weak results, usually involving negations and double negations.

We will provide a short list.

5.2.2. Lemma.

(1) $\vdash \neg\varphi \leftrightarrow \neg\neg\neg\varphi$

(2) $\vdash (\varphi \wedge \neg\psi) \rightarrow \neg(\varphi \rightarrow \psi)$

(3) $\vdash (\varphi \rightarrow \psi) \rightarrow (\neg\neg\varphi \rightarrow \neg\neg\psi)$

(4) $\vdash \neg\neg(\varphi \rightarrow \psi) \leftrightarrow (\neg\neg\varphi \rightarrow \neg\neg\varphi)$

(5) $\vdash \neg\neg(\varphi \wedge \psi) \leftrightarrow (\neg\neg\varphi \wedge \neg\neg\psi)$

(6) $\vdash \neg\neg\forall x\, \varphi(x) \rightarrow \forall x \neg\neg\varphi(x)$

In order to abbreviate derivations we will use the notation $\frac{\Gamma}{\overline{\psi}}$ in a derivation when there is a derivation for $\Gamma \vdash \psi$ (Γ has 0,1 or 2 elements).

Proof. (1) $\neg\varphi \rightarrow \neg\neg\neg\psi$ follows from lemma 5.2.1.(7)
For the converse we again use 5.2.1.(7)

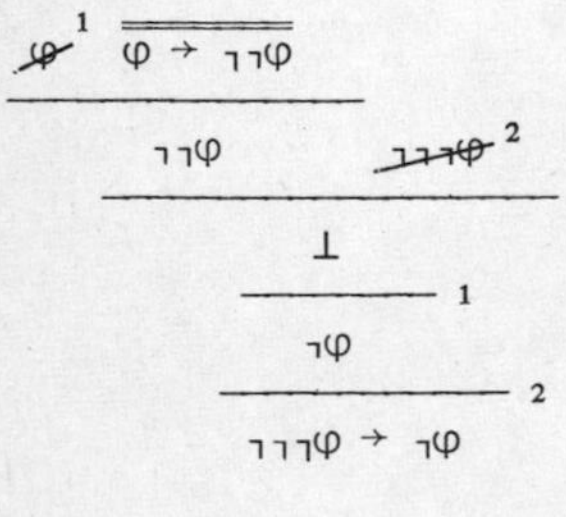

(2)

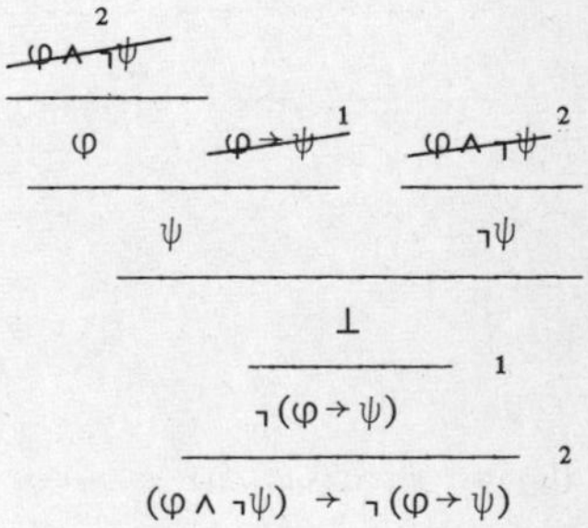

(3)

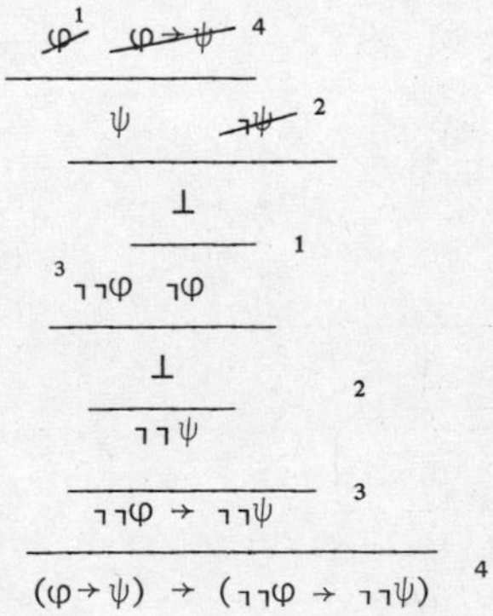

Prove (3) also by using (14) and (15) from 5.2.1.

(4) Apply the intuitionistic half of the contra position (lemma 5.2.1(14)) to (2):

$$\dfrac{\dfrac{\dfrac{\dfrac{\dfrac{\dfrac{\dfrac{[\neg\neg(\varphi\to\psi)]^4}{\neg(\varphi\wedge\neg\psi)} \qquad \dfrac{[\varphi]^1 \quad [\neg\psi]^2}{\varphi\wedge\neg\psi}}{\bot}}{\neg\varphi}\,1 \qquad [\neg\neg\varphi]^3}{\bot}}{\neg\neg\psi}\,2}{\neg\neg\varphi\to\neg\neg\psi}\,3}{\neg\neg(\varphi\to\psi)\to(\neg\neg\varphi\to\neg\neg\psi)}\,2$$

For the converse we apply some facts from 5.2.1.

$$D \left\{ \begin{array}{l} \dfrac{\dfrac{[\neg(\varphi\to\psi)]^1}{\neg(\neg\varphi\vee\psi)}\ \text{5.2.1.(13) and (14)}}{\neg\neg\varphi\wedge\neg\psi}\ \text{5.2.1.(11)} \end{array} \right.$$

$$\dfrac{\dfrac{\dfrac{\dfrac{\neg\neg\varphi \qquad [\neg\neg\varphi\to\neg\neg\psi]^2}{\neg\neg\psi} \qquad \dfrac{D^1}{\neg\psi}}{\bot}}{\neg\neg(\varphi\to\psi)}\,1}{(\neg\neg\varphi\to\neg\neg\psi)\to\neg\neg(\varphi\to\psi)}\,2$$

(5) $\to$: Apply (3) to $\varphi\wedge\varphi\to\varphi$ and $\varphi\wedge\psi\to\psi$

$\leftarrow$:

$$\dfrac{\dfrac{\dfrac{\dfrac{[\neg\neg\varphi\wedge\neg\neg\psi]^4}{\neg\neg\psi} \qquad \dfrac{\dfrac{\dfrac{\dfrac{[\neg(\varphi\wedge\psi)]^3 \qquad \dfrac{[\varphi]^1 \quad [\psi]^2}{\varphi\wedge\psi}}{\bot}}{\neg\varphi}\,1 \qquad \dfrac{[\neg\neg\varphi\wedge\neg\neg\psi]^4}{\neg\neg\varphi}}{\bot}}{\neg\psi}\,2}{\bot}}{\neg\neg(\varphi\wedge\psi)}\,3}{(\neg\neg\varphi\wedge\neg\neg\psi)\to\neg\neg(\varphi\wedge\psi)}\,4$$

(6) $\vdash \exists x \neg\varphi(x) \rightarrow \neg\forall x\varphi(x)$, 5.2.1.(20)

so $\vdash \neg\neg\forall x\varphi(x) \rightarrow \neg\exists x\neg\varphi(x)$, 5.2.1.(14)

hence $\vdash \neg\neg\forall x\varphi(x) \rightarrow \forall x\neg\neg\varphi(x)$. 5.2.1.(19)

Most of the straightforward meta-theorems of propositional and predicate logic carry over to intuitionistic logic. The following theorems can be proved by a tedious but routine induction.

5.2.3. Substitution theorem for derivations.

If D is a derivation and P a propositional atom, then $D[\varphi/P]$ is a derivation if the free variables of φ do not occur bound in D.

5.2.4. Substitution theorem for derivability.

If $\Gamma \vdash \sigma$ and P is a propositional atom, then $\Gamma[\varphi/P] \vdash \sigma[\varphi/P]$, where the free variables of φ do not occur bound in the derivation of σ from Γ.

5.2.5. Substitution theorem for equivalence.

$\Gamma \vdash \varphi_1 \leftrightarrow \varphi_2 \Rightarrow \Gamma \vdash \psi[\varphi_1/P] \leftrightarrow \psi[\varphi_2/P]$, where P is an atomic proposition, the free variables of φ_1 and φ_2 do not occur bound in Γ or ψ and the bound variables of ψ do not occur free in Γ.

The proofs of the above theorems are left to the reader. Theorems of this kind are always suffering from unaesthetic variable-conditions. In practical applications one always renames bound variablesm or considers only closed hypoth´-eses, so that there is not much to worry. For precise formulations cf. Kleene, Introd. to Metamathematics (which is, however, not based on natural deduction).

The reader will have observed from the heuristics that $\vee$ and $\exists$ carry most of the burden of constructiveness. We will demonstrate this once more in an informal argument.

There is an effective procedure to compute the decimal expansion of π (3, 1415927....). Let us consider the statement φ_n := in the decimal expansion of π there is a sequence of n consecutive sevens.
Clearly $\varphi_{100} \rightarrow \varphi_{99}$ holds, but there is no evidence whatsoever for $\neg\varphi_{100} \vee \varphi_{99}$.

The fact that $\wedge, \rightarrow, \forall, \perp$ do not ask for the kind of decisions that $\vee$ and $\exists$ require, is more or less confirmed by the following

5.2.6. Lemma. If φ does not contain $\vee$ or $\exists$ and all atoms in φ are negated, then $\vdash \varphi \leftrightarrow \neg\neg\varphi$.

Proof. Induction on φ.
We leave the proof to the reader. (Hint: apply 5.2.2.) □

By definition the intuitionistic predicate (propositional) logic is a subsystem of the corresponding classical systems. Gödel and Gentzen have shown, however, that by interpreting the classical disjunction and existence quantifier in a weak sense, we can embed classical logic into intuitionistic logic. For this purpose we introduce a suitable translation:

5.2.7. Definition. The mapping $^{\circ}$: FORM → FORM is defined by

(*i*) $\bot^{\circ} := \bot$ and
$\varphi^{\circ} := \neg\neg\varphi$ for atomic φ distinct from $\bot$.

(*ii*) $(\varphi \wedge \psi)^{\circ} := \varphi^{\circ} \wedge \psi^{\circ}$

(*iii*) $(\varphi \vee \psi)^{\circ} := \neg(\neg\varphi^{\circ} \wedge \neg\psi^{\circ})$

(*iv*) $(\varphi \to \psi)^{\circ} := \varphi^{\circ} \to \psi^{\circ}$

(*v*) $(\forall x\, \varphi(x))^{\circ} := \forall x\, \varphi^{\circ}(x)$

(*vi*) $(\exists x\, \varphi(x))^{\circ} := \neg\forall x \neg\varphi^{\circ}(x)$

The mapping $^{\circ}$ is called the *Gödel translation*. We define $\Gamma^{\circ} = \{\varphi^{\circ} \mid \varphi \in \Gamma\}$. The relation between classical derivability ($\vdash_c$) and intuitionistic derivability ($\vdash_i$) is given by

5.2.8. Theorem. $\Gamma \vdash_c \varphi \Leftrightarrow \Gamma^{\circ} \vdash_i \varphi^{\circ}$.

Proof. It follows from the preceding chapters that $\vdash_c \varphi \leftrightarrow \varphi^{\circ}$, therefore ⇐ is an immediate consequence of $\Gamma \vdash_i \varphi \Rightarrow \Gamma \vdash_c \varphi$.
For the converse implication, we use induction on the derivation D of φ from Γ.

(1) $\varphi \in \Gamma$, then also $\varphi^{\circ} \in \Gamma^{\circ}$ and hence $\Gamma^{\circ} \vdash_i \varphi^{\circ}$.

(2) the last rule of D is a propositional introduction or elimination rule.
We consider two cases.

→I
$$\dfrac{\begin{array}{c}[\varphi]\\ \mathcal{D}\\ \psi\end{array}}{\varphi \to \psi}$$

Induction hypothesis $\Gamma^{\circ}, \varphi^{\circ} \vdash_i \psi^{\circ}$.
By →I $\Gamma^{\circ} \vdash_i \varphi^{\circ} \to \psi^{\circ}$, and so by definition $\Gamma^{\circ} \vdash_i (\varphi \to \psi)^{\circ}$.

∨∃
$$\dfrac{\begin{array}{c}\\ \mathcal{D}\\ \varphi \vee \psi\end{array} \quad \begin{array}{c}[\varphi]\\ \mathcal{D}_1\\ \sigma\end{array} \quad \begin{array}{c}[\psi]\\ \mathcal{D}_2\\ \sigma\end{array}}{\sigma}$$

Induction hypothesis: $\Gamma^{\circ} \vdash_i (\varphi \vee \psi)^{\circ}$, $\Gamma^{\circ}, \varphi^{\circ} \vdash_i \sigma^{\circ}$, $\Gamma^{\circ}, \psi^{\circ} \vdash_i \sigma^{\circ}$ (where Γ contains all uncancelled hypotheses involved).

$\Gamma^{\circ} \vdash_i \neg(\neg\varphi^{\circ} \wedge \neg\psi^{\circ})$, $\Gamma^{\circ} \vdash_i \varphi^{\circ} \to \sigma^{\circ}$, $\Gamma^{\circ} \vdash_i \psi^{\circ} \to \sigma^{\circ}$.

The result follows from the derivation below

$$\dfrac{\dfrac{\neg(\neg\varphi^\circ\wedge\neg\psi^\circ) \qquad \dfrac{\dfrac{\dfrac{\dfrac{\overset{1}{\varphi^\circ}\quad \varphi^\circ\to\sigma^\circ}{\sigma^\circ}\qquad \overset{3}{\neg\sigma^\circ}}{\bot}}{\neg\varphi^\circ}\,1 \qquad \dfrac{\dfrac{\dfrac{\overset{2}{\psi^\circ}\quad \psi^\circ\to\sigma^\circ}{\sigma^\circ}\qquad \overset{3}{\neg\sigma^\circ}}{\bot}}{\neg\psi^\circ}\,2}{\neg\varphi^\circ\wedge\neg\psi^\circ}}{\dfrac{\bot}{\neg\neg\sigma^\circ}\,3}}{}$$

$$\dfrac{\neg\neg\sigma^\circ}{\sigma^\circ}\ \text{lemma 5.2.6.}$$

The remaining rules are left to the reader.

(3) the last rule of D is the falsum rule. This case is obvious.

(4) the last rule of D is a quantifier introduction or elimination rule. Let us consider two cases.

$\forall I$: $\dfrac{\begin{matrix}D\\ \varphi(x)\end{matrix}}{\forall x\,\varphi(x)}$ Induction hypothesis: $\Gamma^\circ \vdash_i \varphi(x)^\circ$.
By $\forall I$ $\Gamma^\circ \vdash_i \forall x\,\varphi(x)^\circ$, so $\Gamma^\circ \vdash_i (\forall x\,\varphi(x))^\circ$.

$\exists E$: $\dfrac{\begin{matrix}D\\ \exists x\,\varphi(x)\end{matrix}\qquad \begin{matrix}[\varphi(x)]\\ D_1\\ \sigma\end{matrix}}{\sigma}$ Induction hypothesis: $\Gamma^\circ \vdash_i (\exists x\,\varphi(x))^\circ$,
$\Gamma^\circ, \varphi(x)^\circ \vdash_i \sigma^\circ$.

$\Gamma^\circ \vdash_i \neg\forall x\neg\varphi(x)^\circ$, $\Gamma^\circ \vdash_i \forall x\ \varphi(x)^\circ \to \sigma^\circ$

$$\dfrac{\neg\forall x\neg\varphi(x)^\circ \qquad \dfrac{\dfrac{\dfrac{\dfrac{\overset{1}{\varphi(x)^\circ}\qquad \dfrac{\forall x\,(\varphi(x)^\circ\to\sigma^\circ)}{\varphi(x)^\circ\to\sigma^\circ}}{\sigma^\circ}\qquad \overset{2}{\neg\sigma^\circ}}{\bot}\,1}{\neg\varphi(x)^\circ}}{\forall x\neg\varphi(x)^\circ}}{\dfrac{\bot}{\neg\neg\sigma^\circ}\,2}$$

$$\dfrac{\neg\neg\sigma^\circ}{\sigma^\circ}\ \text{lemma 2.5.6.}$$

We now get $\Gamma^\circ \vdash_i \sigma^\circ$.

(5) the last rule of D is RAA.

$$\dfrac{\begin{array}{c}\not{\neg\varphi}\\ \mathcal{D}\\ \bot\end{array}}{\varphi}$$

Induction hypothesis $\Gamma^\circ, (\neg\varphi)^\circ \vdash_i \bot$, so $\Gamma^\circ \vdash_i \neg\neg\varphi^\circ$, and hence by lemma 2.5.6. $\Gamma^\circ \vdash_i \varphi^\circ$. □

Let us call formulas in which all atoms occur negated, and which contain only the connectives $\wedge, \to, \forall, \bot$, *negative*.
The special role of $\vee$ and $\exists$ is underlined by

5.2.9. Corollary. Classical predicate (propositional) logic is conservative over intuitionistic predicate (propositional) logic with respect to negative formulae, i.e. $\vdash_c \varphi \Leftrightarrow \vdash_i \varphi$ for negative φ.

Proof. φ°, for negative φ, is obtained by replacing each atom p by $\neg\neg p$. Since all atoms occur negated we have $\vdash_i \varphi^\circ \leftrightarrow \varphi$ (apply 5.2.2.(1) and 5.2.5.). The result now follows from 5.2.8. □

In some particular theories (e.g. arithmetic) the atoms are *decidable*, i.e. $T \vdash \varphi \vee \neg\varphi$ for atomic φ. For such theories one may simplify the Gödel translation by putting $\varphi^\circ := \varphi$ for atomic φ.

Observe that corollary 5.2.9. tells us that intuitionistic logic is consistent iff classical logic is so (a not very surprising result!).

For propositional logic we have a somewhat stronger result than 5.2.8.

5.2.10. Glivenko's theorem. $\vdash_c \varphi \Leftrightarrow \vdash_i \neg\neg\varphi$.

Proof. Show by induction on φ that $\vdash_i \varphi^\circ \leftrightarrow \neg\neg\varphi$ (use 5.2.2.), and apply 5.2.8. □

5.3. KRIPKE'S SEMANTICS

There are a number of (more or less formalized) semantics for intuitionistic logic that allow for a completeness theorem. We will concentrate here on the semantics introduced by Kripke since it is convenient for applications and it is fairly simple.

Heuristic motivation. Think of an idealized mathematician (in this context traditionally called the *creative subject*) who extends both his knowledge and his universe of objects in the course of time. At each moment k he has a stock Σ_k of sentences, which he by some means has established, and a stock A_k of objects which he has constructed (or created). Since at every moment k the idealized mathematician has various choices for his future activities (he may even stop alltogether), the stages of his activity must be thought of as being *partially ordered*, and not necessarily linearly ordered. How will the idealized mathematician interprete the logical connectives ? Evidently the interpretation of a composite statement must depend on the interpretation of its parts, e.g. the idealized mathematician has established φ or (and) ψ at stage k if he has established φ at stage k or (and) ψ at stage k. The implication is more cumbersome, since $\varphi \rightarrow \psi$ may be known at stage k without φ or ψ being known. Clearly, the idealized mathematician knows $\varphi \rightarrow \psi$ at stage k if he knows that if at any future stage (including k) φ is established, also ψ is established. Similarly $\forall x \varphi(x)$ is established at stage k if at any future stage (including k) for all objects a that exist at that stage $\varphi(\bar{a})$ is established. Evidently we must in case of the universal quantifier take the future into account since *for all elements* means more than just "for all elements that we have constructed so far"! Existence, on the other hand, is not relegated to the future. The idealized mathematician knows at stage k that $\exists x \varphi(x)$ if he has constructed an object a such that at stage k he has established $\varphi(\bar{a})$. Of course, there are many observations that could be made, for example that it is reasonable to add "in principle" to a number of clauses. This takes care of large numbers, choice sequences etc. Think of $\forall xy \exists z (z = x^y)$, does the idealized mathematician really construct 10^{10} as a succession of units ? For this and similar questions the reader is referred to the literature.

We will now formalize the above sketched semantics.
It is for a first introduction convenient to consider a language without functions symbols. Later it will be simple to extend the language.

We consider models for some language L.

5.3.1. Definition. A *Kripke model* is a quadruple $K = \langle P, \Sigma, C, D \rangle$, where P is a (non-empty) partially ordered set, C a function defined on the constants of L, D a set valued function on P, Σ a function on P such that

$C(c) \in D(k)$ for all k

$D(k) \neq \emptyset$ for all $k \in P$,

$\Sigma(k) \subseteq At_k$ for all $k \in P$,

where At_k is the set of all atomic sentences of L with constants for the elements of D(k).

(i) $k \leqslant l \Rightarrow D(k) \subseteq D(l)$.

(ii) $\perp \notin \Sigma(k)$, for all k.

(iii) $k \leqslant l \Rightarrow \Sigma(k) \subseteq \Sigma(l)$.

D(k) is called the *domain* of *K* at k, the elements of P are called *nodes* of *K*. Instead of "φ has auxilliary constants for elements of D(k)" we say for short "φ has parameter in D(k)".

Σ assigns to each node the 'basic facts' that hold at k, the conditions (i), (ii), (iii) merely state that the collection of available objects does not decrease in time, that a falsity is never established and that a basic fact that once has been established remains true in later stages. The constants are interpreted by the same elements in all domains (they are *rigid designators*).

Note that D and Σ together determine at each node k a classical structure $\mathfrak{A}(k)$ (in the sense of 2.1.1.). The universe of $\mathfrak{A}(k)$ is D(k) and the relations of $\mathfrak{A}(k)$ are given by $\Sigma(k)$ as the positive diagram: $\langle \vec{a} \rangle \in R^{\mathfrak{A}(k)}$ iff $R(\vec{a}) \in \Sigma(k)$. The conditions (i) and (iii) above tell us that the universes are increasing:

$$k \leqslant l \Rightarrow |\mathfrak{A}(k)| \subseteq |\mathfrak{A}(l)|$$

and that the relations are increasing:

$$k \leqslant l \Rightarrow R^{\mathfrak{A}(k)} \subseteq R^{\mathfrak{A}(l)}.$$

Furthermore $c^{\mathfrak{A}(k)} = c^{\mathfrak{A}(l)}$ for all k and l.

In $\Sigma(k)$ there are also propositions, something we did not allow in classical predicate logic. Here it is convenient for treating propositional and predicate logic simultaneously.

The function Σ tells us which atoms are "true" in k. We now extend Σ to all sentences.

5.3.2. Lemma. Σ has a unique extension to a function on P such that $\Sigma(k) \subseteq Sent_k$, the set of all sentences with parameters in D(k), satisfying

(i) $\varphi \vee \psi \in \Sigma(k) \Leftrightarrow \varphi \in \Sigma(k)$ or $\psi \in \Sigma(k)$

(ii) $\varphi \wedge \psi \in \Sigma(k) \Leftrightarrow \varphi \in \Sigma(k)$ and $\psi \in \Sigma(k)$

(iii) $\varphi \rightarrow \psi \in \Sigma(k) \Leftrightarrow$ for all $l \geqslant k$ $(\varphi \in \Sigma(l) \Rightarrow \psi \in \Sigma(l))$

(vi) $\exists x \varphi(x) \in \Sigma(k) \Leftrightarrow$ there is an $a \in D(k)$ such that $\varphi(\bar{a}) \in \Sigma(k)$

(v) $\forall x \varphi(x) \in \Sigma(k) \Leftrightarrow$ for all $l \geqslant k$ and for all $a \in D(l)$ $\varphi(\bar{a}) \in \Sigma(l)$.

Proof. Immediate, we clearly define $\varphi \in \Sigma(k)$ for all $k \in P$ simultaneously by induction on φ. □

Notation: we write $k \Vdash \varphi$ for $\varphi \in \Sigma(k)$, pronounce '*k forces* φ'.

Exercise for the reader: reformulate (i) - (v) above in terms of forcing.

5.3.3. <u>Corollary</u>. $k \Vdash \neg\varphi \Leftrightarrow$ for all $\ell \geqslant k$ $\ell \nVdash \varphi$.

Proof. $k \Vdash \neg\varphi \Leftrightarrow k \Vdash \varphi \rightarrow \perp \Leftrightarrow$ for all $\ell \geqslant k$ $(\ell \Vdash \varphi \Rightarrow \ell \Vdash \perp) \Leftrightarrow$ for all $\ell \geqslant k$ $\ell \nVdash \varphi$. □

The monotonicity of Σ (from 5.3.1) is preserved:

5.3.4. <u>Lemma</u>. $k \leqslant \ell$, $k \Vdash \varphi \Rightarrow \ell \Vdash \varphi$ (monotonicity of $\Vdash$).

Proof. induction on φ.
For atomic φ the lemma holds by definition 5.3.1.

$\varphi = \varphi_1 \wedge \varphi_2$. Let $k \Vdash \varphi_1 \wedge \varphi_2$ and $k \leqslant \ell$, then $k \Vdash \varphi_1 \wedge \varphi_2 \Leftrightarrow k \Vdash \varphi_1$ and $k \Vdash \varphi_2 \Rightarrow$ (ind. hyp.) $\ell \Vdash \varphi_1$ and $\ell \Vdash \varphi_2 \Leftrightarrow \ell \Vdash \varphi_1 \wedge \varphi_2$.
$\varphi = \varphi_1 \vee \varphi_2$. Mimic the conjunction.
$\varphi = \varphi_1 \rightarrow \varphi_2$. Let $k \Vdash \varphi_1 \rightarrow \varphi_2$, $\ell \geqslant k$. Suppose $p \geqslant \ell$ and $p \Vdash \varphi_1$ then, since $p \geqslant k$, $p \Vdash \varphi_2$. Hence $\ell \Vdash \varphi_1 \rightarrow \varphi_2$.
$\varphi = \exists x \varphi_1(x)$. Immediate.
$\varphi = \forall x \varphi_1(x)$. Let $k \Vdash \forall x \varphi_1(x)$ and $\ell \geqslant k$. Suppose $p \geqslant \ell$ and $a \in D(p)$, then, since $p \geqslant k$, $p \Vdash \varphi_1(\bar{a})$. Hence $\ell \Vdash \forall x \varphi_1(x)$. □

5.3.5. <u>Lemma</u>. $k \vdash \neg\neg\varphi \Leftrightarrow$ for all $\ell \geqslant k$ there is a $p \geqslant \ell$ such that $p \Vdash \varphi$.

Proof: $k \Vdash \neg\neg\varphi \Leftrightarrow$ for all $\ell \geqslant k$ $\ell \nVdash \neg\varphi \Leftrightarrow$
for all $\ell \geqslant k$ not (for all $p \geqslant \ell$ $p \nVdash \varphi$) $\Leftrightarrow$
for all $\ell \geqslant k$ there is a $p \geqslant \ell$ such that $p \Vdash \varphi$. □

We will now present some examples. It suffices to indicate which atoms are forced at each node. We will simplify the presentation by drawing the partially ordered set and indicate the atoms forced at each node. For propositional logic no domain function is required (equivalently, a constant one, say $D(k) = \{0\}$), so we simplify the presentation accordingly.

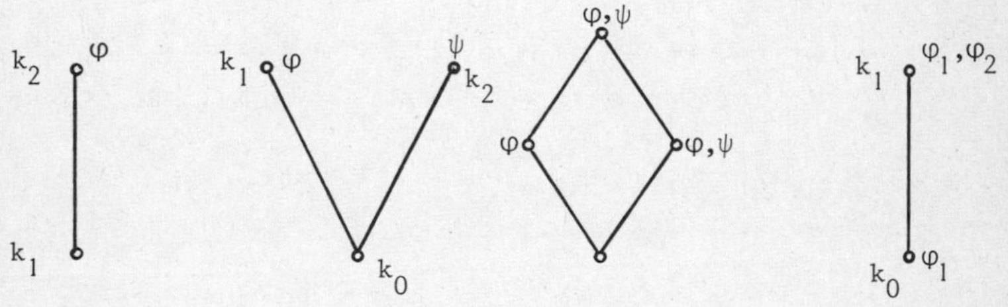

a b c d

a. In the bottom node no atoms are known, in the second one only φ, to be precise $k_0 \nVdash \varphi$, $k_1 \Vdash \varphi$. By 5.3.5 $k_0 \Vdash \neg\neg\varphi$, so $k_0 \nVdash \neg\neg\varphi \rightarrow \varphi$. Note, however, that $k_0 \nVdash \neg\varphi$, since $k_1 \Vdash \varphi$. So $k_0 \nVdash \varphi \vee \neg\varphi$.

b. $k_i \nVdash \varphi \wedge \psi$ $(i = 0,1,2)$, so $k_0 \Vdash \neg(\varphi \wedge \psi)$. However, $k_0 \Vdash \neg\varphi \vee \neg\psi \Leftrightarrow k_0 \Vdash \neg\varphi$ or $k_0 \Vdash \neg\psi$. The first is false, since $k_1 \Vdash \varphi$, and the latter is false, since $k_2 \Vdash \psi$. Hence $k_0 \nVdash \neg\varphi \vee \neg\psi$, and so $k_0 \nVdash \neg(\varphi \wedge \psi) \rightarrow \neg\varphi \vee \neg\psi$.

c. the bottom node forces $\psi \rightarrow \varphi$, but it does not force $\neg\psi \vee \varphi$ (Why ?). So it does not force $(\varphi \rightarrow \psi) \rightarrow (\neg\varphi \vee \psi)$.

d. In the bottom node the following implications are forced: $\varphi_2 \rightarrow \varphi_1, \varphi_3 \rightarrow \varphi_2$, $\varphi_3 \rightarrow \varphi_1$, but none of the converse implications is forced, hence $k_0 \nVdash (\varphi_1 \leftrightarrow \varphi_2) \vee (\varphi_2 \leftrightarrow \varphi_3) \vee (\varphi_3 \leftrightarrow \varphi_1)$.

We will analyse this example a bit further. Consider a Kripke model with two nodes as in d, with some assignment Σ of atoms. We will show that for four arbitrary propositions $\sigma_1,\sigma_2,\sigma_3,\sigma_4$ $\quad k_0 \Vdash \bigvee\limits_{1 \leqslant i < j \leqslant 4} \sigma_i \leftrightarrow \sigma_j$, i.e. from any four propositions at least two are equivalent. There are a number of cases. (1) At least two of σ_1, $\sigma_2,\sigma_3,\sigma_4$ are forced in k_0. Then we are done. (2) Just one σ_i is forced in k_0. Then of the remaining propositions, either two are forced in k_1, or two of them are not forced in k_1. In both cases there are two $\sigma_j, \sigma_{j'}$, such that $k_0 \Vdash \sigma_j \leftrightarrow \sigma_{j'}$. (3) No σ_i is forced in k_0. Then we may repeat the argument under (2).

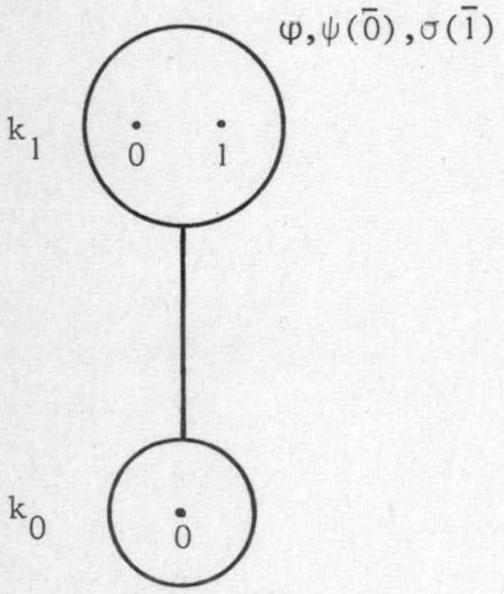

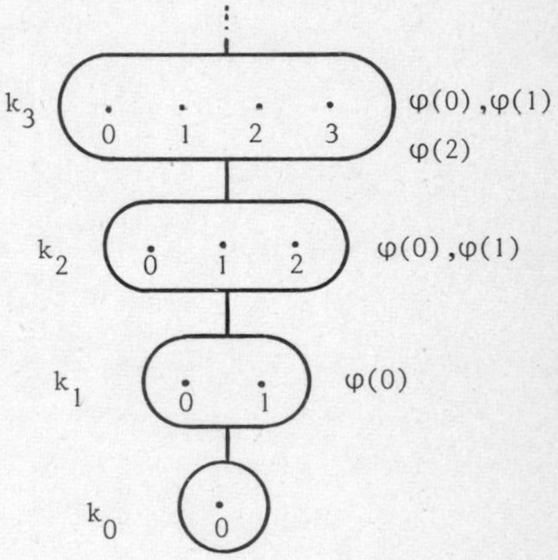

e. (i) $k_0 \Vdash \varphi \rightarrow \exists x\, \sigma(x)$, for the only node that forces φ is k_1, and indeed $k_1 \Vdash \sigma(\bar{1})$, so $k_1 \Vdash \exists x\, \sigma(x)$. Now suppose $k_0 \Vdash \exists x(\varphi \rightarrow \sigma(x))$, then -since $D(k_0) = \{0\}$- $k_0 \Vdash \varphi \rightarrow \sigma(\bar{0})$. But $k_1 \Vdash \varphi$ and $k_1 \nVdash \sigma(\bar{0})$. Contradiction. Hence $k_0 \nVdash (\varphi \rightarrow \exists x\, \sigma(x)) \rightarrow \exists x(\varphi \rightarrow \sigma(x))$.

<u>Remark</u>: $(\varphi \rightarrow \exists x\, \sigma(x)) \rightarrow \exists x(\varphi \rightarrow \sigma(x))$ is called the *independence of premise principle*. It is not surprising that it fails in some Kripke models, for $\varphi \rightarrow \exists x\, \sigma(x)$ tells us that the required element a for $\sigma(\bar{a})$ may depend on the proof of φ (in our

heuristic interpretation); while in $\exists x(\varphi \to \sigma(x))$, the element a must be found independently of φ. So the right hand side is stronger.

(ii) $k_0 \Vdash \neg\forall x\,\psi(x) \Leftrightarrow k_i \nVdash \forall x\,\psi(x) \quad (i = 0,1)$.
$k_0 \nVdash \psi(\bar{0})$ and $k_1 \nVdash \psi(\bar{1})$, so we have shown $k_0 \Vdash \neg\forall x\,\psi(x)$.
$k_0 \Vdash \exists x \neg\psi(x) \Leftrightarrow k_0 \Vdash \neg\psi(\bar{0})$. However, $k_1 \Vdash \psi(\bar{0})$, so $k_0 \nVdash \exists x\neg\psi(x)$.
Hence $k_0 \nVdash \neg\forall x\,\psi(x) \to \exists x\neg\psi(x)$.

(iii) A similar argument shows
$k_0 \nVdash (\forall x\,\psi(x) \to \tau) \to \exists x(\psi(x) \to \tau)$, where τ is not forced in k_0 or k_1.

f. $D(k_i) = \{0,\dots,i\}$, $\Sigma(k_i) = \{\varphi(0),\dots,\varphi(i-1)\}$
$k_0 \Vdash \forall x\neg\neg\varphi(x) \Leftrightarrow$ for all i $k_i \Vdash \neg\neg\varphi(j)$, $j \leq i$.
The latter is true since for all $p > i$ $k_p \Vdash \varphi(j)$, $j \leq i$.
Now $k_0 \Vdash \neg\neg\forall x\,\varphi(x) \Leftrightarrow$ for all i there is a $j \geq i$ such that $k_j \Vdash \forall x\,\varphi(x)$.
But no k_j forces $\forall x\,\varphi(x)$. So $k_0 \nVdash \forall x\neg\neg\varphi(x) \to \neg\neg\forall x\,\varphi(x)$.

Remark. We have seen that $\neg\neg\forall x\,\varphi(x) \to \forall x\neg\neg\varphi(x)$ is derivable -and the reader may check that it holds in all Kripke models (or he may wait for the soundness theorem)- the converse fails, however, in some models. The schema $\forall x\neg\neg\varphi(x) \to \neg\neg\forall x\,\varphi(x)$ is called the *double negation shift* (DNS).

The next thing to do is to show that Kripke semantics is sound for intuitionistic logic.

We define a few more notions for sentences:

(i) $K \Vdash \varphi$ if $k \Vdash \varphi$ for all $k \in P$.

(ii) $\Vdash \varphi$ if $K \Vdash \varphi$ for all K.

For formulas containing free variables we have to be more careful. Let φ contain free variables, then we say that $k \Vdash \varphi$ iff $k \Vdash Cl(\varphi)$ (the universal closure). For a set Γ and a formula φ with free variables $x_{i_0}, x_{i_1}, x_{i_2}, \dots$ (which we will denote by $\vec{x}$), we define $\Gamma \Vdash \varphi$ by: for all K and $k \in P$, for all $\vec{a} \in D(k)$, $[k \Vdash \psi(\vec{a})$ for all $\psi \in \Gamma \Rightarrow k \Vdash \varphi(\vec{a})]$. ($\vec{a} \in D(k)$ is a convenient abuse of language).

Before we proceed we introduce an extra abuse of language which will prove extremely useful: we will freely use quantifiers in our metalanguage. It will have struck the reader that the clauses in the definition of the Kripke semantics abound with expressions like "for all $\ell \geq k$", for all $a \in D(k)$". It saves quite a bit of writing to use "$\forall \ell \geq k$", "$\forall a \in D(k)$" instead, and it increases systematic readability to boot. By now the reader is well used to the routine phrases of our semantics, so he will have no difficulty to avoid a confusion of quantifiers in the meta language and the object language.

By way of example we will reformulate the preceding definition:
$\Gamma \Vdash \varphi := (\forall K)(\forall k \in P)(\forall \vec{a} \in D(k))[\forall \psi \in \Gamma(k \Vdash \psi(\vec{a})) \Rightarrow k \Vdash \varphi(\vec{a})]$.

There is a useful reformulation of this "semantic consequence" notion

5.3.6. Lemma. Let Γ be finite, then $\Gamma \Vdash \varphi \Longleftrightarrow \Vdash Cl(\bigwedge(\Gamma \to \varphi))$ (where $Cl(X)$ is the universal closure of X).

Proof. Left to the reader. □

5.3.7. Soundness Theorem. $\Gamma \vdash \varphi \Rightarrow \Gamma \Vdash \varphi$.

Proof. Use induction on the derivation D of φ from Γ. We will abbreviate "$k \Vdash \psi(\bar{a})$ for all $\psi \in \Gamma$" by "$k \Vdash \Gamma(\vec{a})$". The model K is fixed in the proof.

(1) D consists of just φ, then obviously $k \Vdash \Gamma(\vec{a}) \Rightarrow k \Vdash \varphi(\vec{a})$ for all k and $\vec{a} \in D(k)$.

(2) D ends with an application of a derivation rule.

($\wedge$I) Induction hypothesis: $\forall k \quad \forall \vec{a} \in D(k)\ (k \Vdash \Gamma(\vec{a}) \Rightarrow k \Vdash \varphi_j(\vec{a}))$, for $i = 1,2$. Now choose a $k \in P$ and $\vec{a} \in D(k)$ such that $k \Vdash \Gamma(\vec{a})$, then $k \Vdash \varphi_1(\vec{a})$ and $k \Vdash \varphi_2(\vec{a})$, so $k \Vdash (\varphi_1 \wedge \varphi_2)(\vec{a})$.

Note that the choice of $\vec{a}$ did not really play a role in this proof. To simplify the presentation we will suppress reference to $\vec{a}$, when it does not play a role.

($\wedge$E) Immediate.

($\vee$I) Immediate.

($\vee$E) Induction hypothesis: $\forall k(k \Vdash \Gamma \Rightarrow k \Vdash \varphi \vee \psi)$, $\forall k(k \Vdash \Gamma, \varphi \Rightarrow k \Vdash \sigma)$, $\forall k(k \Vdash \Gamma, \varphi \Rightarrow k \Vdash \sigma)$. Now let $k \Vdash \Gamma$, then by i.h. $k \Vdash \varphi \vee \psi$, so $k \Vdash \varphi$ or $k \Vdash \psi$. In the first case $k \Vdash \Gamma, \varphi$, so $k \Vdash \sigma$. In the second case $k \Vdash \Gamma, \psi$, so $k \Vdash \sigma$. In both cases $k \Vdash \sigma$, so we are done.

($\to$I) Induction hypothesis: $(\forall k)(\forall \vec{a} \in D(k))(k \Vdash \Gamma(\vec{a}), \varphi(\vec{a}) \Rightarrow k \Vdash \psi(\vec{a}))$. Now let $k \Vdash \Gamma(\vec{a})$ for some $\vec{a} \in D(k)$. We want to show $k \Vdash (\varphi \to \psi)(\vec{a})$, so let $\ell \geqslant k$ and $\ell \Vdash \varphi(\vec{a})$. By monotonicity $\ell \Vdash \Gamma(\vec{a})$, and $\vec{a} \in D(\ell)$, so the ind. hyp. tells us that $\ell \Vdash \psi(\vec{a})$. Hence $\forall \ell \geqslant k(\ell \Vdash \varphi(\vec{a}) \Rightarrow \ell \Vdash \psi(\vec{a}))$, so $k \Vdash (\varphi \to \psi)(\vec{a})$.

($\to$E) Immediate.

($\perp$) Induction hypothesis $\forall k(k \Vdash \Gamma \Rightarrow k \Vdash \perp)$. Since, evidently, no k can force Γ, $\forall k(k \Vdash \Gamma \Rightarrow k \Vdash \varphi)$ is correct.

($\forall$I) The free variables in Γ are $\vec{x}$, and z does not occur among the sequence $\vec{x}$. Induction hypothesis: $(\forall k)(\forall \vec{a}, b \in D(k))(k \Vdash \Gamma(\vec{a}) \Rightarrow k \Vdash \varphi(\vec{a}, b))$. Now let $k \Vdash \Gamma(\vec{a})$ for some $\vec{a} \in D(k)$, we must show $k \Vdash \forall z\, \varphi(\vec{a}, z)$. So let $\ell \geqslant k$ and $b \in D(\ell)$. By monotonicity $\ell \Vdash \Gamma(\vec{a})$ and $\vec{a} \in D(\ell)$, so by the ind. hyp. $\ell \Vdash \varphi(\vec{a}, b)$. This shows $(\forall \ell \geqslant k)(\forall b \in D(\ell))(\ell \Vdash \varphi(\vec{a}, b))$, and hence $k \Vdash \forall z\, \varphi(\vec{a}, z)$.

($\forall\exists$) Immediate.

($\exists$I) Immediate.

($\exists$E) Induction hypothesis: $(\forall k)(\forall \vec{a} \in D(k))(k \Vdash \Gamma(\vec{a}) \Rightarrow k \Vdash \exists z\, \varphi(\vec{a},z))$ and $(\forall k)(\forall \vec{a}, b \in D(k))(k \Vdash \varphi(\vec{a},b),\ k \Vdash \Gamma(\vec{a}) \Rightarrow k \Vdash \sigma(\vec{a}))$.

Here the variables in Γ and σ are $\vec{x}$, and z does not occur among the sequence $\vec{x}$. Now let $k \Vdash \Gamma(\vec{a})$, for some $\vec{a} \in D(k)$, then $k \Vdash \exists z\, \varphi(\vec{a},z)$. So let $k \Vdash \varphi(\vec{a},b)$ for some $b \in D(k)$. By the induction hypothesis $k \Vdash \sigma(\vec{a})$. □

For the completeness theorem we need some notions and a few lemma's.

5.3.8. Definition. A set of sentences Γ is a *prime theory* with respect to a language L if (i) Γ is closed under $\vdash$

(ii) $\varphi \vee \psi \in \Gamma \Rightarrow \varphi \in \Gamma$ or $\psi \in \Gamma$

(iii) $\exists x\, \varphi(x) \in \Gamma \Rightarrow \varphi(c) \in \Gamma$ for some constant c in L.

The following is analogue of the Henkin construction combined with a maximal consistent extension.

5.3.9. Lemma. Let Γ and φ be closed, then if $\Gamma \nvdash \varphi$, there is a prime theory Γ' extending Γ such that $\Gamma' \nvdash \varphi$.

In general one has to extend the language L of Γ by a suitable set of 'witnessing' constants.

Proof. Extend the language L of Γ by a denumerable set of constants to a new language L'. The required theory Γ' is obtained by series of extensions $\Gamma_0 \subseteq \Gamma_1 \subseteq \Gamma_2 \subseteq \ldots$. We put $\Gamma_0 := \Gamma$.

Let Γ_k be given such that $\Gamma_k \nvdash \varphi$ and Γ_k contains only finitely many new constants. We consider two cases. *k is even.* Look for the first existential sentence $\exists x\, \psi(x)$ in L' that has not yet been treated, such that $\Gamma_k \vdash \exists x\, \psi(x)$. Let c be the first new constant not in Γ_k. Now put $\Gamma_{k+1} := \Gamma_k \cup \{\psi(c)\}$.

k is odd. Look for the first disjunctive sentence $\psi_1 \vee \psi_2$ with $\Gamma_k \vdash \psi_1 \vee \psi_2$ that has not yet been treated. Note that not both $\Gamma_1, \psi_1 \vdash \varphi$ and $\Gamma_2, \psi_2 \vdash \varphi$. for then by $\vee$E $\Gamma_k \vdash \varphi$. Now we put

$$\Gamma_{k+1} := \begin{cases} \Gamma_k \cup \{\psi_1\} & \text{if } \Gamma_k, \psi_1 \nvdash \varphi \\ \Gamma_k \cup \{\psi_2\} & \text{otherwise.} \end{cases}$$

Finally $\Gamma' := \bigcup_{k \geqslant 0} \Gamma_k$.

There are a few things to be shown.

(1) $\Gamma' \nvdash \varphi$.

We first show $\Gamma_i \nvdash \varphi$ by induction on i.
For $i = 0$ $\Gamma_0 \nvdash \varphi$ holds by assumption. The duction step is obvious for i is odd. For i even we suppose $\Gamma_{i+1} \vdash \varphi$. Then $\Gamma_i, \psi(c) \vdash \varphi$. Since $\Gamma_i \vdash \exists x\,\psi(x)$, we get $\Gamma_i \vdash \varphi$ by $\exists$E, which contradicts the induction hypothesis. Hence $\Gamma_{i+1} \nvdash \varphi$, and therefore by complete induction $\Gamma_i \nvdash \varphi$ for all i.
Now, if $\Gamma' \vdash \varphi$, then $\Gamma_i \vdash \varphi$ for some i. Contradiction.

(2) Γ is a prime theory.

(a) Let $\psi_1 \vee \psi_2 \in \Gamma'$ and let k be the least number such that $\Gamma_k \vdash \psi_1 \vee \psi_2$. Clearly $\psi_1 \vee \psi_2$ has not been treated before stage k, and $\Gamma_h \vdash \psi_1 \vee \psi_2$ for $h \geqslant k$. Eventually $\psi_1 \vee \psi_2$ has to be treated at some stage $h \geqslant k$, so then $\psi_1 \in \Gamma_{h+1}$ or $\psi_2 \in \Gamma_{h+1}$, and hence $\psi_1 \in \Gamma'$ or $\psi_2 \in \Gamma'$.

(b) Let $\exists x\,\psi(x) \in \Gamma'$, and let k be the least number such that $\Gamma_k \vdash \exists x\,\psi(x)$. For some $h \geqslant k$ $\exists x\,\psi(x)$ is treated, and hence $\psi(c) \in \Gamma_{h+1} \subseteq \Gamma'$ for some c.

(c) Γ' is closed under $\vdash$.
If $\Gamma' \vdash \psi$, then $\Gamma' \vdash \psi \vee \psi$, and hence by (a) $\psi \in \Gamma'$.

Conclusion: Γ' is a prime theory containing Γ, such that $\Gamma' \nvdash \varphi$. □

The next step is to construct for closed Γ and φ with $\Gamma \nvdash \varphi$, a Kripke model, with $\mathcal{K} \Vdash \Gamma$ and $k \nVdash \varphi$ for some $k \in P$.

5.3.10. Model Existence Lemma.

If $\Gamma \nvdash \varphi$ then there is a Kripke model $\mathcal{K}$ with a bottom node k_0 such that $k_0 \Vdash \Gamma$ and $k_0 \nVdash \varphi$.

Proof. Let $\{c^i_m \mid i \geqslant 0, m \geqslant 0\}$ be a set of constants not in L, so that we have a denumerable family of denumerable sets of constants, C^i.
We first extend Γ to a suitable prime theory Γ_0 such that $\Gamma_0 \nvdash \varphi$. Now for any finite sequence $\vec{n}$ ($= \langle n_0, \ldots, n_{k-1} \rangle$) of natural numbers we consider a language $L(\vec{n})$, obtained from the original language L by adding the set of constants $C(\vec{n}) = C^0 \cup C^1 \cup \ldots \cup C^{k-1}$ (where k is the length of $\vec{n}$).
We now define the required Kripke model. The underlying partially ordered set consists of all finite sequences of natural numbers (including the empty sequence $\langle\ \rangle$). Now define $D(\vec{n}) := C(\vec{n})$. ($D(\langle\ \rangle)$ is the set of constants from the language of Γ_0).

$$\Sigma(\langle\ \rangle) := \Gamma_0 \cap At$$

We define $\Sigma(\vec{n})$ by induction on the length. Suppose $\Sigma(\vec{n})$ has already been defined. Consider an enumeration $\langle \sigma_0, \tau_0 \rangle, \langle \sigma_1, \tau_1 \rangle, \ldots$ of pairs of sentences in $L(\vec{n})$ such that $\Sigma(\vec{n}), \sigma_i \nvdash \tau_i$. Now apply for each i lemma 5.3.9 to $\Sigma(\vec{n}) \cup \{\sigma_i\}$ and τ_i, this yields a prime theory Γ_i. Now we put $\Sigma(\langle n_0,\ldots,n_{k-1}\rangle) := \Gamma_i \cap At$. We first remark that all conditions for a Kripke model are met. The model reflects (like the model of 3.1.1.) very much the nature of the prime theories involved.

Claim: $\vec{n} \Vdash \psi \iff \Sigma(\vec{n}) \vdash \psi$

We prove the claim by induction on ψ.

For atomic ψ the equivalence holds by definition.

$\psi = \psi_1 \wedge \psi_2$ - immediate.

$\psi = \psi_1 \vee \psi_2$. (a) $\vec{n} \Vdash \psi_1 \vee \psi_2 \iff \vec{n} \Vdash \psi_1$ or $\vec{n} \Vdash \psi_2 \Rightarrow$ (ind. hyp.) $\Sigma(\vec{n}) \vdash \psi_1$ or $\Sigma(\vec{n}) \vdash \psi_2 \Rightarrow \Sigma(\vec{n}) \vdash \psi_1 \vee \psi_2$.

(b) $\Sigma(\vec{n}) \vdash \psi_1 \vee \psi_2 \Rightarrow \Sigma(\vec{n}) \vdash \psi_1$ or $\Sigma(\vec{n}) \vdash \psi_2$, since $\Sigma(\vec{n})$ is a prime theory (in the right language). So, by induction hypothesis, $\vec{n} \Vdash \psi_1$ or $\vec{n} \Vdash \psi_2$, and hence $\vec{n} \Vdash \psi_1 \vee \psi_2$.

$\psi = \psi_1 \to \psi_2$. (a) $\vec{n} \Vdash \psi_1 \to \psi_2$. Suppose $\Sigma(\vec{n}) \nvdash \psi_1 \to \psi_2$, then $\Sigma(\vec{n}), \psi_1 \nvdash \psi_2$, by the definition of the model there is an extension $\vec{m} = \langle n_0,\ldots,n_{k-1},i\rangle$ of $\vec{n}$ such that $\Sigma(\vec{n}) \cup \{\psi_1\} \subseteq \Sigma(\vec{m})$ and $\Sigma(\vec{m}) \nvdash \psi_2$. By induction hypothesis $\vec{m} \Vdash \psi_1$ and by $\vec{m} \geqslant \vec{n}$ and $\vec{n} \Vdash \psi_1 \to \psi_2$, $\vec{m} \Vdash \psi_2$. Applying the induction hypothesis once more we get $\Sigma(\vec{m}) \vdash \psi_2$. Contradiction. Hence $\Sigma(\vec{n}) \vdash \psi_1 \to \psi_2$.

(b) The converse is simple, it is left to the reader.

$\psi = \forall x \psi_1(x)$. (a) $\vec{n} \Vdash \forall x \psi_1(x) \Rightarrow$ for all $\vec{m} \geqslant \vec{n}$ and $c \in C(\vec{m})$ $\vec{m} \Vdash \psi_1(c)$. Choose a constant c that belongs to a language one node higher than $\vec{n}$, but not to $L(\vec{m})$, suppose $\Sigma(\vec{n}) \nVdash \psi_1(c)$. By definition there is an extension $\vec{m} = \langle n_0,\ldots,n_{k-1},i\rangle$ such that $\Sigma(\vec{m}) \nVdash \psi_1(c)$ (think of the pair $\langle T,\psi_1(c)\rangle$), and so by induction $\vec{m} \nVdash \psi_1(c)$. Contradiction. Hence $\Sigma(\vec{n}) \vdash \psi_1(c)$. By replacing c by a variable and applying $\forall I$ we now get $\Sigma(\vec{n}) \vdash \forall x \psi_1(x)$.

(b) The converse is immediate.

$\psi = \exists x \psi_1(x)$.

The implication from left to right is obvious. For the converse we use the fact that $\Sigma(\vec{n})$ is a prime theory. The details are left to the reader.

We now can finish our proof. The bottom node forces Γ and φ is not forced. □

We can get some extra information from the proof of the model existence lemma: (i) the underlying partially ordered set is a *tree*, (ii) all sets $D(m)$ are denumerable.

From the model existence lemma we easily derive the following

5.3.11. Completeness Theorem. (Kripke) $\Gamma \vdash_i \varphi \iff \Gamma \Vdash \varphi$ (Γ and φ closed).

Proof. We have already shown $\Rightarrow$. For the converse we assume $\Gamma_i \nVdash \varphi$ and apply 5.3.10., which yields a contradiction. □

Actually we have proved the following refinement: intuitionistic logic is complete for countable models over trees.

The above results are completely general (safe for the cardinality restriction on L), so we may as well assume that Γ contains the identity axioms $I_1,\ldots,I_4$ (2.6). May we also assume that the identity predicate is interpreted by the real equality in each world ? The answer is no, this assumption constitutes a real restriction, as the following theorem shows.

5.3.12. <u>Theorem</u>. If for all $k \in P$ $k \Vdash \bar{a} = \bar{b} \Rightarrow a = b$ for $a,b \in D(k)$ then $\mathcal{K} \Vdash \forall xy(x = y \vee x \neq y)$.

Proof. Let $a,b \in D(k)$ and $k \nVdash \bar{a} = \bar{b}$, then $a \neq b$, not only in $D(k)$, but in all $D(\ell)$ for $\ell \geqslant k$, hence for all $\ell \geqslant k$, $\ell \nVdash \bar{a} = \bar{b}$, so $k \Vdash \bar{a} \neq \bar{b}$. □

For a kind of converse, cf. exercise 18.

The fact that the relation $a \sim_k b$ in $\mathfrak{A}(k)$, given by $k \Vdash \bar{a} = \bar{b}$, is not the identity relation is definitely embarrassing for a language with function symbols. So let us see what we can do about it. We assume that a function symbol F is interpreted in each k by a function F_k. We require $k \leqslant \ell \Rightarrow F_k \subseteq F_\ell$.
F has to obey I_4: $\forall \vec{x}\vec{y}(\vec{x} = \vec{y} \to F(\vec{x}) = F(y))$. For more about functions see exercise 34.

5.3.13. <u>Lemma</u>. The relation $\sim_k$ is a congruence relation on $\mathfrak{A}(k)$, for each k.

Proof. Straightforward, by interpreting $I_1 - I_4$. □
For convenience we usually drop the index k.

We now may define new structures by taking equivalence classes:
$\mathfrak{A}^*(k) := \mathfrak{A}(k)/\sim$, i.e. the elements of $|\mathfrak{A}^*(k)|$ are equivalence classes $a/\sim$ of elements $a \in D(k)$, and the relations are canonically determined by
$R^*_k(a/\sim,\ldots) \Leftrightarrow R_k(a,\ldots)$, similarly for the functions $F^*_k(a/\sim,\ldots) = F_k(a,\ldots)/\sim$.
The inclusion $\mathfrak{A}(k) \subseteq \mathfrak{A}(\ell)$, for $k \leqslant \ell$, is now replaced by a map $f_{k\ell} : \mathfrak{A}^*(k) \to \mathfrak{A}^*(\ell)$, where $f_{k\ell}$ is defined by $f_{k\ell}(a) = \bar{a}^{\mathfrak{A}^*(\ell)}$ for $a \in |\mathfrak{A}^*(k)|$. To be precise:
$a/\sim_k \longmapsto a/\sim_\ell$, so we have show $a \sim_k a' \Rightarrow a \sim_\ell a'$ to ensure the well-definedness of $f_{k\ell}$. This, however, is obvious, since $k \Vdash \bar{a} = \bar{a}' \Rightarrow \ell \Vdash \bar{a} = \bar{a}'$.

Claim. $f_{k\ell}$ is a homomorphism.

Proof. We will treat one case, a binary relation.

$R_k^*(a/\sim,b/\sim) \iff R_k(a,b) \iff k \Vdash R(a,b) \Rightarrow \ell \Vdash R(a,b) \iff R_\ell(a,b) \iff R_\ell^*(a/\sim,b/\sim)$.

The case of an operation is left to the reader.

The result is that we can define a modified notion of Kripke model.

5.3.14. Definition. A modified Kripke model for a language L is a triple $\mathcal{K} = \langle P,\mathfrak{A},f\rangle$ such that P is a partially ordered set, $\mathfrak{A}$ and f are mappings such that for $k \in P$, $\mathfrak{A}(k)$ is a structure for L and for $k,\ell \in P$ with $k \leqslant \ell$ $f(k,\ell)$ is a homomorphism from $\mathfrak{A}(k)$ to $\mathfrak{A}(\ell)$.

Notation: we write $f_{k\ell}$ for $f(k,\ell)$, and $k \Vdash^* \varphi$ for $\mathfrak{A}(k) \models \varphi$, for atomic φ.

From this point one may mimic the development presented for the original notion of Kripke semantics.

In particular the connection between the two notions is given by

5.3.15. Lemma. Let $\mathcal{K}^*$ be the modified Kripke model obtained from $\mathcal{K}$ by dividing out $\sim$. Then $k \Vdash \varphi(\vec{a}) \iff k \Vdash^* \varphi(\vec{a}/\sim)$ for all $k \in P$.

Proof. Left to the reader. □

5.3.16. Corollary. Intuitionistic logic is complete with respect to modified Kripke semantics.

Proof. Apply 5.3.10 and 5.3.15. □

We will usually work with ordinary Kripke models, but for convenience we will often replace inclusions of structures $\mathfrak{A}(k) \subseteq \mathfrak{A}(\ell)$ by inclusion mappings $\mathfrak{A}(k) \hookrightarrow \mathfrak{A}(\ell)$.

5.4. Some model theory.

We will give some simple applications of Kripke's semantics. The first ones concern the so-called *disjunction* and *existence properties*.

5.4.1. Definition. A set of sentences Γ has the

(i) *disjunction property* (DP) if $\Gamma \vdash \varphi \vee \psi \Rightarrow \Gamma \vdash \varphi$ or $\Gamma \vdash \psi$

(ii) *existence property* (EP) if $\Gamma \vdash \exists x\, \varphi(x) \Rightarrow \Gamma \vdash \varphi(t)$ for some closed term t.

(where $\varphi \vee \psi$ and $\exists x\, \varphi(x)$ are closed).

In a sense DP and EP reflect the constructive character of the theory Γ (in the frame of intuitionistic logic), since it makes explicit the clause 'if we have a proof of $\exists x\, \varphi(x)$, then we have a proof of a particular instance', similarly for disjunction.

Classical logic does not have DP or EP, for consider in propositional logic $\varphi = p_0 \vee \neg p_0$. Clearly $\vdash_c p_0 \vee \neg p_0$, but neither $\vdash_c p_0$ nor $\vdash_c \neg p_0$!

5.4.2. Theorem. Intuitionistic propositional and predicate logic without functions symbols have DP.

Proof. Let $\vdash \varphi \vee \psi$, and suppose $\nvdash \varphi$ and $\nvdash \psi$, then there are Kripke models K_1 and K_2 with bottom nodes k_1 and k_2 such that $k_1 \nVdash \varphi$ and $k_2 \nVdash \psi$. It is no restriction to suppose that the partially ordered sets P_1, P_2 of K_1 and K_2 are disjoint.

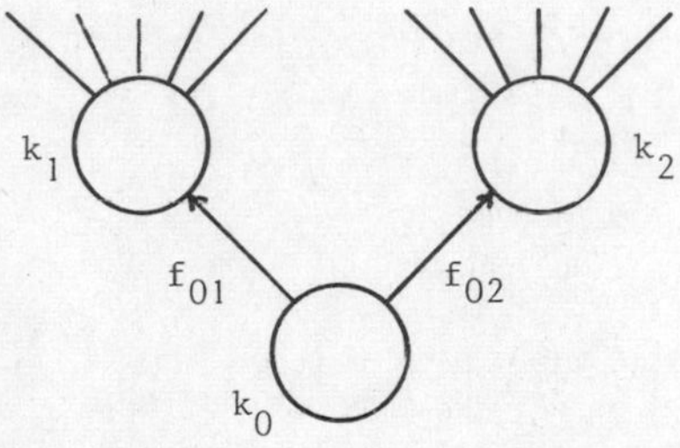

We define a new Kripke model with $P = P_1 \cup P_2 \cup \{k_0\}$ where $k_0 \notin P_1 \cup P_2$. We define

$$\mathfrak{A}(k) = \begin{cases} \mathfrak{A}_1(k) & \text{for } k \in P_1 \\ \mathfrak{A}_2(k) & \text{for } k \in P_2 \\ \mathfrak{L} & \text{for } k = k_0, \end{cases}$$

where $|\mathfrak{L}|$ consists of all the constants of L, if there are any, otherwise $|\mathfrak{L}|$ contains only one element α. The inclusion mapping for $\mathfrak{A}(k_0) \hookrightarrow \mathfrak{A}(k_i)$ $(i = 1,2)$ is defined by $c \mapsto c^{\mathfrak{A}(k_i)}$ if there are constants, if not we pick $a_i \in \mathfrak{A}(k_i)$ arbitrarily and define $f_{01}(\alpha) = a_1$, $f_{02}(\alpha) = a_2$.
$\mathfrak{A}$ satisfies the definition of a Kripke model.

The models K_1 and K_2 are 'submodels' of the new model in the sense that the forcing induced on K_i by that of K is exactly its old forcing, cf. exercise 10. By the completeness theorem $k_0 \Vdash \varphi \vee \psi$, so $k_0 \Vdash \varphi$ or $k_0 \Vdash \psi$. If $k_0 \Vdash \varphi$, then $k_1 \Vdash \varphi$. Contradiction. If $k_0 \Vdash \psi$, then $k_2 \Vdash \psi$. Contradiction. So $\nvdash \varphi$ and $\nvdash \psi$ is not true, hence $\vdash\varphi$ or $\vdash\psi$. □

Observe that this proof can be considerably simplified for propositional logic, all we have to do is put an extra bottom node under k_1 and k_2 in which no atom is forced (cf. exercise 19).

5.4.3. Theorem. Let the language of intuitionistic predicate logic contain at least one constant and no function symbols, then EP holds.

Proof. Let $\vdash \exists x\varphi(x)$ and $\nvdash \varphi(c)$ for all constants c. Then for each c there is a Kripke model $\mathcal{K}_c$ with bottom node k_c such that $k_c \nVdash \varphi(c)$. Now mimic the argument of 5.4.2 above, by taking the disjoint union of the $\mathcal{K}_c$'s and adding a bottom node k_0. Use the fact that $k_0 \Vdash \exists x\varphi(x)$. □

The reader will have observed that we reason about our intuitionistic logic and model theory in a classical metatheory. In particular we use the principle of the excluded third in our meta-language. This indeed detracts from the constructive nature of our considerations. For the present we will not bother to make our arguments constructive, it may suffice to remark that classical arguments can often be circumvented, cf. *Troelstra*, 1973, 1977.

In constructive mathematics one often needs stronger notions than some classical ones. A paradigm is the notion of *inequality*. E.g. in the case of the real numbers it does not suffice to know that a number is unequal (i.e. not equal) to 0 in order invert it. The procedure that constructs the inverse for a given Cauchy sequence requires that there exists a number n such that the distance of the given number to zero is greater than 2^{-n}. Instead of a negative notion we need a positive one, this was introduced by Brouwer and formalized by Heyting.

5.4.4. Definition. A binary relation $\#$ is called an *apartness relation* if

(i) $\forall xy(x = y \leftrightarrow \neg x \# y)$

(ii) $\forall xy(x \# y \rightarrow y \# x)$

(iii) $\forall xyz(x \# y \rightarrow x \# z \vee y \# z)$

Examples. (1) For rational numbers the inequality is an apartness relation.

(2) If the equality relation on a set is decidable (i.e. $\forall xy(x = y \vee x \neq y)$), then $\neq$ is an apartness relation (exercise 22).

(3) For real numbers the relation $\exists n(|a-b| > 2^{-n})$ is an apartness relation (cf. *Heyting*, p. 19, 20).

We call the theory with axioms (i), (ii), (iii) of 5.4.4. AP, the theory of apart-ness (of course the obvious identity axiom $x_1 = x_2 \wedge y_1 = y_2 \wedge x_1 \# y_1 \rightarrow x_2 \# y_2$ is included).

5.4.5. Theorem. $AP \vdash \forall xy(\neg\neg x = y \rightarrow x = y)$.

Proof. Observe that
$$\begin{aligned}\neg\neg x = y &\leftrightarrow \neg\neg\neg x \# y\\ &\leftrightarrow \neg x \# y\\ &\leftrightarrow x = y. \qquad \square\end{aligned}$$

We call an equality relation that satisfies the condition $\forall xy(\neg\neg x = y \rightarrow x = y)$ *stable*. Note that *stable* is essentially weaker than *decidable* (exercise 19).

In the passage from intuitionistic theories to classical ones by adding the prin'-ciple of the excluded third usually a lot of notions are collapsed, e.g. $\neg\neg x = y$ and $x = y$. Or conversely, when passing from classical theories to intuitionistic ones (by deleting the principle of the excluded third) there is a choice of the right notions. Usually (but not always) the strongest notions fare best. An example is the notion of *linear order*.

The theory of linear order, LO, has the following axioms

(*i*) $\forall xyz(x < y \wedge y < z \rightarrow x < z)$

(*ii*) $\forall xyz(x < y \rightarrow z < y \vee x < z)$

(*iii*) $\forall xyz(x = y \leftrightarrow \neg x < y \wedge \neg y < x)$.

One might wonder why we did not choose the axiom $\forall xy(x < y \vee x = y \vee y < x)$ instead of (ii), it certainly would be stronger! There is a simple reason: the axiom is *too* strong, it does not hold e.g. for the reals.

We will next investigate the relation between linear order and apartness.

5.4.6. Theorem. The relation $x < y \vee y < x$ is an apartness relation.

Proof. An exercise in logic. $\square$

Conversely we can in every Kripke model over a tree of AP introduce an order re-lation, as we will show.

Let $\mathcal{K} \Vdash AP$, then in each D(k) the following is an equivalence relation: $k \nVdash a \# b$.

(a) $k \Vdash a = a \leftrightarrow \neg a \# a$, since $k \Vdash a = a$ we get $k \Vdash \neg a \# a$ and hence $k \nVdash a \# a$.

(b) $k \Vdash a \# b \leftrightarrow b \# a$, so obviously $k \nVdash a \# b \Longleftrightarrow k \nVdash b \# a$.

(c) let $k \nVdash a \# b$, $k \nVdash b \# c$ and suppose $k \Vdash a \# c$, then by axiom (iii)

$k \Vdash a \# b$ or $k \Vdash c \# b$ which contradicts the assumptions. So $k \nVdash a \# c$.

Observe that this equivalence relation contains the one induced by the identity: $k \Vdash a = b \Rightarrow k \nVdash a \# b$. The domains $D(k)$ are thus split up in equivalence classes, which can be linearly ordered in the classical sense. Since we want to end up with a Kripke model, we have to be a bit careful.
Observe that equivalence classes may be split by passing to a higher node, e.g. if $k < \ell$ and $k \nVdash a \# b$ then $\ell \Vdash a \# b$ is very well possible, but $\ell \nVdash a \# b \Rightarrow k \nVdash a \# b$.
We take an arbitrary ordering of the equivalence classes of the bottom node (using the axiom of choice in our metalanguage if necessary). Next we indicate how to order the equivalence classes in an immediate successor ℓ of k.

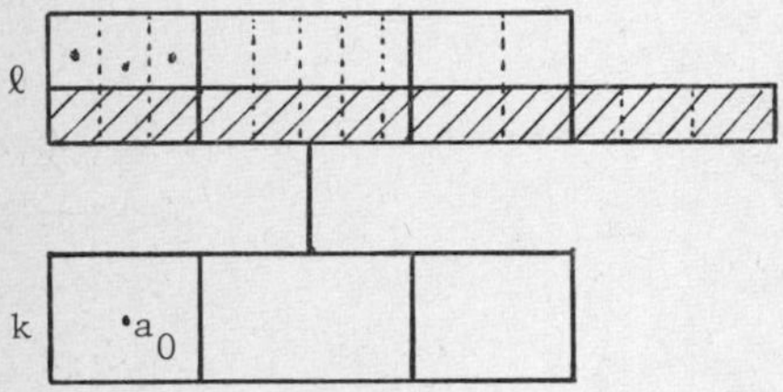

The 'new' elements of $D(\ell)$ are indicated by the shaded part.
(i) Consider an equivalence class $[a_0]_k$ in $D(k)$, and look at the corresponding class $\hat{a}_0 := \cup\{[a]_\ell \mid a \in [a_0]_k\}$.

This class splits in a number of classes, we order those linearly. Denote the equivalence classes of $\hat{a}_0$ by a_0b (where b is a representative). Now the classes belonging to the b's are ordered, and we order all the classes in $\cup\{\hat{a}_0 \mid a_0 \in D(k)\}$ lexicographically according to the representation a_0b. (ii) Finally we consider the new equivalence classes, i.e. of those that are not equivalent to any b in $\cup\{\hat{a}_0 \mid a_0 \in D(k)\}$. We order those classes and put them in the order behind the classes of case (i).

Under this procedure we order all equivalence classes in all nodes.

We now define a relation R_k for each k: $R_k(a,b) := [a]_k < [b]_k$, where $<$ is the ordering defined above. By our definition $k < \ell$ and $R_k(a,b) \Rightarrow R_\ell(a,b)$. We leave it to the reader to show that I_4 is valid, i.e. in particular $k \Vdash \forall xy(x = x' \wedge x < y \to \to x' < y)$, where $<$ is interpreted by R_k.

Observe that in this model the following holds

$$(\#) \qquad \forall xy(x \# y \leftrightarrow x < y \vee y < x),$$

for in all nodes k, $k \Vdash a \# b \Leftrightarrow k \Vdash a < b$ or $k \Vdash b < a$.
We must check now the axioms of linear order.
(i) *transitivity*. $k_0 \Vdash \forall xyz(x < y \wedge y < z \to x < z) \Leftrightarrow$ for all $k \geq k_0$, for all $a,b,c \in D(k)$ $k \Vdash a < b \wedge b < c \to a < c \Leftrightarrow$ for all $k \geq k_0$, for all $a,b,c \in D(k)$ and for all $\ell \geq k$ $\ell \Vdash a < b$ and $\ell \Vdash b < c \Rightarrow \ell \Vdash a < c$.

So we have to show $R_\ell(a,b)$ and $R_\ell(b,c) \Rightarrow R_\ell(a,c)$, but that is indeed the case by the linear ordering of the equivalence classes.

(ii) *(weak) linearity*. We must show $k_0 \Vdash \forall xyz(x<y \to z<y \vee x<z)$. Since in our model $\forall xy(x \# y \leftrightarrow x<y \vee y<x)$ holds the problem is reduced to pure logic: show: $AP + \forall xyz(x<y \wedge y<z \to x<z) + \forall xy(x \# y \leftrightarrow x<y \vee y<x) \vdash$

$$\forall xyz(x<y \to z<y \vee x<z).$$

We leave the proof to the reader.

(iii) *anti-symmetry*. We must show $k_0 \Vdash \forall xy(x=y \leftrightarrow \neg x<y \wedge \neg y<x)$. As before the problem is reduced to logic. Show

$AP + \forall xy(x \# y \leftrightarrow x<y \vee y<x) \vdash \forall xy(x=y \leftrightarrow \neg x<y \wedge \neg y<x)$.

Now we have finished the job, we have put a linear order on a model with an apartness relation. We can now draw some conclusions.

5.4.7. Theorem. $AP + LO + \langle\#\rangle$ is conservative over LO.

Proof. Immediate, by theorem 5.4.6. □

5.4.8. Theorem. $AP + LO + \langle\#\rangle$ is conservative over AP.

Proof. Suppose $AP \nvdash \varphi$, then by the model existence lemma there is a tree model K of AP such that the bottom node k_0 does not force φ.

We now carry out the construction of a linear order on K, the resulting model K^* is a model of $AP + LO + \langle\#\rangle$, and, since φ does not contain $<$, $k_0 \nVdash \varphi$. Hence $AP + LO + \langle\#\rangle \nvdash \varphi$. This shows the conservative extension result: $AP + LO + \langle\#\rangle \vdash \varphi \Rightarrow AP \vdash \varphi$, for φ in the language of AP. □

We end this chapter by giving some examples of models with surprising properties.

1.

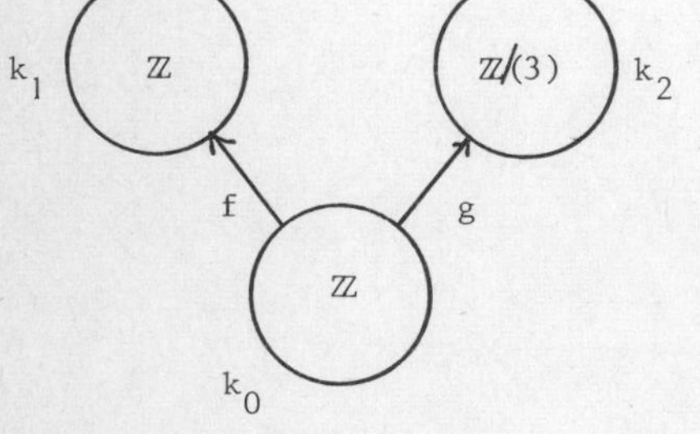

f is the identity and g is the canonical ring homomorphism $\mathbb{Z} \to \mathbb{Z}/(2)$.
K is a model of the ring axioms (p. 88).

Note that $k_0 \Vdash 3 \neq 0$, $k_0 \nVdash 2 = 0$, $k_0 \nVdash 2 \neq 0$ and $k_0 \nVdash \forall x(x \neq 0 \to \exists y(xy = 1))$, but also $k_0 \nVdash \exists x(x \neq 0 \wedge \forall y(xy \neq 1))$. Hence K is a commutative ring in which not all non-zero elements are invertible, but in which it is impossible to exhibit a non-invertible, non-zero element.

2.

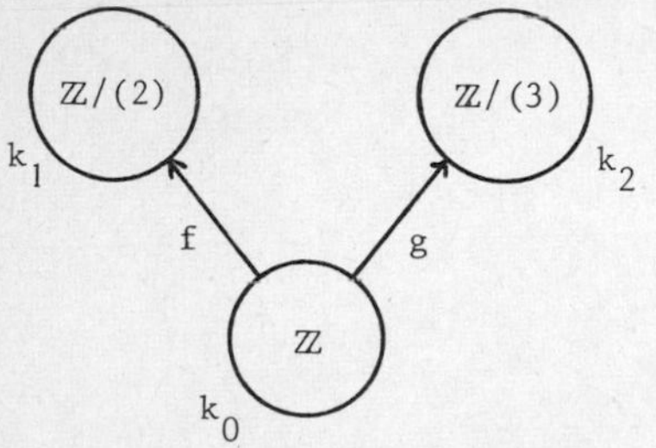

Again f and g are the canonical homomorphisms.
K is an intuitionistic, commutative ring, as one easily verifies.

K has no zero-divisors: $k_0 \Vdash \neg\exists xy(x \neq 0 \wedge y \neq 0 \wedge xy = 0) \Longleftrightarrow$ for all i $k_i \nVdash \exists xy(x \neq 0 \wedge y \neq 0 \wedge xy = 0)$. (1)
For $i = 1,2$ this is obvious, so let us consider $i = 0$.
$k_0 \Vdash \exists xy(x \neq 0 \wedge y \neq 0 \wedge xy = 0) \Longleftrightarrow k_0 \Vdash \bar{m} \neq 0 \wedge \bar{n} \neq 0 \wedge \bar{m}\bar{n} = \bar{n}$ for some m,n. So $m \neq 0$, $n \neq 0$, $mn = 0$. Contradiction. This proves (1).

The cardinality of the model is rather undetermined. We know $k_0 \Vdash \exists xy(x \neq y)$ - take 0 and 1, and $k_0 \Vdash \neg\exists x_1x_2x_3x_4 \bigwedge_{1 \leq i<j \leq 4} x_i \neq x_j$. But note that

$k_0 \nVdash \exists x_1x_2x_3 \bigwedge_{1 \leq i<j \leq 3} x_i \neq x_j$, $k_0 \nVdash \forall x_1x_2x_3x_4 \bigvee_{1 \leq i<j \leq 4} x_i = x_j$ and

$k_0 \nVdash \neg\exists x_1x_2x_3 \bigwedge_{1 \leq i<j \leq 3} x_i \neq x_j$.

Observe that the equality relation in K is not stable: $k_0 \Vdash \neg\neg 0 = 6$, but $k_0 \nVdash 0 = 6$.

3.

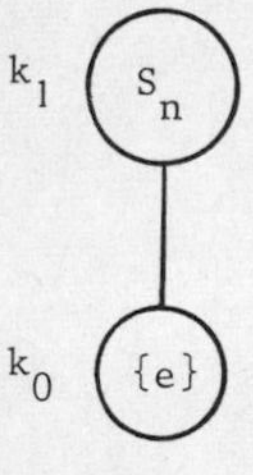

S_n is the (classical) symmetric group on n elements. Choose $n \geq 3$. k_0 forces the group axioms (p. 86). $k_0 \Vdash \neg\forall xy(xy = yx)$, but $k_0 \nVdash \exists xy(xy \neq yx)$, and $k_0 \nVdash \forall xy(xy = yx)$. So this group is not commutative, but one cannot indicate non-commuting elements.

So this intuitionistic group is non-commutative but we cannot find non-commuting elements.

4.

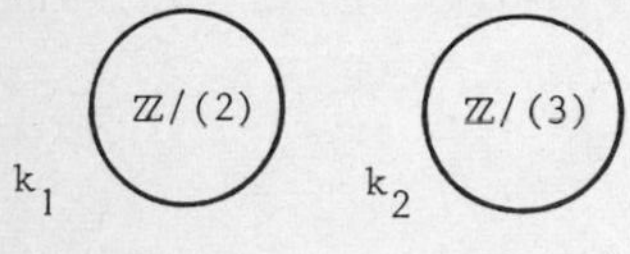

Define an apartness relation by $k_1 \Vdash a \# b \Longleftrightarrow a \neq b$ in $\mathbb{Z}/(2)$, idem for k_2.
Then $K \Vdash \forall x(x \# 0 \to \exists y xy = 1)$.

This model is an intuitionistic field, but we cannot determine its characteristic. $k_1 \vdash \forall x(x+x = 0)$, $k_2 \Vdash \forall x(x+x+x = 0)$. All we know is $K \Vdash \forall x(6.x = 0)$.

In the short introduction to intuitionistic logic that we have presented we have only been able to scratch the surfaces. We have intentionally simplified the issues such that a reader can get a rough impression of the problems and methods without going into the finer philosophical details. In particular we have treated intuitionistic logic in a classical metamatics, e.g. we have freely applied proof by contradiction (cf. 5.3.11). Obviously this does not do justice to constructive mathematics as an alternative mathematics in its own right. For this and related issues the reader is referred to the literature.

EXERCISES.

1. (informal mathematics). Let $\varphi(n)$ be a decidable property of natural numbers such that neither $\exists n\,\varphi(n)$, nor $\forall n \neg\varphi(n)$ has been established (e.g. n is the largest number such that n and n+2 are prime). Define a real number a by the cauchy sequence

$$a_n := \begin{cases} \sum_{i=1}^{n} 2^{-i} & \text{if } \forall k < n\ \neg\varphi(k) \\ \sum_{i=1}^{k} 2^{-i} & \text{if } k < n \text{ and } \varphi(k) \text{ and } \neg\varphi(i) \text{ for } i < k. \end{cases}$$

Show that: "$\neg\neg$a is rational", but there is no evidence for "a is rational".

2. Prove $\vdash \neg\neg(\varphi\to\psi) \to (\varphi\to\neg\neg\psi)$; $\vdash \neg\neg(\varphi \vee \neg\varphi)$; $\vdash \neg(\varphi\wedge\neg\varphi)$
$\vdash \neg\neg(\neg\neg\varphi\to\varphi)$; $\neg\neg\varphi,\ \neg\neg(\varphi\to\psi) \vdash \neg\neg\psi$;
$\vdash (\neg\neg\varphi\to\psi) \to \neg(\varphi\wedge\neg\psi)$; $\vdash \neg(\varphi\vee\psi) \leftrightarrow \neg(\neg\varphi\to\psi)$

3. (a) $\varphi\vee\neg\varphi,\ \psi\vee\neg\psi \vdash (\varphi\,\square\,\psi) \vee \neg(\varphi\,\square\,\psi)$, where $\square \in (\wedge,\vee,\to)$
(b) let the proposition φ have atoms $p_0,\ldots,p_n$, show $\bigwedge\!\!\!\bigwedge p_i \vee \neg p_i \vdash \varphi\vee\neg\varphi$.

4. Define the double negation translation $\varphi^{\neg\neg}$ of φ by placing $\neg\neg$ in front of each subformula. Show $\vdash_i \varphi^\circ \leftrightarrow \varphi^{\neg\neg}$ and $\vdash_c \varphi \Leftrightarrow \vdash_i \varphi^{\neg\neg}$.

5. Show that for propositional logic $\vdash_i \neg\varphi \Leftrightarrow \vdash_c \neg\varphi$.

6. Intuitionistic arithmetic HA (Heyting's arithmetic) is the first-order intuitionistic theory with the axioms of page 89 as mathematical axioms. Show $HA \vdash \forall xy(x = y \vee x \neq y)$ (use the principle of induction). Show that the Gödel translation works for arithmetic, i.e. $PA \vdash \varphi \Leftrightarrow HA \vdash \varphi^\circ$. (where PA is Peano's (classical) arithmetic).

7. Show that PA is conservative over HA with respect to formula's not containing $\vee$ and $\exists$.

8. Show that $HA \vdash \varphi \vee \psi \leftrightarrow \exists x((x=0 \rightarrow \varphi) \wedge (x \neq 0 \rightarrow \psi))$.

9. (a) Show $\nvdash (\varphi \rightarrow \psi) \vee (\psi \rightarrow \varphi)$; $\nvdash \neg\varphi \vee \neg\neg\varphi$;
$\nvdash (\neg\neg\varphi \rightarrow \varphi) \rightarrow (\varphi \vee \neg\varphi)$; $\nvdash (\neg\varphi \rightarrow \psi \vee \sigma) \rightarrow [(\neg\varphi \rightarrow \psi) \vee (\neg\varphi \rightarrow \sigma)]$
$\nvdash \bigvee_{1 \leqslant i < j \leqslant n} (\varphi_i \leftrightarrow \varphi_j)$, for all $n > 2$.

(b) Use the completeness theorem to establish the following theorems
(*i*) $\varphi \rightarrow (\psi \rightarrow \varphi)$
(*ii*) $(\varphi \vee \varphi) \rightarrow \varphi$
(*iii*) $\forall xy\, \varphi(x,y) \rightarrow \forall yx\, \varphi(x,y)$
(*iv*) $\exists x \forall y\, \varphi(x,y) \rightarrow \forall y \exists x\, \varphi(x,y)$

(c) Show $k \Vdash \forall xy\, \varphi(xy) \iff \forall \ell \geqslant k\ \forall a,b \in D(\ell)\ \ell \Vdash \varphi(\bar{a},\bar{b})$.
$k \nVdash \varphi \rightarrow \psi \iff \exists \ell \geqslant k (\ell \Vdash \varphi$ and $\ell \nVdash \psi)$.

10. Give the simplified definition of a Kripke model for (the language of) propositional logic by considering the special case of def. 5.3.1. with $\Sigma(k)$ consisting of propositional atoms only, and $D(k) = \{0\}$ for all k.

11. Give an alternative definition of Kripke model based on the "structure-map" $\mathfrak{A}(k)$ and show the equivalence with definition 5.3.1. (without propositional atoms).

12. Prove the soundness theorem using lemma 5.3.6.

13. A subset P' of a partially ordered set P is closed (under $\leqslant$) if $k \in P'$, $k \leqslant \ell \Rightarrow \ell \in P$. If P' is a closed subset of the underlying partially ordered set P of a Kripke model K, then P' determines a Kripke model K' over P' with $D'(k) = D(k)$ and $k \Vdash' \varphi \iff k \Vdash \varphi$ for $k \in P'$ and φ atomic. Show $k \Vdash' \varphi \iff k \Vdash \varphi$ for all φ with parameters in $D(k)$, for $k \in P'$ (i.e. it is the future that matters, not the past).

14. Give a modified proof of the model existence lemma by taking as nodes of the partially ordered set prime theories that extend Γ and that have a language with constants in some set $C^0 \cup C^1 \cup \ldots \cup C^{k-1}$ (cf. proof of 5.3.9) (note that the resulting partially ordered set need not (and, as a matter of fact, is not) a tree, so we lose something).

15. (a) Show that $(\varphi \to \psi) \vee (\psi \to \varphi)$ holds in all linearly ordered Kripke models for propositional logic.
    (b) By applying the construction of exercise 10, show that $LC \nvdash \sigma \Rightarrow$ there is a linear Kripke model of LC in which σ fails, where LC is the propositional theory axiomatized by the schema $(\varphi \to \psi) \vee (\psi \to \varphi)$. Hence LC is complete for linear Kripke models (Dummett).

16. Each Kripke model with bottom node k_0 can be turned into a model over a tree as follows: P_t consists of all finite increasing sequences $\langle k_0, k_1, \ldots, k_n \rangle$, $k_i < k_{i+1}$ $(0 \leq i < n)$, and $\mathfrak{A}_t(\langle k_0, \ldots, k_n \rangle) := \mathfrak{A}(k_n)$. Show $\langle k_0, \ldots, k_n \rangle \Vdash_t \varphi \Leftrightarrow k_n \Vdash \varphi$, where $\Vdash_t$ is the forcing relation in the tree model.

17. Consider a propositional Kripke model K, where the Σ function assigns only subsets of a finite set Γ of propositions, which is closed under subformulas. We may consider the sets of propositions forced at a node instead of the node: define $[k] = \{\varphi \in \Gamma \mid k \Vdash \varphi\}$. The set $\{[k] \mid k \in P\}$ is partially ordered by inclusion define $\Sigma_\Gamma([k]) := \Sigma(k) \cap At$, show that the conditions of a Kripke model are satisfied; call this model K_Γ, and denote the forcing by $\Vdash_\Gamma$. We say that K_Γ is obtained by *filtration* from K.
    (a) Show $[k] \Vdash_\Gamma \varphi \Leftrightarrow k \Vdash \varphi$, for $\varphi \in \Gamma$.
    (b) Show that K_Γ has a finite partially ordered set.
    (c) Show that $\vdash \varphi \Leftrightarrow \varphi$ holds in all finite Kripke models.
    (d) Show that intuitionistic propositional logic is *decidable* (i.e. there is a decision method for $\vdash \varphi$), apply 3.3.18.

18. Consider a Kripke model K for decidable equality (i.e. $\forall xy(x = y \vee x \neq y)$). For each k the relation $k \Vdash \bar{a} = \bar{b}$ is an equivalence relation. Define a new model K' with the same partially ordered set as K, and $D'(k) = \{[a]_k \mid a \in D(k)\}$, where $[a]$ is the equivalence class of a. Replace the inclusion of $D(k)$ in $D(\ell)$, for $k < \ell$, by the corresponding canonical embedding $[a]_k \longmapsto [a]_\ell$.
Define for atomic φ $k \Vdash' \varphi := k \Vdash \varphi$ and show $k \Vdash' \varphi \Leftrightarrow k \Vdash \varphi$ for all φ.

19. Prove DP for propositional logic directly by simplifying the proof of 5.4.2.

20. Show that HA has DP and EP, the latter in the form: $HA \vdash \exists x \varphi(x) \Rightarrow HA \vdash \varphi(\bar{n})$ for some $n \in \mathbb{N}$. (Hint, show that the model, constructed in 5.4.2. and in 5.4.3., is a model of HA).

21. Consider predicate logic in a language without function symbols and constants. Show $\vdash \exists x \varphi(x) \Rightarrow \vdash \forall x \varphi(x)$. (Hint, add an auxilliary constant c, apply 5.4.3,

and replace it by a suitable variable).

22. Show $\forall xy(x = y \vee x \neq y) \vdash \bigwedge AP$, where AP consists of the three axioms of the apartness relation, with $x \# y$ replaced by $\neq$.

23. Show $\forall xy(\neg\neg x = y \to x = y) \nvdash \forall xy(x = y \vee x \neq y)$.

24. If k is a maximal node in a Kripke model, show that $k \Vdash \varphi \vee \neg\varphi$, and $\Sigma(k) = Th(\mathfrak{A}(k))$ (in the classical sense). So "the logic in a maximal node is classical."

25. Give an alternative proof of Glivenko's theorem, using exercises 17(c) and 24.

26. Consider a Kripke model with two nodes k_0, k_1; $k_0 < k_1$ and $\mathfrak{A}(k_0) = \mathbb{R}$, $\mathfrak{A}(k_1) = \mathbb{C}$. Show $k_0 \nVdash \neg\forall x(x^2 + 1 \neq 0) \to \exists x(x^2 + 1 = 0)$.

27. Let $\mathbb{D} = \mathbb{R}[X]/X^2$ be the ring of dual numbers. $\mathbb{D}$ has a unique maximal ideal, generated by X. Consider a Kripke model with two nodes k_0, k_1; $k_0 < k_1$ and $\mathfrak{A}(k_0) = \mathbb{D}$, $\mathfrak{A}(k_1) = \mathbb{R}$, with $f: \mathbb{D} \to \mathbb{R}$ the canonical map $f(a + bX) = a$. Show that the model is an intuitionistic field, define the apartness relation.

28. Show that $\forall x(\varphi \vee \psi(x)) \to (\varphi \vee \forall x\psi(x))$ $(x \notin FV(\varphi))$ holds in all Kripke models with constant domain function (i.e. $\forall k\ell(D(k) = D(\ell))$.

29. This exercise will establish the undefinability of propositional connectives in terms of other connectives. To be precise the connective $\square_1$ is not definable by $\square_2, \dots, \square_n$ if there is no formula φ containing the connectives $\square_2, \dots, \square_n$ and the atoms p_0, p_1 such that $\vdash p_0 \square_1 p_2 \leftrightarrow \varphi$.

   (*i*) $\vee$ is not definable by $\to, \wedge, \bot$.
   Hint: suppose φ defines $\vee$, apply the Gödel translation.

   (*ii*) $\wedge$ is not definable in $\to, \vee, \bot$.
   Consider the Kripke model with three nodes k_1, k_2, k_3 and $k_1 < k_3, k_2 < k_3$, $k_1 \Vdash p, k_2 \Vdash q, k_3 \Vdash p, q$. Show that all $\wedge$-free formulas are either equiv'-alent to $\bot$ or are forced in k_1 or k_2.

   (*iii*) $\to$ is not definable in $\wedge, \vee, \neg, \bot$.
   Consider the Kripke model with three nodes k_1, k_2, k_3 and $k_1 < k_3, k_2 < k_3$, $k_1 \Vdash p, k_3 \Vdash p, q$. Show that for all $\to$-free formulas $k_2 \Vdash \varphi \Rightarrow k_1 \Vdash \varphi$.

30. We consider here only propositions with a single atom p. Define a sequence of formulas by $\varphi_0 := \bot$, $\varphi_1 := p$, $\varphi_2 := \neg p$, $\varphi_{2n+3} := \varphi_{2n+1} \vee \varphi_{2n+2}$, $\varphi_{2n+4} := \varphi_{2n+2} \to \varphi_{2n+1}$ and an extra formula $\varphi_\infty := \top$. There is a specific set of implications among the φ_i, indicated in the diagram on the left.

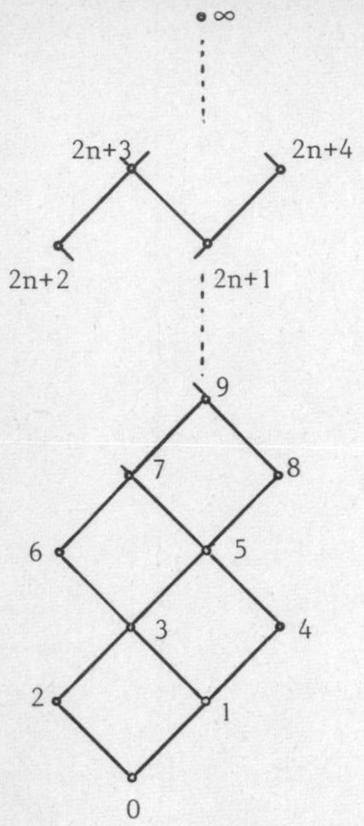

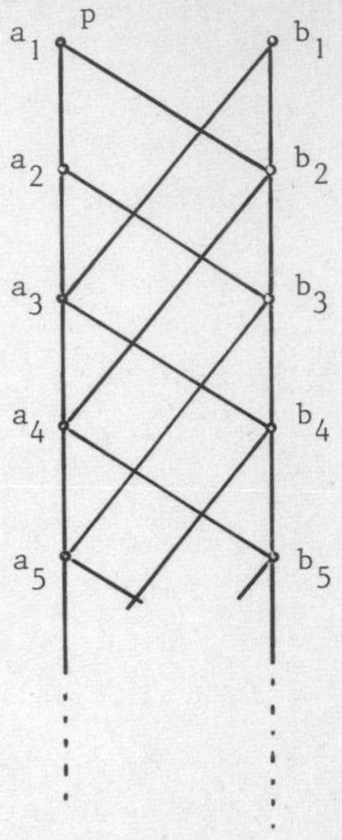

(*i*) Show that the implications hold: $\vdash \varphi_{2n+1} \to \varphi_{2n+3}$, $\vdash \varphi_{2n+1} \to \varphi_{2n+4}$, $\vdash \varphi_{2n+2} \to \varphi_{2n+3}$, $\vdash \varphi_0 \to \varphi_n$, $\vdash \varphi_n \to \varphi$.

(*ii*) Show that the following 'identities' hold: $\vdash (\varphi_{2n+1} \to \varphi_{2n+2}) \leftrightarrow \varphi_{2n+2}$ $\vdash (\varphi_{2n+2} \to \varphi_{2n+4}) \leftrightarrow \varphi_{2n+4}$. $\vdash (\varphi_{2n+3} \to \varphi_{2n+1}) \leftrightarrow \varphi_{2n+4}$, $\vdash (\varphi_{2n+4} \to \varphi_{2n+1}) \leftrightarrow \varphi_{2n+6}$, $\vdash (\varphi_{2n+5} \to \varphi_{2n+1}) \leftrightarrow \varphi_{2n+1}$, $\vdash (\varphi_{2n+6} \to \varphi_{2n+1}) \leftrightarrow \varphi_{2n+4}$, $\vdash (\varphi_k \to \varphi_{2n+1}) \leftrightarrow \varphi_{2n+1}$ for $k \geqslant 2n+7$, $\vdash (\varphi_k \to \varphi_{2n+2}) \leftrightarrow \varphi_{2n+2}$ for $k \geqslant 2n+3$. Determine identities for the implications not covered above.

(*iii*) Determine all possible identities for conjunctions and disjunctions of φ_i's (look at the diagram).

(*iv*) Show that each formula in p is equivalent to some φ_i.

(*v*) In order to show that there are no other implications than those indicated in the diagram (and the compositions of course) it suffices to show that no φ_n is derivable. Why ?

(*vi*) Consider the Kripke model indicated in the diagram on the right.

$a_1 \Vdash p$ and no other node forces p. Show

$$\forall a_n \exists \varphi_i \forall k (k \Vdash \varphi_i \Leftrightarrow k \geqslant a_n)$$

$$\forall b_n \exists \varphi_j \forall k (k \Vdash \varphi_j \Leftrightarrow k \geqslant b_n)$$

Clearly the $\varphi_i (\varphi_j)$ is uniquely determined, call it $\varphi(a_n)$, resp. $\varphi(b_n)$.

Show $\varphi(a_1) = \varphi_1$, $\varphi(b_1) = \varphi_2$, $\varphi(a_2) = \varphi_4$, $\varphi(b_2) = p_6$,

$$\varphi(a_{n+2}) = [(\varphi(a_{n+1}) \vee \varphi(b_n)) \to (\varphi(a_n) \vee \varphi(b_n))] \to (\varphi(a_{n+1}) \vee \varphi(b_n)),$$

$$\varphi(b_{n+2}) = [(\varphi(a_{n+1}) \vee \varphi(b_{n+1})) \to (\varphi(a_{n+1}) \vee \varphi(b_n))] \to (\varphi(a_{n+1}) \vee \varphi(b_{n+1})).$$

(*vii*) Show that the diagram on the left contains all provable implications.

Remark. The diagram of the implications is called the *Rieger-Nishimura lattice* (it actually is the free Heyting algebra with one generator).

31. Consider intuitionistic predicate logic without function symbols. Prove the following extension of the existence property:

$$\vdash \exists y \varphi(x_1, \ldots, x_n, y) \Leftrightarrow \vdash \varphi(x_1, \ldots, x_n, t),$$

where t is a constant or one of the variables $x_1, \ldots, x_n$. (Hint: replace $x_1, \ldots, x_n$ by new constants $a_1, \ldots, a_n$).

32. Let $Q_1 x_1 \ldots Q_n x_n \varphi(\vec{x}, \vec{y})$ be a prenex formula (without function symbols), then we can find a suitable substitution instance φ' of φ obtained by replacing the existentially quantified variables by certain universally quantified variables or by constants, such that $\vdash Q_1 x_1 \ldots Q_n x_n \varphi(\vec{x}, \vec{y}) \Leftrightarrow \vdash \varphi'$ (use ex. 31).

33. Show that $\vdash \varphi$ is decidable for prenex φ. (use ex. 32, 17).

Remark. Combined with the fact that intuitionistic predicate logic is undecidable, this shows that not every formula is equivalent to one in prenex normal form.

34. Consider a language with identity and function symbols, and interprete a n-ary symbol F by a function $F_k : D(k)^n \to D(k)$ for each k in a given Kripke model K. We require *monotonicity*: $k \leqslant \ell \Rightarrow F_k \subseteq F_\ell$ and *preservation of equality*: $\vec{a} \sim_k \vec{b} \Rightarrow F_k(\vec{a}) \sim_k F_k(\vec{b})$.

(*i*) Show $K \Vdash \forall \vec{x} \exists ! y (F(\vec{x}) = y)$

(*ii*) Show $K \Vdash I_4$.

(*iii*) Let $K \Vdash \forall\vec{x}\exists!y\,\varphi(\vec{x},y)$, show that we can define for each k an F_k satisfying the above requirements such that $K \Vdash \forall\vec{x}\,\varphi(\vec{x},F(\vec{x}))$.

(*iv*) Show that one can conservatively add definable Skolem functions.

Note that we have shown how to introduce functions in Kripke models, when they are given by "functional" relations. So, strictly speaking, Kripke models with just relations are good enough.

LITERATURE

L.E.J. Brouwer. *Collected Works I*. (Ed. A. Heyting). North-Holland Publ. Co. Amsterdam 1975.

——— *Brouwer's Cambridge Lectures on Intuitionism*. (Ed. D. van Dalen). Cambridge University Press. Cambridge 1981.

D. van Dalen. Intuitionistic Logic. In *Philosophical Logic*, Vol. III (eds. D.M. Gabbay, F. Guenthner) Reidel. Dordrecht. To appear.

M. Dummett. *Elements of Intuitionism*. Oxford University Press. Oxford 1977.

D.M. Gabbay. *Semantical investigations in Heyting's intuitionistic logic*. Reidel. Dordrecht 1981.

A. Heyting. *Intuitionism. An introduction*. North-Holland Publ. Co. Amsterdam 1956.

S.C. Kleene. *Introduction to Meta-mathematics*. North-Holland Publ. Co. Amsterdam 1952.

D. Prawitz. *Natural Deduction. A proof theoretical study*. Almqvist & Wiksell. Stockholm 1965.

A.S. Troelstra (ed.). *Metamathematical Investigations of Intuitionistic Arithmetic and Analysis*. SLN # 344. Springer Verlag. Berlin 1973.

——— *Choice Sequences. A chapter of intuitionistic mathematics*. Oxfords University Press. Oxford 1977.

A.S. Troelstra, D. van Dalen. *Principles of Intuitionism*, to appear.

6. Appendix

At various points we have introduced classes by inductive definitions, e.g. the sets of propositions, terms, formulas, derivations. For these classes we have employed a principle of definition by recursion which we, as yet, have to justify. There is a general theory of inductive definitions, but our present discussion deals only with a very simple special case.

Our inductive definitions are of the form:

X_∞ is the smallest set X satisfying

(*i*) $S \subseteq X$

(*ii*) $x_1,\ldots,x_{n_i} \in X \Rightarrow f_i(x_1,\ldots,x_{n_i}) \in X$,

for $i = 1,\ldots,m$ and given functions f_i.

As a matter of fact the functions f_i are of a special sort, as we will see in a moment.

X_∞ can be obtained "from below" in the following way:

$$X_0 = S$$

$$X_{n+1} = \{f_i(x_1,\ldots,x_{n_i}) \mid x_1,\ldots,x_{n_i} \in X_n;\ i \leqslant m\} \cup X_n$$

and $X_\infty = \bigcup_{n \geqslant 0} X_n$

The proof of this fact is simple and we leave it to the reader. In the cases where we apply inductive definitions in this book we also have $f_i(x_1,\ldots,x_{n_i}) \notin X_n$ for $x_1,\ldots,x_{n_i} \in X_n - X_{n-1}$; moreover the f_i's all are injective and have disjoint ranges.

We now describe the definition by recursion for the general case:

Let H, $H_i (i \in m)$ be functions such that

$$\begin{cases} H : S \to W, \\ H_i : W^{n_i} \to W. \end{cases}$$

Then there is one and only one function G such that

$$* \begin{cases} G(x) = H(x) \text{ for } x \in S, \\ G(f_i(x_1,\ldots,x_{n_i})) = H_i(G(x_1),\ldots,G(x_{n_i})), \text{ for } x_1,\ldots,x_{n_i} \in X_\infty. \end{cases}$$

We will "approximate" G by functions G_n on the X_n's.

(0) $G_0 = H_0$. Clearly G is the unique function on X_0 that satisfies *.

(n+1) Suppose that G_n is defined on X_n and that it is the unique solution to * on X_n.

Define: $G_{n+1} = G_n \cup \{\langle f_i(x_1,\ldots,x_{n_i}),\ H_i(G_n(x),\ldots,G_n(x_{n_i}))\rangle \mid x_1,\ldots,x_{n_i} \in X_n;\ i \leqslant m\}$.

(N.B. the function value is followed by the argument).

Since $f_i(x_1,\ldots,x_{n_i}) \notin X_n$, we only have to check functionality for the new pairs. Because of the extra conditions, we have $f_i(x_1,\ldots,x_{n_i}) \neq f_j(y,\ldots,y_{n_j})$ for $i \neq j$, and $f_i(x_1,\ldots,x_{n_i}) \neq f_i(y,\ldots,y_{n_i})$ for $\langle x_1,\ldots,x_{n_i}\rangle \neq \langle y_1,\ldots,y_{n_i}\rangle$. But then the functionality follows immediately from the functionality of the H_i's.

By definition, and by the induction hypothesis on G_n, G_{n+1} satisfies *.

Put $G = \bigcup_{n \leqslant 0} G_n$, then it follows immediately that G is a function on X_∞ and that G satisfies *.

Now suppose G' also satisfies *, then one easily shows that G and G' coincide on all X_n's by induction on n. Hence G' = G.

There is one case which is not covered by the "definition by recursion", namely the satisfaction definition for predicate calculus. In order to define $v(\forall x\varphi(x))$ we need (in general) infinitely many values of "earlier" sentences $\varphi(\overline{a})$. So we need a function, operating on a function from $|\mathfrak{A}|$ to W.

Consider therefore one function $H' : W^{|\mathfrak{A}|} \to W$ and add to * the equation $G(f'(x)) = H'(\lambda a.G(g(x,a)))$ (think of $f'(\varphi)$ as $\forall z\varphi$ and $g(\varphi,a) = [\overline{a}/z]$).

We consider the case

$$(n+1).\ G_{n+1} = G_n \cup \{\langle f_i(x_1,\ldots,x_{n_i}),\ H_i(G_n(x_1),\ldots,G_n(x_{n_i}))\rangle \mid x_1,\ldots,x_{n_i} \in X_n,\ i \leqslant m\} \cup \{\langle f'(x),\ H'(\lambda a.G_n(g(x,a)))\rangle \mid x \in X_n\}.$$

Again the functionality of G_{n+1} is an immediate consequence of that of G_n and the properties of the f_i, H_i, f', H', g. Likewise one obtains the uniqueness.

It is fairly easy to show that the above theorems actually cover the applications made in the text. The most interesting case is that of definition 2.4.2. The functions that generate FORM are simple and one immediately recognizes that they satisfy our assumptions.

Define $H(\varphi)$ for atoms as in 2.4.2, e.g. $H_\to(i.j) = \mathrm{Max}(1-i,j)$.

For $H_\forall$ and $H_\exists$ we have

$H_\forall(f) = \min\{f(a) \mid a \in |\mathfrak{A}|\}$,

$H_\exists(f) = \max\{f(a) \mid a \in |\mathfrak{A}|\}$, where $f \in \{0,1\}^{|\mathfrak{A}|}$,

For 2.4.2 (iv) we get

$$v(\forall x\varphi) = H_{\forall}(\lambda a.v(g(\varphi,a))),$$

where $g(\varphi,a) = \varphi[\bar{a}/x]$, so $v(\forall x\varphi) = \min\{v(\varphi(\bar{a})) \mid a \in |\mathfrak{A}|\}$.

The above definitions are all cases of the so-called "definition by recursion on a well-founded relation" in set theory (cf. *van Dalen, Doets, de Swart*, p. 157). Clearly, the relations "φ is a subformula of ψ" or "D is a subderivation of D" are well founded.

7. Bibliography

The following books are recommended for further reading.

C.C. Chang, H.J. Keisler. *Model Theory*. North-Holland Publ. Co, Amsterdam 1973.

A. Church, *Introduction to Mathematical Logic*. Princeton Un. Press, Princeton 1956.

J. Barwise, *Handbook of Mathematical Logic*. North-Holland Publ. Co., Amsterdam 1977.

D. van Dalen, H.C. Doets, H.C.M. de Swart, *Sets, Naiv, axiomatic and applied*, Pergamon Press, Oxford 1978.

M. Davis, *Computability & Unsolvability*, New York 1958.

D. Hilbert, P. Bernays, *Grundlagen der Mathematik I, II*. Springer-Verlag, Berlin 1934, 1939, second edition 1970.

S.C. Kleene, *Introduction to meta mathematics*. North-Holland Publ. Co., Amsterdam-New York 1952.

G. Kreisel, J.L. Krivine, *Elements of Mathematical Logic*. North-Holland Publ. Co., Amsterdam 1967.

Y.I. Manin, *A course in Math. Logic*. Springer-Verlag, Berlin 1977.

D. Prawitz, *Natural Deduction*. Almqvist & Wiksell, Stockholm 1965.

J.W. Robbin, *Mathematical Logic*, W.A. Benjamin, New York 1969.

A. Robinson, *Non-standard Analysis*. North-Holland Publ. Co., Amsterdam 1966.

G. Sacks, *Saturated Model Theory*. W. A. Benjamin, New York 1972.

J.R. Shoenfield, *Mathematical Logic*, Addison & Wesley, Reading 1967.

K.D. Stroyan, W.A.J. Luxemburg, *Introduction to the theory of infinitesimals*. Academic Press, New York 1976.

8. Gothic Alphabet

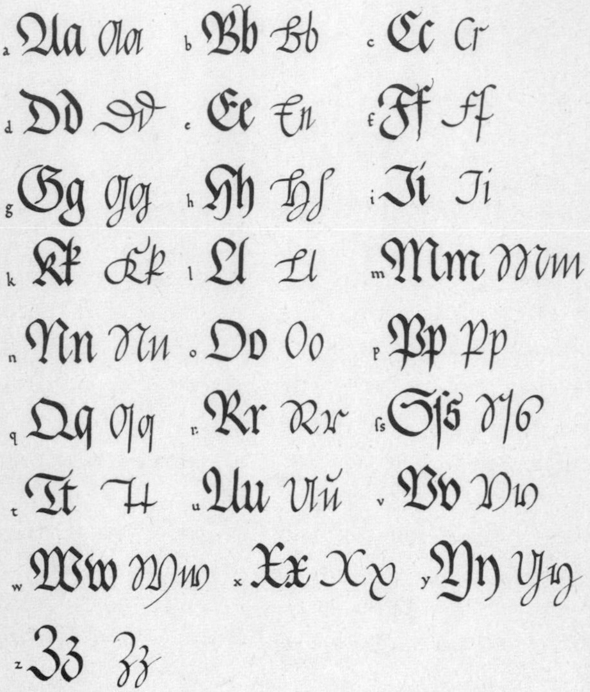

9. Index